Vampires from Another World

ALSO OF INTEREST AND FROM McFARLAND

The Transmedia Vampire: Essays on Technological Convergence and the Undead, edited by Simon Bacon (2021)

Eco-Vampires: The Undead and the Environment, Simon Bacon (2020)

Dracula as Absolute Other: The Troubling and Distracting Specter of Stoker's Vampire on Screen, Simon Bacon (2019)

Growing Up with Vampires: Essays on the Undead in Children's Media, edited by Simon Bacon and Katarzyna Bronk (2018)

To Boldly Go: Essays on Gender and Identity in the Star Trek *Universe,* edited by Nadine Farghaly and Simon Bacon (2017)

Vampires from Another World

*The Cinematic Progeny
of H.G. Wells'* The War of the Worlds
and Bram Stoker's Dracula

SIMON BACON

McFarland & Company, Inc., Publishers
Jefferson, North Carolina

LIBRARY OF CONGRESS CATALOGUING-IN-PUBLICATION DATA

Names: Bacon, Simon, 1965– author.
Title: Vampires from another world : the cinematic progeny of H.G. Wells' The war of the worlds and Bram Stoker's Dracula / Simon Bacon.
Description: Jefferson, North Carolina : McFarland & Company, Inc., Publishers, 2021 | Includes bibliographical references and index.
Identifiers: LCCN 2021021161 |
ISBN 9781476678733 (paperback : acid free paper) ∞
ISBN 9781476642307 (ebook)
Subjects: LCSH: Vampire films—History and criticism. | Other (Philosophy) in motion pictures. | Wells, H. G. (Herbert George), 1866–1946. War of the worlds. | Wells, H. G. (Herbert George), 1866–1946—Film adaptations. | Stoker, Bram, 1847–1912. Dracula. | Stoker, Bram, 1847–1912—Film adaptations. | BISAC: PERFORMING ARTS / Film / Genres / Horror | PERFORMING ARTS / Film / Genres / Science Fiction & Fantasy
Classification: LCC PN1995.9.V3 B38 2021 | DDC 791.43/675—dc23
LC record available at https://lccn.loc.gov/2021021161

BRITISH LIBRARY CATALOGUING DATA ARE AVAILABLE

ISBN (print) 978-1-4766-7873-3
ISBN (ebook) 978-1-4766-4230-7

© 2021 Simon Bacon. All rights reserved

No part of this book may be reproduced or transmitted in any form or by any means, electronic or mechanical, including photocopying or recording, or by any information storage and retrieval system, without permission in writing from the publisher.

Front cover image from *Lifeforce*, 1985
(Cannon Film Distributors/Photofest)

Printed in the United States of America

*McFarland & Company, Inc., Publishers
Box 611, Jefferson, North Carolina 28640
www.mcfarlandpub.com*

For the never-ending patience
of Mrs. Mine, Eben and Majki
and the support of Mam i Tata Bronk

Acknowledgments

Heartfelt thanks as always to my two partners in crime for this book, Andy (Andrew M.) Boylan and Hadas Elber-Aviram. Andy, who is the go-to person for all things vampire, and whose help in getting the original proposal together and for suggestions for additional films/books to look at were (and are) invaluable. He also runs a blog that I cannot recommend highly enough for anyone interested in, or researching vampires in any media (https://taliesinttlg.blogspot.com). And Hadas, who is the most amazingly patient and kind person I know, and who sped through the manuscript leaving a trail of priceless comments, suggestions, and very amusing notes. I highly recommend her amazing book on urban fantasy, *Fairy Tales of London: British Urban Fantasy, 1840 to the Present* (Bloomsbury: 2021). As always, I cannot thank my wonderful Always Mrs. Mine (Katarzyna Bronk-Bacon) enough for her continual help, support and encouragement, and our, not so little, two monsters, Seba and Majki, who are always "helpful" by just being themselves. I na koniec, bardzo dziękuję Mam i tacie za wsparcie … i "sernik Magdy."

Table of Contents

Acknowledgments vi

Introduction 1

---

1. *The War of the Worlds* 15
2. *Planet of the Vampires* 49
3. *Lifeforce* 84
4. *Underworld* 116
5. *The Thing from Another World* 148

Filmography 181

Bibliography 185

Index 189

Introduction

This book was in part inspired by the realization that the vampire stories of both Bram Stoker and H.G. Wells were originally published in the same year.[1] This suggests that there exists a curious equivalence between Transylvania, Mars, and London as worlds/locations linked by the body of the vampire seeing the undead creature as both manifestation of this alien world (Mars/Transylvania) but equally a bridge between it and our own—this is an idea that emerges again and again throughout this volume.

More fundamentally, though, vampires would seem to be creatures inherently rooted to their homeland/world. Even though a vampire can transform into many different forms, "bats ... wolf ... elemental mist" (Stoker: 1997, 258),[2] to name but a few, it needs to return to the earth every day to rest. In some versions the soil that makes its bed should be from its homeland, as seen in Chelsea Quinn Yarboro's *Saint-Germain* series (1978–2014) or even its own grave, as in Bram Stoker's *Dracula* (1897) (Stoker: 1997, 52). However, the need for sustenance, more often than not human blood or life force, often sees vampires leaving their homes to find a new one that is "younger ... stronger and more virile ... [to] fasten on it and drain it dry" (*Son of Dracula*, Siodmak: 1942). Indeed, they appear to be constantly on the move, which may not be so surprising for creatures that often profess to be tired of their homes. Jeffrey Weinstock notes that vampires "always appear to be coming from someplace else" (2012, 11), at least in relation to places they seem to end up in, i.e., Victorian England, 1990s New York, or early 21st-century New Zealand. This becomes more complicated when the destinations are no longer located on Earth but are extraterrestrial or

1. Although *The War of the Worlds* was not published as a book until 1898, when it was serialized in *Pearson's Magazine* in 1897.
2. Interestingly Van Helsing suggests that the vampire cannot rest in "soil barren of holy memories" (Stoker: 1997, 260), yet Dracula insists on putting earth from the chapel in his own castle into boxes and taking with him to England where he is dependent upon them for his survival.

even inter-dimensional, as is discussed later. This last, in fact, begins to explain the curious anomalies or impossibilities that surround the figure of the vampire in its ability to connect its "home" to ours and to seemingly move to where and when it likes. Something of this is hinted at in Weinstock's description of "vampire space," which he sees as "a smooth space in which thought overcomes distance and movement [and] is unimpeded by either material obstacles or national boundaries" (13). There is a correlation here between the idea of the inter-dimensional and that of human thought or consciousness, so that vampires only exist as soon as one becomes become aware of them, so that they have the ability to be anywhere and everywhere. Brian Stableford captures the mystical aspects of this when he describes the "innerspace," as that place/space where "real" vampires can exist. While being rather confusing—Count Dracula is nothing if not an essentially difficult character—it does begin to suggest the complications inherent within the figure of the vampire that is simultaneously dependent on its home, but constantly traveling; a spirit of the ether yet reliant on the mundanity of the dirt; and a superhuman monster that is disintegrated in the light of the sun.

This reinforces the notion of the vampire as a transitional entity that connects the cognitive space where they are "real," as noted by Stableford, with the real-world place where they find physical form. These correlations between "inner" and "outer" space in terms of the human psyche—a mirroring between the events in the real world with our consciousness—can be extrapolated to further suggest a linkage between outer space and that which happens here on Earth, intimating a form of mirroring or over-laying worlds or dimensions which exist concurrently with our own. Something of this is captured in the two novels that form the main points of comparison here, Bram Stoker's *Dracula* and H.G. Wells' *The War of the Worlds*, which feature extremely different vampires from vastly different locations but manage to simultaneously exist in 1897 London. There is much to suggest that Transylvania and Mars are not just culturally and geographically distant locations but manifestations of the "dark side" of Victorian London—Jeffrey Cohen's volume on *Monster Theory* (1996) confirms as much in its reading of the Victorian Gothic novel—seeing them as much part of the mental landscape as they are of the physical one. This mental or psychic aspect goes some way to explain the predilection of vampires from other worlds for human energies around dreaming, excessive emotional states and/or sexual arousal.

Unsurprisingly, then, there are many correlations between Wells' *The War of the Worlds* and Stoker's *Dracula* in terms of cultural anxieties with each of them centering on outside invaders planning to overthrow the British Empire, demonstrating the same kind of wanton colonization of land that typified British Imperialism—for Wells, British Imperialism found its worst expression in relation to Tasmania while for Stoker it was more a general reverse colonialism.[3] Both stories also posit that the inherent strength of the land or nation will save the world from the alien invader, bacteria in the case of *War of the Worlds*, and the virility of British manhood in *Dracula*, while expressing an ongoing anxiety over the imminent decline of civilization and empire. The alien others inevitably come from a land/world that is vastly different from our own: Mars, like Transylvania, is seen as an almost dreamlike land as far away from civilization in distance as it is in time—the Martians are a future, devolved version of humanity,[4] while Dracula is humanity risen from the depths of time, both greedily eyeing the fecundity and life force of the present.

Unsurprisingly, much of what typified these two novels, and particularly the themes they have in common, have been used and adapted by a large number of the "vampires from other worlds" narratives that have followed. This book looks at a range of films (and a couple of television shows) to show how the tropes from both narratives have evolved since the end of the 19th century until the start of the 21st. Thus we shall look at films as varied as *Nosferatu* (Murnau: 1922), *Not of This Earth* (Corman: 1957), *Dark City* (Proyas: 1998), *Day of the Triffids* (Copus: 2009), *Interstellar* (Nolan: 2014), and *Stranger Things* (Duffer Brothers: 2016–present), to see what anxieties they might be embodying that can only find form as blood-sucking, energy draining vampires from another world.

Across the Gulf of Space…

One of the key points in *War of the Worlds* is the way that the Earth saves humanity. Humans themselves have no answer to the creatures from outer space; science, weaponry, human endeavor provide no answer to the superior alien other from outside our world. Indeed, it sets up something of a Manichean binary between the Earth and all that is not-of-this-Earth, configuring space itself as an alien and dangerous entity that is intent on our destruction and wants to, quite literally, suck the life out of us. This is an idea that is carried forward in many cinematic texts that feature vampiric creatures from other worlds, even those that

---

3. See Arata: 1996.
4. Constructing the Martians as future humans frames them as being as much from another dimension as it does from Mars seeing them not only cross space but time itself to reach late 19th century England. See Frank McConnell: 1981, 128, 130.

4   Introduction

construct other worlds or dimensions themselves as vampiric entities in their own right.[5]

Unsurprisingly, the first of these comes at a time when flying into outer space was increasingly becoming a possibility. With the commencement of the Space Race between America and the USSR in 1955, the push to be the first nation into space increased dramatically, with the Soviet Union claiming the first victory in October 1957, sending *Sputnik 1* into orbit. This was followed by the successful manned space mission of Yuri Gagarin in April 1961. America seemed only able to respond by extolling the dangers of outer space as seen in the B-movie *The Monster from Green Hell* (Crane: 1957), which starts with the flight control team discussing the impending mission with intense trepidation. Their anxiety derives mainly from their lack of knowledge regarding the effects of space-travel on any life-form, let alone human and their suspicion that just leaving the Earth's atmosphere might cause irreparable damage to any form of biological life. Despite these worries, they still send the astronauts, a guinea pig and some insects into space with the predictable results that they return as mutated monsters. This sequence of events paints a picture of how space was viewed, and indeed to some measure still is, as an environment where the rules of normal life no longer apply. In fact, space is seen as beyond life, a black abyss that is death-like, a dark mirror that not only reflects back at us all that is monstrous in humanity, but actively wants to consume it.[6] Space itself is then seen as an almost vampiric entity where just entering it, however marginally or briefly, can have disastrous effects.[7] This is dramatically seen in *First Man into Space* (Day: 1959)[8] where an astronaut/pilot briefly leaves the Earth's atmosphere and is immediately attacked by a mysterious meteor shower that literally coats him in a layer of "space" making him a monster on his return to the planet. He immediately becomes an abject creature on his return to Earth, forced to try and drink blood to cure himself but killing nearly everyone he comes into contact with. Although his former colleague tries to recreate the conditions of space on Earth to save him, he is too foreign, too contaminated by outer space to survive.

   5. Aliens and alien worlds become an easy shorthand for the cultural dangerous Other of choice with the postwar movies particularly correlating it with the USSR.
   6. There is much here that correlates to the series *The Quatermass Experiment* (Cartier: 1953) and its many iterations that see a mysterious entity from outer space with vampiric intentions upon the Earth.
   7. The film *Vampire Wars: Battle for the Universe* [aka Bloodsuckers] (Hastings: 2005) sees literally every alien race/species that humans come into contact with outer space as vampires in some way.
   8. As human exploration increases, this notion becomes extended into the idea of the "unknown" making new lifeforms, worlds, galaxies, and latterly black holes and unexplored phenomena equivalently vampiric and deadly.

Many of the B-movies of the 1950s construct an interesting cosmology where the Earth and outer space are opposites, with the Earth representing life and outer space representing death, with the result that anyone who travels between them is almost instantly a third thing, not alive, not dead, but undead—this also relates to space creatures that take residence on the Earth, as in say *Invasion of the Body Snatchers* (Siegel: 1956) where the aliens draw the life essence from their human victims and take on their form, but they are not really human (alive), nor dead, but something else. The body snatchers are caught between two worlds and therefore carry something of both but can never be truly at home in either. The alien thus emerges as kin to the vampire, a being that exists in the gaps, a between entity that is not one thing or the other, but something else (see Showalter: 1992). It is this "something else" that destroys the cognitive integrity of the human world, seeing its otherworldly invaders as not just dangerous but intent on sucking the very life out of the Earth itself.

Part of this idea of being caught between two physical spaces is also that of temporal difference as well; that the vampire's otherness is not just its resistance to spatial categorization but is similarly so in relation to time. This is seen in *The War of the Worlds*, where the Martians that look greedily on the Earth can be seen as embodying our own future of evolutionary exhaustion; a vision of what we will become if our consumerism and colonial intent remain unchecked—a space vampire version of Scrooge's "ghost of Christmas yet to come" that is trying to get us to mend our ways (Dickens, *A Christmas Carol*: 1843). In similar fashion, Count Dracula, and vampires in general, often represent a distant, darker, human past that wants to drain the present of its vitality. In this reading the present is life, the source of energy and life force which the vampires of the distant past and the future (often embodying forms of exhaustion and/or extreme consumption) want to consume to reinvigorate themselves. Be they aliens or vampires, hailing from the past or the future, these creatures are out of time and not of the now; not really "alive" in the sense of being an integral part of the present. Something of this is seen in the 1982 adaptation of *The Thing* (Carpenter: 1982) where the creature's temporal origins remain ambiguous—it hails from either the past or the future in this version, unlike the original. The spacecraft in which it is found suggests futurity, but its burial in ice conversely constructs it as coming from the Earth's past. The Thing takes on the form of the victims it eats and thus it literally consumes the present. However, when the alien is killed, the victims it has eaten are seemingly released from its body, which we see represented when the dying entity goes through enforced bodily transformations revealing the victims' faces; literally vomiting out the present—vampires often go through a similar process when they die, releasing the youthful energy they have consumed in the form of blood, deflating like a temporal balloon and rapidly aging until their body returns to their real age.[9]

Parallel worlds are quite often a key characteristic of narratives about vampires from another world. Here, a world often similar to our own but usually with some twist or other exists alongside it. While kept apart, these worlds can exist without troubling each other, as seen in the early films of the *Underworld* series (2003–16), but more often than not the parallel world functions as a doppelgänger, or dark other that is intent on the destruction of "our" world or its consumption. This doubling of worlds often constructs the alien other, or double, as non-human or anti-human in some way—where "human" is seen as an inhabitant of our world and so inherently more deserving of life. Aliens from mirror/parallel worlds are accordingly configured as creatures of darkness or the shadows, adding to their vampire-like qualities/characteristics. Extraterrestrial monsters in films of the 1950s and 1960s are often shadowy and, like Orlok from Murnau's *Nosferatu* (1922) before them, they seem to exist as much in the insubstantial darkness they cast and/or produce as in their own physical bodies. This crepuscular portrayal has persisted into more modern vampiric alien entities such as the xenomorphs from the *Alien* film series (1979–2017), and even the *Predator* franchise (1987–2018)—unsurprisingly both are connected. The xenomorph virtually coalesces out of the darkness that forms its natural habitat, using humans as living incubators to sustain its progeny through birth. The Predator is invisible even in daylight and only given substance by the same human aggression and fear that also gives it life. Indeed, many alien vampires do not require blood as such but its energy—an almost mystical substance that brings together the ideas of the galvanizing or life-giving properties of blood and the human will/soul/psychic strength as most obviously seen in Tobe Hooper's *Lifeforce* (1985)—or affective equivalents such as dreams, sexual energy and strong emotions.[10] All of these texts hinge on the construction of a binary of "us" and "them," which largely delineates the difference between human and non-human—or humans and their alien "doubles." This is seen in both *War of the Worlds* and *Dracula*, notwithstanding that Wells used his "non-human" Martians as physical manifestations, or projections of, the monstrous nature of humanity. Stoker's non-human vampire, while embodying many of the prejudices and anxieties of late–Victorian Britain—anti-Semitism, homophobia, miscegenation, and cultural devolution

9. An interesting example of this transformation is seen at the end of *Vamps* (Heckerling: 2012).
10. The novel *Space Vampires* (1976) by Colin Wilson, on which the film is based, suggests that psychic vampirism is a natural occurrence in humans in both a sexual and predatory manner.

to name but a few[11]—is more easily made monstrous in the novel through his more obvious human appearance being monsterized by his need to drink blood, ability to change into animals, but also his "brides" and their predilection for feasting on babies; the Martians are never anything other than "them" while Dracula's greater monstrosity is that he is equally always "them" but looks like, and pretends to be, "us."

For the space vampire films of the 1950s and '60s, the point of anxiety for America and much of the Western world is most obviously the Soviet Union and the ongoing Cold War that filled cultural consciousness at that time. Ralph Donald applies the term "Great Satan" to stand for the iconic figure that embodies the national and/or ideological threat that is diametrically opposed to America and "democracy" (Donald: 2014). In terms of the notion of parallel/alien worlds and the vampires that inhabit them which underpins this book, space is such a place and symbolizes the USSR which contaminates and (ideologically) alters all who come into contact with it. Springing from the web of suspicion created by McCarthyism in the late 1940s until early 1950s, the fear of contamination from spies in the midst of America gripped the nation and was expressed in films like *Invasion of the Body Snatchers* (Siegel: 1956), and even a film like Mario Bava's *Planet of the Vampires* (1965) is constructed around the idea that those we know and care for might not be who they seem.[12] This becomes more complicated, of course, when it is the "humans" that become the "non-humans" (*Avatar*, Cameron: 2009), or both groups are "humans" (*Snowpiercer*, Bong: 2013).

Each chapter in this study offers a closer examination of particular aspects of these encounters with vampires from other worlds and brings out more nuanced and detailed observations and linkages. The chapters also chart a course from the past into the present, in terms of the date of the films looked at, to assess what points of cultural anxiety are represented by the otherworldly alien/vampires. It is worth noting that while many of the movies examined here are well known and accepted within the sub-genre of space vampires, some of them are less so and some purposely chosen to be provocative—films and series such as *Event Horizon* (Anderson: 1997), *Interstellar* (Nolan: 2014), and *Stranger Things* (Duffer Brothers: 2016–present), for example—in part to cover new territory but also to provide new readings of texts and show that alien vampires from

11. See Malchow, *Gothic Images of Race in Nineteenth-Century Britain*, 1996; Arata, *Fictions of Loss in the Victorian Fin de Siècle*, 1996; Gibson, *Dracula and the Eastern Question: British and French Vampire Narratives of the Nineteenth-Century Near East*, 2006; and Craft, *Another Kind of Love Male Homosexual Desire in English Discourse, 1850–1920*, 1994.

12. This theme continues into the 21st century where sleeper cells, "groomed" and brainwashed fundamentalists, very much form the narrative around the various wars against Al Qaeda and ISIS.

other worlds are not always where we expect them to be and that "[t]here are such beings ... [and] some of us have evidence that they exist" (Stoker: 1997, 255).

With this in mind it is worth quickly qualifying what is considered a vampire within this study as many of them are nothing like the popular conception of Dracula-esque beings that wear capes, have fangs, and drink human blood. This study defines vampires as entities that feed off human life force and/or energies. This can be blood, but can equally be emotional states, dream energy, sexual energy, the "soul" or biological energy—these last two are sometimes equated (see Hooper's *Lifeforce*). Energy vampires may be more well known from the use of the term in contemporary popular culture describing people that seem to leave one feeling emotionally drained or exhausted (see Slate: 2002, and Bernstein: 2012), and as recently represented by Colin Robinson (Mark Proksch) in the hit television series *What We Do in the Shadows* (Clement: 2019–present). However, in literature it has a long history and in the 19th century vampire stories often feature mysterious strangers or entities that drained their victims' energy: Sabine Baring-Gould's *Margery of Quether* (1884) where a creature turned young woman drains the life energy of a male host; Florence Marryat's *Blood of the Vampire* (1897) where a young girl unknowingly kills all those she loves; George Sylvester Viereck's *The House of the Vampire* (1907) where an impresario drains the creative energies of young artists; and other vampiric entities such as a flower in H.G. Wells' "The Flowering of the Strange Orchid" (1894), and a patch of ground in Algernon Blackwood's "The Transfer" (1911). This last naturally leads to the fact that not all vampires are necessarily humanoid in appearance and can be forms of both alien fauna and flora. As such, they can be any entity that knowingly entraps and feeds off humans. In this sense they can be something as basic as a Venus flytrap, that is evolutionarily developed—or genetically engineered—to capture certain kinds of prey, or as advanced as A.I. cyborgs that require humans as energy cells. More so they can be entities that are not usually considered in the purview of vampires, such as patches of ground, or an entire habitat—Dracula was able to exist as a mist or even control the weather—or a planet, and even black holes.

The Earth Under the Martians

This study is divided into five chapters that deal with respective issues that arise out of the intersections between *The War of the Worlds* and *Dracula*. Rather than just discuss the better known examples of alien vampires on film, they have been used as chapter titles (i.e., Chapter 2 is titled *Planet of the Vampires* after Mario Bava's seminal film from 1965) and the other movies under consideration in that chapter illuminate certain aspects of that film as well as link back to *War of the Worlds* and *Dracula*. Each chapter then looks at five pairs of films in rough chronological order, from the oldest to the most recent, in order to examine the cultural milieu that created them as well as the ways in which the representation of the alien/vampire evolves over time.

Chapter 1, "*The War of the Worlds*," uses one of the central ideas of Wells' novel and focuses on what one might term the consumerist (colonialist) interpretation of the Martians, as greedy for the Earth's resources and embodying anxieties around over-consumption and ideological colonialism. Wells' text shares much with Stoker's *Dracula*, which equally talks of covetous admiration of lands full of vitality and sees the Count wanting to consume and control the empire himself so it becomes his "bountiful wine press for a while" (Stoker: 1997, 311). Of course, both texts see human blood itself as the planet's greatest resource, though the intimate connection between humanity and the planet's ecosystem, as described by Wells, sees the lifeblood of the planet as equally important. This chapter thus aptly begins with an extended look at selected topics from Wells' novel *The War of the Worlds* (1897), particularly in terms of the relationship between humanity and its home and later interpretations of the text. Subsequent comparative readings of films bring out other topics from Wells book while emphasizing their vampiric credentials. *Not of This Earth* (Corman: 1957) and *Species* (Donaldson: 1995) both see the Earth as a last chance for an alien race. Corman's film sees blood as its priority though Donaldson sees human reproduction in general and male semen in particular as the literal life-giving fluid. *Skyline* (The Brothers Strause: 2010) and *Edge of Tomorrow* (Liman: 2014) envision extremely sophisticated alien vampires that seem unstoppable in their domination of the Earth. In these films, it is not a planetary bacterium that saves humanity but rather the "virus" of humans that offers hope against the alien invaders. In both films, the human mind emerges as both food for the aliens and a point of resistance against their assault. *Avatar* (Cameron: 2009) and *Ghosts of Mars* (Carpenter: 2001) shift the location of predation to alien worlds—ironically, Carpenter's film is set on Mars. In each of these films, it is humanity that embodies the alien vampires who are consequently repelled by the alien planet's own, ecological/biological, defense systems. *Prometheus* (Scott: 2012) and *Jupiter Ascending* (The Wachowskis: 2015) return to the Earth, but it is an alternate Earth where humanity is a species that has been created and farmed by alien vampires. The salvation of the planet, and of humanity itself then becomes a matter of ongoing negotiation with and resistance to our alien vampire gods.

Chapter 2, "*Planet of the Vampires,*" follows the thread of Bava's film, which grows more from Stoker's tale than Wells' scientific romance, where aliens take over the body of a human host, much as Dracula partially inhabited all his victims in Stoker's novel. Bava actually bases his story on a planet quite similar to Wells' vision of Mars, one that is exhausted and used up. But rather than launching attacks on other worlds, its inhabitants lure a rescue ship to their planet so they can use the bodies of its crew as their escape pods—not unlike the later *Alien* franchise discussed further on. The film plays upon fears of cultural assimilation, miscegenation, and loss of national identity. *It: The Terror from Beyond Space* (Cahn: 1958) and *Alien* (Scott: 1979) each feature ghost-like entities that haunt the spaces they inhabit and draw energies from the humans in their vicinity. Both films follow the struggles of their respective crews as they desperately try to keep the alien vampires from reaching Earth. The same theme persists in both *Planet of the Vampires* (Bava: 1965) and *Life* (Espinosa: 2017), though here the alien vampires manage to reach their victims' home world, with unknown consequences. *The First Man into Space* (Fay: 1959) and *The Astronaut's Wife* (Ravich: 1999) pick up where the previous films left off, as the alien vampire is unleashed on Earth but contained by the human body to which it attached itself. *The Andromeda Strain* (Wise: 1971) and *The Invasion of the Body Snatchers* (Kaufman: 1978) depict alien vampires in a far more aggressive and rampant mood once released on the planet, with Kaufman's film foreshadowing the impending decimation of humanity. The final pairing features the human body as a shell or exoskeleton for the alien vampires. In *The Host* (Niccol: 2013), the vampires arrive from outer space, while *Get Out* (Peele: 2017) constructs a parallel world and thereby foreshadows the next chapter.

Chapter 3, "*Lifeforce,*" focuses in on the different types of human energy, other than blood, that vampires from other worlds need to survive. These encompass many varieties of life essence from vital organs galvanizing bodily energies to psychic or emotional ones, though the most obvious example of this is possibly Tobe Hooper's *Lifeforce* (1985) where aliens from space are "rescued" and brought to Earth where they proceed to suck the life energy out of the humans they encounter leaving them wizened, dried-out husks. The aliens here are exhaustive if rather indiscriminate in their energy requirements, though there is a suggestion that life force on some level equates with the human soul. Other vampires are rather more specific in the kinds of energy, often emotional, that they require usually around excessive states such as arousal, excitement, and fear. The first two media discussed, *Citadel* (Foy: 2012) and *NOS4A2* (O'Brien: 2019–present), see the parallel worlds as spaces within our own world, though ones founded on deprivation and abuse that mirror hidden spaces in societies and inner cities and also see the vampire being drawn to,[13] and feeding off, emotional energy. These two touch on the idea of urban legend, which finds fuller form in the next movies, *Stay Alive* (Bell: 2006) and *Slender Man* (White: 2018). The parallel worlds in these works, while manifesting materially in the physical universe, locate themselves within the virtual spaces of gaming or cyberspace and more pointedly requires human fear to energize the vampires. *Nothing Left to Fear* (Leonardi III: 2013) and *Odd Thomas* (Sommers: 2013) again bring out the idea of an organic, vegetal parallel world trying to break into our own, though that world requires more specialized forms of human energies such as those released at the moment of death. The next pairing continues the idea of very particular kinds of human energies providing sustenance and the equally specialized vampires that require them. *Terminator 3: Rise of the Machines* (Mostow: 2003) and *Predators* (Antal: 2010) respectively sees robots from the future "sampling" humans to become them while alien warriors feed off the act of combat and its associated heightened emotions. Human emotional, psychic states come to the fore in the final pairing with *Event Horizon* (Anderson: 1997) and *Dark City* (Proyas: 1998). *Event Horizon* features a vampiric dimension feasting on human agony and emotional excess while *Dark City* deals in never-ending dreams and nightmares.

Chapter 4, "*Underworld*," focuses on the idea of parallel worlds, specifically ones that exist alongside our own world or mirror it in some way, expressing the kind of simultaneity of vampiric spaces and worlds mentioned above. The *Underworld* series of films are set in the darkness and shadows of our own world, its sewers, underground tunnels and walled in and hidden communities. These spaces fulfill the role of doppelgänger to contemporary societies and many of the more literally parallel worlds discussed herein similarly play on ideas of populations divided through historical, racial and ethnic differences as well as economic and sexual differences. In the films examined in this chapter, these parallel worlds and dimensions no longer serve simply as metaphorical mirrors but become vampiric entities in their own right, intent on consuming our world in order to perpetuate their own existence. *Perfect Creature* (Standring: 2006) and *The Breed* (Oblowitz: 2001) both envision parallel worlds that hark back to the past, but simultaneously highlight the ongoing divisions in contemporary society. *Blood: The Last Vampire* (Nahon: 2009) and *Priest* (Stewart: 2011) depict their parallel worlds through a postcolonial lens and enact what might be called the revenge of indigeneity. In these films, the natives of a world have been exiled to the last man and must fight to reclaim the

---

13. *Let the Right One In* (Lindqvist: 2004, Alfredson: 2008) similarly creates a space of monstrous urban decay which draws the vampire to it.

world of the present. *Ultraviolet* (Wimmer: 2006) and *Aeon Flux* (Kusama: 2005) are set in the super-sophisticated future where difference and poverty consign the abjected to a distant stratum of outsidership and literal undeath. *John Carter* (Stanton: 2012) and *The Matrix* (The Wachowskis: 1999) increase the scale of the alien parallel world as it consumes the life force of entire planets. A scale which continues to expand into the final two examples in this chapter, *Interstellar* (Nolan: 2014) and *The Cloverfield Paradox* (Onah: 2018) These films increase the size of the vampiric parallel world literally beyond the scale of comprehension, as they feature, respectively, a black hole and a mirrored, parallel universe.

The final section, Chapter 5, "*The Thing from Another World*," provides a sustained examination of the permutations of the vegetal component of the Martian invasion in *The War of the Worlds* and the red weed that accompanied the invaders. While not strictly vampiric itself, the red weed is strongly connected to blood, partly in its bright red color but also its proliferation around pits where the Martians drank blood—the 2005 Spielberg film adaptation of *War of the Worlds* shows this quite dramatically. Stoker's novel makes no real reference to vegetation in that way, but its first surviving (unofficial) adaptation into film, *Nosferatu*, directly links the undead to vampiric plants, such as the Venus flytrap. It is something of a combination of these two that informs the film of the chapter title from 1951 by Christian Nyby where an alien is uncovered and retrieved from under the Arctic ice. The monstrous creature from outer space exhibits many strange characteristics; it requires blood to survive; its severed arm is able to survive independently of its body; and it appears to be some kind of plant-based life form.

The films under consideration in this chapter exhibit an increasingly Anthropocene, ecological anxiety where everything not considered human (us) is deadly and must be destroyed. The first pairing of films in this chapter includes *The Thing from Another World* but also the slightly later *Queen of Blood* (Harrington: 1966), two films that envision different forms of intelligent, planet-based life that require human blood to survive or germinate. The next pair of films, *The Relic* (Hyams: 1997) and *The Day of the Triffids* (Sekeley: 1963/Copus: 2009), feature vampires that hail from alien worlds that evoke a colonial past—colonial South America and colonial Africa, respectively. *Relic* is more fauna than flora, but along with the *Day of the Triffids*, it depicts vampires who are as much an environmental immune system as an alien invasion. *Splinter* (Wilkins: 2008) and *Venom* (Fleischer: 2018) feature vampiric life forms that prefer hybridity to destruction, though they still assimilate/absorb their host. Both films center on a form of fungal biological jouissance. *A Quiet Place* (Krasinski: 2018) and *Bird Box* (Bier: 2018) feature a past Earth that is not strictly vegetal but can be read as an environmental defense system that operates by vampiric siphoning of energy. The chapter concludes with a consideration of *Stranger Things* (The Duffer Brothers: 2016–present) and *The Girl with All the Gifts* (McCarthy: 2016) which depict a version of our world that is overrun by alien fauna and flora that, rather than destroy humanity, satiate their appetite through hybridity and evolution, offering a future that we, humanity as it currently is, will not necessarily be part of.

Vampires from other worlds are here even when they are not. As noted in relation to some of the examples listed here, it takes only a certain kind of belief for them to become apparent and reveal the many worlds alongside our own. These "alien" doubles more clearly manifest the darkness that hovers, largely unrecognized, just below the surface of our own. More often than not, they highlight the exploitative and self-interested nature of humanity in times that cannot afford them. This was as true in Wells' time where colonial exploits decimated indigenous populations as it is in our own when stockpiling and breaking quarantine inflict irreparable damage on those around us. This is even more true of our effects on the wider environment around us where willful denial of climate change and exploitation of the eco-system see us as the vampires from Mars that have used the Earth as our bountiful wine-press for too long and with no sign of stopping. In this regard, vampires from another world, as eco-retribution/rejuvenation, might be the only thing that can save humanity.

1

The War of the Worlds

This chapter sees the Martians from *The War of the Worlds* as greedy consumers of the Earth's resources and an embodiment of anxieties around over-consumption and ideological colonialism. Indeed, the vampiric invaders in this scientific romance emblematize a perfect consumer that is never satiated, not unlike the figure of Count Dracula in Franco Moretti's compelling reading of Stoker's novel (2005, 91). Stoker's Dracula expresses covetous admiration for the British Empire, which he views as his "bountiful wine press" (Stoker: 1997, 311). The central difference between Stoker's Dracula and Wells' Martians is their approach to technology, which can be attributed to the alien world from which they hail. Count Dracula can never change and is completely self-sufficient and self-centered, as he configures a continually accruing past—he speaks of his house and the history of his people as a collective "we" of which he is "master"—that wants to remake (transform) the present into a version of himself—"flesh of my flesh; blood of my blood" (311)—so that he incorporates all that he covets[14]; in contrast the Martians are from the future and are utterly dependent upon technology,[15] so much so that they cannot survive without it—"They have become practically mere brains, wearing different bodies [mechanical exoskeletons] according to their needs" (Wells: 2018, 81). Although both require human blood, they actually embody different anxieties in late-Victorian society. Dracula embodies anxiety around miscegenation, sexuality, and male impotence, while the Martians embody a more existential threat—not just the downfall of the empire but the extinction of the

---

14. One can read Count Dracula as a dark, traumatic version of Walter Benjamin's *Angel of History* (2019, 201). Benjamin saw the figure of the angel with its wings spread wide facing the past accumulating the wreckage of the past but unable to see the future at its back. Count Dracula in contrast faces forward, his wings spread wide flying into the future which he continually consumes turning it into the wreckage of his own past.

15. As pointed out to me by Andrew M. Boylan, this makes for an interesting comparison to *Prisoner of the Vampires of Mars* by Gustave Le Rouge, which, only 10 years after Wells' novel, sees a French engineer traveling to Mars via a combination of Brahmin psychic powers and science to discover it is inhabited by three kinds of vampires.

human race.¹⁶ Wells' tale also differs from Stoker's in the helplessness of the human race. Neither technology, nor esoteric knowledge, nor Imperial power can save humanity from its imminent destruction. It is only the planet that we call home, even if we do not treat it as such, that saves us at the eleventh hour. In Wells' original story, though not always in its adaptations, humanity is saved because we belong to the Earth, not because it belongs to us. Wells' story is nothing if not anti-colonial—the empire is powerless to protect itself, and it is ultimately saved by a force that has no interest in it as a global power. In fact, ownership becomes a central theme in the films discussed below, as they adapt the core components of Wells' story to critique not only humanity's treatment of the Earth, but its colonial aspirations beyond the confines of our own world out into space where we become the vampires with "greedy eyes." This chapter ends with the possibility that humanity does not "belong" to the Earth at all and it is serving as a convenient holding pen until our true owners decide what to do with us.

War of the Worlds, H.G. Wells, 1897

One of the many interesting things about Wells' novel is that the start of the Martian invasion goes almost unnoticed. A meteor at night, a brief light in the sky and it is not until the following morning that someone bothers to go out and see what has fallen to Earth. Furthermore, the first Martian cylinder lands in Horsell Common, in the Home County of Surrey. Unlike more recent adaptations where fleets of spaceships hang over the world's capital cities, the aliens appear on the edge of the edge of a suburb thirty miles outside of London—Horsell is on the edge of the suburb of Woking, and Horsell Common is even more remote than that—seeing the effects of such an invasion as being local and almost domestic scale. *The War of the Worlds* is not just about nations and cities, it starts in the home so that all that was once familiar is suddenly unhomely, unheimlich, which is a defining feature of many of the films to be looked at later on in this chapter/study where another world impacts on the domestic space just as much as on the global one.¹⁷ In fact, much of the story affects such small personal spaces, both in terms of familial and marital connections—

16. Curiously with Stoker's novel there is never the suggestion of a vampire apocalypse, even though Dracula suggests the beginnings of a much larger project when he arrives in London. It was not really until after World War II and Richard Matheson's *I Am Legend* (1954) that vampires truly threatened the end of humanity.
17. As an aside, I grew up near Woking and Horsell Common and was always surprised how much my view of the area changed once I read *War of the Worlds*, as though my childhood home had suddenly become exotic and different somehow.

the narrator spends most of the tale trying to return to the domestic space provided by his wife and also spends a significant amount of time confined with a curate in a house in Sheen.

The curate appears out of nowhere, as if conjured up by the invasion, and tags along with the narrator. Where the narrator is depicted as stalwart, rational, manly, and the right material for empire, the curate is nervous to the point of hysteria, embodying the feminization of the British public that could be read as the cause of colonial decline[18]—in this sense the curate acts as a Renfield-figure (from *Dracula*), opening a gateway or point of entry for the alien contagion to take hold. It is not surprising then that when they become trapped in the house in Sheen due to the Martians approaching, the narrator is forced to take extreme action against him. As the Martians begin searching the house, the two men attempt to conceal themselves, but the curate grows increasingly agitated, unable to control himself and endangering them both. Thus, the feminized and hysterical body, as in Renfield's case, becomes an agent of the vampire and facilitates its evil plan, at least in terms of endangering those around him and bringing them to the vampire's attention. The narrator feels he has no option but to silence him, ensuring his own survival, and the survival of the Imperial body, and showing the way forward for the continuance of empire—curiously the 2005 adaptation by Steven Spielberg replaces the curate with a survivalist, as does *10 Cloverfield Lane* (Trachtenberg: 2016),[19] suggesting both are equally selfish and dangerous to the continuation of the "empire" (read American way of life). Wells' *The War of the Worlds* thus sets up a long-lasting correlation in alien vampire stories between saving the empire and protecting the self and the home and envisioning an evolutionary and environmental synergy between all three spheres. Wells further deploys the curate to highlight the delusion of reliance on the Church of England and the wider belief in God in the face of increasing societal conviction around the veracity of Charles Darwin's theory of evolution. Darwin's *On the Origin of Species* was published in 1859 and by the close of the century had gained much traction in the popular imagination (see Burdett: 2014).

Wells' first scientific romance, *The Time Machine* (1895), also took up this evolutionary theme, depicting humanity's evolution (or more precisely, devolution) into two branches of a dystopian future self. *The War of the Worlds* more tacitly implies that the Martians are our distant descendants and that we will inevitably follow in their course, which is a feature often left out of adaptations of the story. *War of the Worlds* culminates in an affirmation of mankind's attachment to the Earth (and the continuing rule of

---

18. Unsurprisingly the curate also criticizes the empire during his many outbursts.
19. Here the Martians are from a different dimension as discussed later in relation to *The Cloverfield Paradox* (Onah: 2018).

empire) that is linked directly to evolutionary factors and the connection to one's "home-world" that is engendered over time—though Wells himself rather disavows religious explanations at the start of the narrative (Wells: 1897, 3).[20] The narrator of *War of the Worlds* further notes after the demise of the Martian invaders that "By the toll of a billion deaths man has bought his birthright of the Earth, and it is his against all comers; it would still be his were the Martians ten times as mighty as they are. For neither do men live nor die in vain" (106). While this assertion strengthens the evolutionary credentials of the narrative, it rather goes against the reality of the colonial experience that inspired Wells to write the tale.

The War of the Worlds was written at a time when it was felt the British Empire was on the wane and that the sun was finally setting on it just as it was on the 19th century. *War of the Worlds* was in the realm of what is considered "invasion literature," works popular toward the end of the 19th century up until World War I in which Western powers imagined invasions by foreign and technologically superior forces (see Wild: 2017, 26). Much of this was predicated on the fear of a weakening of Imperial virility, due to increasing miscegenation and reverse colonialism—a largely xenophobic anxiety over the "purity" (whiteness) of the empire being lost by mixed marriages and communities of immigrants from colonized countries being established in the UK—but also the anxiety over the inherent nature of colonialism itself as a project based on exploiting those weaker than oneself. This last was definitely on Wells' mind when he wrote *War of the Worlds* as it is documented that he knew, through his brother, of the demise of the indigenous people of Tasmania where, before British colonization began in 1803, there were between 3,000 and 15,000 Palawa but within 30 years the native population plummeted to 47.[21] This rather goes against the narrative of the novel as it was the colonialists that brought the deadly diseases, if common ones to them, and not Tasmanian bacteria decimating the British. Although it does intimate a locational/environmental specificity to contagion that sees the colonial imperative as the equivalent

---

20. The Byron Haskin version of *War of the Worlds* from 1953 plays down the evolutionary aspect of the story, as is the wont of many Hollywood films, reasserting the notion that man's (American) superiority is a God given right as seen toward the end of the film where the final act of destruction (blasphemy) by the Martians is to destroy a church while people are seeking sanctuary within it. Directly after this the aliens are struck down by the "plague" of the common cold.

21. Originally this was attributed to disease brought in by the colonizers but since then other commentators have laid the blame with Colonial government, as Matthew Wills notes: "By 1826 there were some 12,600 people of European origin on the island. Their 200,000 sheep threatened to overrun the aboriginal population's hunting grounds. The overwhelmingly male colonialists engaged in wholesale abduction and rape of native women and girls. A brutal war was waged between the invaders and the natives until 1832. Known to Australian history as the 'Black War,' it was the beginning of the end of the original Tasmanian population" (Wills: 2018).

of an epidemic. However, Wells still manages to use this conceit to speak of the fragility of empire, in part by seeing the Martians as a future image of the British Empire and their inevitable disconnection from their "home" and the inherent protection it provides. Consequently, the Martians are used to illustrate the course of empire, whose inevitable downfall is foretold from its inception. As the narrator asserts in the closing pages of *War of the Worlds* "directly these invaders arrived, directly they drank and fed, our microscopic allies began to work their overthrow. Already when I watched them, they were irrevocably doomed, dying and rotting even as they went to and fro. It was inevitable" (106).

In this sense, as soon as the Martians landed on the Earth they were virtually the walking dead, which in part explains their need for blood, but also highlights the vampiric nature of their entire endeavor, and which constitutes the next point of particular note for this volume in the story. Wells never actually mentions the word "vampire" in the story and yet vampire tropes abound—at the start of the 19th century the word "vampire" largely denoted the vampire bat; however, by century's end it had become, as observed by Kevin Dodd, "naturalized" so that it also included psychic vampires that beguiled, seduced, transfused, or scientifically altered the human "life force" (2019, 125). Indeed, there is little about the Martian invaders that cannot be described as vampiric in some way. Most obviously, they need blood to survive. In Wells' story this is not strictly limited to human blood, but human blood is nevertheless their main source of sustenance on Earth. It would appear that on Mars they had evolved into enormous heads, doing away with the time and energy consumed by other bodily functions such as digestion, as the narrator describes: "Entrails they had none. They did not eat, much less digest. Instead, they took the fresh, living blood of other creatures, and injected it into their own veins" (78). Curiously the narrator appreciates the efficiency of such a process, referring to "the tremendous waste of human time and energy occasioned by eating and the digestive process" (78), and oddly almost sympathizes with their position: "The bare idea of this is no doubt horribly repulsive to us, but at the same time I think that we should remember how repulsive our carnivorous habits would seem to an intelligent rabbit" (78), implying that such evolutionary vampirism is a matter of perspective rather than inherently transgressive. One might view it as a kind of apologetics for colonialism, which is of course itself a form of vampirism which sees the enforced consumption of an environment, sucking out its Life blood as it were. This connection between vampirism and colonialism is more explicitly expressed in the 1943 film *Son of Dracula* (Siodmak) where America, "a younger country, stronger and more virile," is about to be "colonized" by unwelcome Europeans in the shape of Count Dracula, who "will fasten on it and drain it dry" (Siodmak: 1943). The wanton exploitation of a land often forms the vampirism of the alien invaders in many of the adaptations discussed below, where the decimation of one species fuels the insatiable "hunger" of the colonial endeavor.

Indeed, the technological augmentations become part of the Martian's body while its identity still remains separate from it—in the same way Dracula remains separate from his shape whether it's wolf, bat, or mist. This vampiric nature informs most of the adaptations of Wells' story seeing various kinds of alien entities/consciousnesses augmented by all manner of cyborg frameworks and attachments. This too is part of the evolutionary construction of the aliens seeing the present-day vampiric aspects of colonialism eventually develop into completely vampiric bodies in the future. A final aspect of *The War of the Worlds* that ties it to late 20th-century alien vampire stories does not appear in Wells' novel but is a component that has become associated with the story since, and that is the reverse invasion of Mars by humans. *War of the Worlds* ends with humanity rebuilding and preparing to defend itself—even if the first attempt was something of a failure—creating a sense of anxiety over the future that is noted by the narrator:

> whether we expect another invasion or not, our views of the human future must be greatly modified by these events. We have learned now that we cannot regard this planet as being fenced in and a secure abiding place for Man; we can never anticipate the unseen good or evil that may come upon us suddenly out of space [112].

While this might be the expected response from an empire on the wane, America still saw itself as "young and virile" and so something of a riposte story by Garrett P. Serviss called *Edison's Conquest of Mars* appeared in 1898—this was actually a sequel to Garrett's *Fighters from Mars* which was an unauthorized version of *War of the Worlds* (it appeared as a serial in *Cosmopolitan* between April and December 1897)—which saw Thomas Edison leading a retaliatory strike on Mars after the earlier attack on the Earth. Interestingly in terms of other texts looked at later, the Martians had previously been on Earth thousands of years previously and built the pyramids and the Sphinx in Giza as well as abducting humans to enslave on their home-world. As the story draws to a close a truce is called between the two worlds and Edison returns home victorious, with the Earth safe once again. Edison accomplishes these feats through superior technology as designed and constructed by a team of scientists he has put together. Suddenly humanity has acquired spaceships, advanced weapons and even a disintegration ray making it as destructive and vampiric as the Martians, and potentially on the cusp of becoming worse than its enemies. In fact, it is as much Serviss' story as it is Wells' that inspires later texts such as *Starship Troopers* (Heinlein, 1959/Vorhoeven: 1997), *Avatar* (Cameron: 2009), and

Predators (Antal: 2010), and *Independence Day: Resurgence* (Emmerich: 2016) and others that reveal alien intervention at the heart of human civilization like *Jupiter Ascending* (The Wachowskis: 2015) and *Prometheus* (Scott: 2012). Wells' story allows for a myriad of adaptations and reinterpretations, and that does not even include those that wear its influence on their proverbial sleeves, with titles such as *War of the Worlds* (Haskins: 1953)—set in America—*War of the Worlds* (Spielberg: 2005)—again set in America—*War of the Worlds* (Latt: 2005)—low budget version followed by a sequel *War of the Worlds 2: The Next Wave* (Howell: 2008), both set in America—and the television series *War of the Worlds* (Strangis: 1988–90)—the Martians, that were killed in 1953 America (connecting to the Haskins version), are reanimated when radiation destroys the bacteria that killed them and they can now take control of humans—*War of the Worlds* (Viveiros: 2019-19)—period remake in London, and *War of the Worlds* (Overman: 2019–present)—a post-apocalyptic tale in the style of *The Walking Dead* again set in London. In an age where ideas around the Anthropocene and human colonialism in general and ecological/environmental responses have come more to the fore, it is not surprising that Wells' tale remains relevant and popular, maybe even more so due to the increasing necessity that humanity might need to leave its "exhausted" home world in search of a "young, virile" new one. The following pairings of films touch on these topics, amongst many others. The first two movies examined below are not obvious adaptations of *War of the Worlds*, but, as will be explained, they are deeply indebted to the genre tropes laid down by it. In these films, there are no invading hordes from outer space but rather a discrete alien advance force looking to change the world forever.

Not of This Earth, Roger Corman, 1957/ *Species*, Roger Donaldson, 1995

Roger Corman's *Not of This Earth* captures the Cold War anxieties of its time, while typifying the rejuvenation of the traditional vampire in the Hammer productions of *Dracula* that began in 1958. The vampire in *Not of This Earth* is itself something of a rejuvenation, but of Wells' greedy Martians, though here it is an alien race that blends almost seamlessly into our own. The aliens, from the planet Davanna, resemble humans in appearance, but they have blank, white eyes, and a very different internal anatomy. Moreover, there is more than a suggestion that this is an assumed form, not unlike the alien vampires from *Invasion of the Body Snatchers* (Siegel, 1956) where pods land on Earth and literally suck the life and identity out of humans in their vicinity, creating a vegetable doppelgänger to replace them. A similar process appears to be at work in *Not of This Earth* as the human copies appear to "eat" directly through their stomachs—one of the later versions shows a big mouth-like orifice just below the chest cavity with large teeth.[22] These vampiric aliens also have acutely sensitive hearing and therefore quickly become disoriented at the sound of police sirens. They can control humans and communicate among themselves telepathically—this last being typical of more conventional vampires. The story follows a single representative from Davanna, Mr. Johnson (Paul Birch), who arrives on Earth to find a cure for a blood disorder that is killing the inhabitants of his home world—it is suggested that the disorder stems from radiation poisoning due to a war on the planet, oddly reminiscent of similar anxieties after World War II here on Earth. Mr. Johnson seems to be quite wealthy and has rented a large house and hired a handyman who doubles as a bodyguard, Jeremy (Jonathan Haze), to look after him. Their relationship echoes Count Dracula buying Carfax Abbey and then hiring an assistant, Renfield, to take care of him—this featured in the stage play of the story which was then closely followed in John Badham's *Dracula* (1979). Mr. Johnson goes to a blood specialist to find a cure for his condition and hire a private nurse, Nadine Storey (Beverley Garland), to administer the blood transfusions he requires. In part it is due to the findings of the specialist, Dr. F.W. Rochelle (William Roerick), that Mr. Johnson discovers that it is human blood that will save his species.

Mr. Johnson relays this information to representatives from his planet through a communications portal in his home and through which objects can also be transported, heightening the impression of two parallel worlds that are not separated by millions of light years of space, but a veil that can be easily penetrated by those with sufficiently advanced technology. Curiously the portal only seems to allow for travel to Earth, but not back to Davanna—any humans they send back die—suggesting that the population of the alien world will need to come to the Earth, inevitably draining it of its vitality. Initially, it seems that Mr. Johnson has come alone to Earth to search out a solution, but soon more aliens arrive, resonating with *The War of the Worlds* where the Martians represent humanity's possible otherworldly future requiring sustenance from an earlier version of themselves.[23] The suggestion that the Davannians follow this pattern and represent an advanced version of humanity is reinforced by the transfusion

---

22. There have been two remakes of the film one by Jim Wynorski (1988) and the other by Terence H. Winkless (1995), each becoming slightly more salacious in its depictions of Mr. Johnson's nurse and his handy man.

23. There is a sense here, and in some of the other narratives mentioned later (*The Day the Earth Stood Still* [Derrickson: 2008] being an obvious example), that the future versions of humanity have returned to a key point in humanoid evolution before humankind irrevocably lost touch with its environment and became an enemy to its own environment.

equipment that they utilize as well as by the "bio-weapon" they use to kill humans that deem to be a threat. Their transfusion equipment consists of a silver briefcase containing a highly advanced version of the human equivalent of pumps, tubes and bottles, which allows the alien to quickly drain the blood from its victims into bottles from which it can transfuse itself—this particular kind of "vampiric" blood collection presages a similar procedure in *Let the Right One In* (Alfredson: 2008) which involves the vampire's assistant collects blood using tubes and bottles. The "bio-weapon" is a curious bat-umbrella-like creature that is energized by the Earth's atmosphere which then causes it to pursue those that threaten the "future humans" plan, enveloping them in its "wings" and killing them[24]—the later versions of the film make more of this kind of bio-technology aligning them to later versions of *The War of the Worlds* such as *Independence Day* (Emmerich, 1996) and *The Recall* (Borelli, 2017).

The alien nature of the bat-like bioweapon—the case it is contained in suggests that it might have been bioengineered to serve as a purpose-built weapon—reinforces the idea that the Davannians, not unlike Wells' Martians, embody some form of evolved humanity, and one that has exploited their home world. Their subsequent journey to the Earth to save themselves further intimates that, as with the Martians, their own world can no longer sustain them.

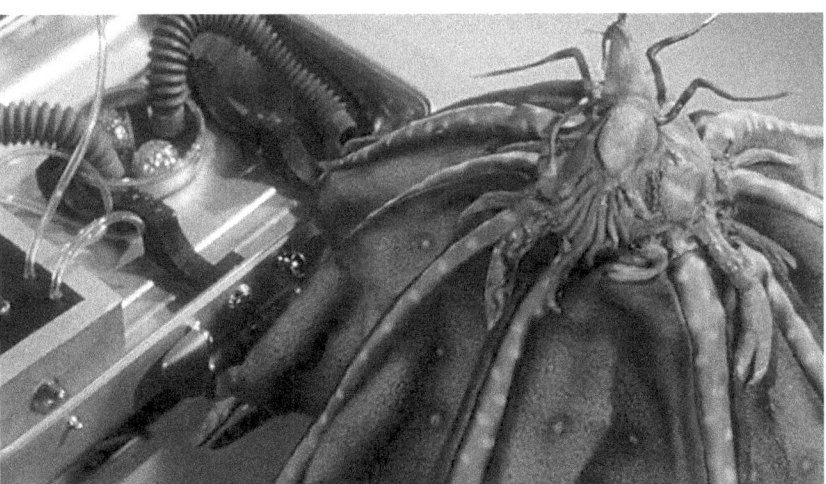

Figure 1. Vampire bioweapons. *Not of This Earth*. Directed by Roger Corman (Allied Artists: 1957).

24. The creatures oddly prefigure the vampiric flying-sea-mantis seen in *Bering Sea Beast* (FauntLeRoy: 2013).

Mr. Johnson's experiments have proved successful and human blood appears to have highly restorative effects on his own system, with results which are reproduced in other aliens on his homeworld. However, it seems that only certain people on Davanna are receiving the supplies and, unsurprisingly, other aliens begin appearing on Earth. The first of these is an unnamed female alien whose appearance resembles a human woman (Anna Lee Carroll), that Mr. Johnson recognizes and enlists her to help in his mission, but when he takes her to get some blood to restore herself, she is mistakenly given some from a rabid dog which has catastrophic effects on her physiognomy and kills her. The film uses this scene to express the otherness of the aliens as well as suggesting the same kind of biological attack on their bodies that Wells' invaders suffered. Indeed, it is the death of his female colleague that arouses the suspicion of the humans around Mr. Johnson, alerting the authorities, who act as the planet's immune system in this instance, and ultimately cause his death in a car crash. This would appear to draw a close to the invasion, and as the film draws to a close the alien's former nurse stands by a headstone with the inscription "Here lies a man who was not of this earth" upon it. As she turns and leaves another suited figure appears wearing sunglasses and carrying a silver suitcase walking toward the grave. The threat from Davanna itself might have passed but the vampires from another world are here and walking amongst us.

What *Not of This Earth* adds to the threat of invasion by alien vampires is their ability to blend in with humanity, thus avoiding the planetary immune system that destroyed Wells' Martians, but also seeing them as covert spies or terrorists of some sort—*Invasion of the Body Snatchers* (Siegel: 1956) achieves the same thing, and like *Not of This Earth* can be seen to express Cold War anxieties around a Soviet invasion of America. The next film also shows an invader from another world, though without Cold War associations, that mixes perfectly with their surroundings, though unlike Mr. Johnson, seems totally unaware of who or what they are.

Species, on the surface at least, seems a very different film from *Not of This Earth*, yet there is much that links them; both films depict an alien life form that assumes a human form during its mission that will lead to it inevitably taking over the Earth; each is also oddly predicated on a similar kind of exploitation and sexual lasciviousness—Corman's *Not of This Earth* uses sex, not just for sensational purposes, but to show how humans are different from the nonsexual aliens while Donaldson's *Species* uses hypersexualization as a marker of monstrosity. However, *Species* has a very different starting point from *Not of This Earth*, positing that the alien invasion is a direct result of humanity's attempts to contact extraterrestrial life. The narrative opens with a SETI (the Search for Extraterrestrial Intelligence) research station receiving two communications from an unknown source in outer space. The first message supplies a formula to produce endless supplies of energy and the second provides instructions on how to splice together human and alien DNA.[25] Despite the spuriousness of the second message, government scientists are convinced this is a good idea given the success of the first message. They combine the DNA with a human ovum with immediate and rapid results with a girl being "born" who develops into the equivalent of a 12-year-old in a matter of months. Concerned by what might happen if she matures into an adult, they decide to terminate the experiment but just as they are about to kill her, the girl breaks out of her containment cell and escapes into the world. She boards a train to Los Angeles and while onboard eats a large amount of sugary food, fueling her metamorphosis into a large gluttonous chrysalis from which a full grown adult female emerges whose sole mission appears to be to get pregnant as quickly as possible.[26] The train journey is framed as an almost Freudian transformation into womanhood with scenes of the young girl greedily scooping chocolate pudding into her mouth, dreamlike images of the train intercut with flashes of mysterious organic/biological transformations, a huge chrysalis with a vagina-like opening (which "eats" the female train guard), and concluding with the birth of a naked, fully grown woman. This extended scene is pivotal in reading the body of the alien, Sil (Natasha Henstridge), both as a vampire and in relation to her as a doorway between worlds.

Sil is certainly not a vampire in what would be considered the "traditional" way—the blood-sucking Dracula-esque variety—but much about her "hunger" and desire is. The scene on the train is the only time we see her in human form actually eat food. Here she has raided the snack bar of the VIP area on the train and taken her illicit bounty back to her private carriage where she consumes all of it before becoming a huge chrysalis hanging from the ceiling in the compartment.[27] After this point Sil does not eat food but becomes far more vampiric in her needs. A female guard enters the carriage and before she can do anything a large tendril/tongue-like appendage shoots out of the vagina-like opening in the chrysalis/birthing sac and grabs the woman pulling her toward it. We next see the guard dead on the floor after Sil has been "born," intimating that the human has helped power her emergence into the world. There is an inference that the energy supplied by the guard could be on two parts; blood is certainly involved

---

25. The slightly later film *Contact* (Zemeckis: 1997) uses a similar idea of aliens sending information to a Earth to facilitate contact of some kind.
26. The film very much plays on ideas of female containment and control and the monstrosity of unrestrained feminine sexuality.
27. For possible sexual interpretations of children and gorging food see Daniel: 2006.

though not in large amounts and there is an emotional element involved as well. The pod is "awakened" by the extreme response of the guard upon seeing it in the carriage and when she is "swallowed" by it there is a sudden cut-shot to a scene suggesting the alien life form inside her with a close up shot of alien limbs moving showing some form of inner transformation. In fact, this is repeated a few times in the film and often when Sil has killed someone; a man in a bathroom whom she kisses and thrusts her tongue through his head[28]; a man she tries to mate with in a swimming pool but is interrupted and so thrusts her tongue down his throat; and when she finally mates she kills the man as soon as she realizes she is impregnated. Each time the scene cuts to the alien entity inside of her—it is never clear whether this is physical reality or purely psychological or a combination of both—it is as though it has suddenly been energized by something such as the excess emotional or sexual energies or even the extreme fear expressed by Sil's victims. Indeed, the narratives use of an empath, Dan Smithson (Forest Whitaker), to track the alien reinforces the idea that strong emotional energies are at play here. Smithson's almost violent responses to Sil's proximity infers that she has a strong connection to psychic and/or emotional energy casting her as an energy vampire of some kind[29]—aliens as energy vampires is not an uncommon trope seen in films such as *It: The Terror from Outerspace*, *Lifeforce*, and *Dark City*—and while in her human form she seems driven by the need for semen, the alien vampire within her actually survives via feeding off human emotional energy.[30]

Another aspect of interest in the film is the idea of Sil as a doorway between worlds. It is not made explicit in the film, but there is much to suggest that this is the case. The start of the film shows that Sil is born of a combination of human and alien DNA creating some kind of hybrid, except she is not really a mixture of two creatures but rather an interface between human and alien worlds. Not unlike the Martians in Wells' story that use machines to live in the human world, the alien entity uses the human body of Sil to exist on Earth. However, as she grows older this becomes increasingly unacceptable to the entity that now wants to exist in the human world as itself, and feed directly from human emotions. This constructs Sil's skin, her exterior surface, as a door between the reptilian, alien environment we are shown in the cut-shots and the human world that Sil exists in—this

28. This one is interesting as she had intended to mate with the man but sensed he was chronically ill, he was diabetic, so did not want to imbibe his semen, oddly resonating with the contaminated blood scene from *Not of This Earth*.
29. There is much crossover here between energy vampires and the figures of the incubus (male) and succubus (female) that also feed upon human energies, often during sleep.
30. There are actually non-hardcore porn vampire films that use this idea of feeding on semen, a version of Jess Franco's *Female Vampire* (1973) features this as well as *Siren X* (Jôjô: 2008).

also explains why the space in which the alien sequences exist appears so immense, as it is an environment beyond time and space, at least as humans know it. This further explains the curious deformed shapes and protuberances that appear in Sil's skin, first seen when she was a child while having nightmares but increasingly more pronounced when she kills people and feeds off their emotional energy. As the psychic energy empowers the alien world within it projects Sil's true form into the human world so that by the time she has been impregnated she can completely exist as her alien self in the human environment. Unsurprisingly, once she is established in her real vampiric form, she shuns the daylight and goes underground into the sewers (the preferred home of many vampire hybrids as seen in *Blade II* [del Toro: 2002] and *Underworld* [Wiseman: 2003]). Now that the divide between the worlds has fallen, Sil gives birth to a child that appears superficially human but quickly begins to transform into its true alien appearance with spikes coming out of its skull and spine, long spider-like limbs and a large tongue that it uses to kill prey—we see it use its tongue to kill and eat a rat. However, as with Corman's film although the human world rallies against the outside invaders and conspires to kill them the door is never totally slammed shut at film's end. As the closing credits finish, the movie resumes and we see a rat consuming a piece of alien flesh left behind and the rodent begins to mutate, intimating the doorway between worlds is still open—a point that is strongly reinforced by the subsequent three sequels.[31]

Alien/human hybridity is an increasingly common feature of many reworkings of Wells' story, seeing the introduction of the kind of miscegenation that formed a central anxiety in *Dracula*. While *Species* begins a move toward that, the next pairing explores that idea a little more positively and reveals it as a way of humanity achieving forms of resistance and agency against the vampires from another world.

Skyline, The Brothers Strause, 2010/ *Edge of Tomorrow*, Doug Liman, 2014

Skyline is more closely based on *The War of the Worlds*, as it is premised on a mass alien invasion of Earth with now familiar scenes of huge spaceships hovering over the planet's capital cities ready to launch a coordinated and crushing attack on the human population below. The alien technology is vastly superior to humanity's and the film also deploys the trope of aliens in the shape of massive brains supported by mechanical exoskeletons

---

31. *Species II* (Medan: 1998), *Species III* (Turner: 2004), and *Species: The Awakening* (Lyon: 2007).

that enable movement between various kinds of machines. Indeed, it would appear that the "brains" would be unable to exist in any environment without the support of technology constructing a very cyborg orientated version of posthumanism where life revolves around organic consciousness and little else—though in this version the notion of individuality seems to be redundant as all the machines are guided by a central, controlling influence located in the Mothership (the King Vampire controlling its minions). The benefit of this is that the aliens are able to live anywhere as there is always a barrier between themselves and whatever environment they find themselves in. As we later discover, human brains seem perfectly suited to integration into these exoskeletons, suggesting that the invaders were once humanoids and represent a possible evolutionary path for humanity, much like Wells' Martians.

Skyline follows a young couple, Jarrod (Eric Balfour) and Elaine (Scottie Thompson), traveling to Los Angeles to visit their childhood friend Terry (Donald Faison) who is doing extremely well for himself working for a special effects company. Terry tries to persuade Jarrod to move to Los Angeles and work with him, a proposition that introduces opposing worlds well before the aliens arrive on the scene. The film opens with Jarrod and Elaine in New York, which is depicted less as a bustling metropolis and more as a couple's home, permeated by an atmosphere of security and homeliness. Jarrod and Elaine live in a smallish, cozy New York apartment that serves as a visual contrast with Los Angeles, which is represented as money-orientated, "fake" and ostentatious. Furthermore, while visiting Terry, Elaine discovers that she is pregnant, upon which she yearns for home in order to raise their child in "safety." The superficiality of Los Angeles is exposed in their visit to Terry's opulent home in a penthouse, surrounded by hangers-on, and he seems to be having an affair with his assistant, Denise (Crystal Reed), while his marriage to his wife Candice (Brittany Daniel) appears to be unraveling. Indeed, Terry seems brainwashed by his new life in the entertainment industry, quite literally losing his mind to it, cutting a poor figure in comparison to the person he was when he knew Jarrod back in New York. The film thus depicts Jarrod as caught between worlds, his old secure life and family and a new one of adventure and pleasure. It is unsurprising then that it is at this moment that the aliens attack, literalizing the theme of an entertainment culture that threatens the sanity of its workers as creatures that literally seek to steal the minds of their victims—the film sets up a clear correlation between the mind stealing of L.A. and that of the alien invaders.

In the early hours of the morning after celebrating Terry's birthday, Elaine and Jarrod wake up to noises outside, and on closer inspection they see the sky ablaze with falling blue lights. They go up onto the roof to take stock of their surroundings and see people being lifted into the sky by an alien craft. Jarrod becomes transfixed by the lights which seem to cause dark blue veins to radiate from his eyes and across his body. Elaine drags him away from the lights, but it is clearly a painful process, though once clear of its influence the veins begin to subside. They begin to realize that the lights coming from the alien craft act as a form of glamoring (vampire mind control) causing those caught in its glare to become infected with a contagion that makes them subservient to the alien vampires who then harvest them with the aid of the many drones that fly over the city. This marks a curious reversal of conventional vampire tropes, as it is the humans who hide in the shadows to protect themselves from daylight so that they are safe from the contagious gaze of the space vampires.

In *Skyline*, rather than requiring blood, the extraterrestrial invaders require human brains. These brains are not required as sustenance but as "pilots" for the worker clones on the main spacecraft. However, the brains are "infected" or processed in such a way that they become part of the alien community, not unlike Dracula's victims who become part of his "body" once infected with his blood.[32] The aliens also farm humans on their spacecraft though in *Skyline* this is a little more specialized in that they only collect pregnant women to put through this procedure so that they can collect the babies' brains once they are born.

Like nearly all the previous adaptations of Wells' *The War of the Worlds*, human technology and military might prove unavailing when faced with the superior capabilities of the invaders from outer space and the aliens appear unstoppable. *Independence Day* (Emmerich: 1996) bucks this trend by showing human technology, in the form of a computer virus, being superior to that of the aliens and it is not the Earth's natural defenses but man's intelligence that saves the world.

At the conclusion of *Skyline*, Jarrod and Elaine are captured by the aliens. Elaine awakens to find herself in a dark chamber covered in gooey slime. Large tentacles are extracting the brains from the people around her and sliding them through tubes into another part of the craft, with the bodies of the dead dropped into a large pool of fluid below—potentially a protein soup that fuels the aliens not unlike that seen in *The Matrix* (The Wachowskis: 1999). One of the tentacles grabs Elaine but quickly realizes she is pregnant and so releases her, allowing another tube to suck her up and expel her into a room full of other pregnant women. Meanwhile, Jarrod's brain has been carried through tubes to a room where it is inserted into a newly made clone. Most of the brains here glow with a blue/green

---

32. There is also much correlation here with the Borg in the *Star Trek* Universe that effectively "reprogrammed" their victims to become part of the collective body of the species.

light which ignites the "eyes" of their respective clones with a similar hue. However, Jarrod's brain is reddish-orange and when it is placed in a body it convulses violently as the human consciousness seems to violently override the vestiges of alien intelligence within it. The scene cuts back to Elaine, where she scans the room, watching the pregnant women as they are prodded by tentacles assessing when they might be able to remove the baby and process its mother. Upon hearing her voice, the Jarrod-Clone enters the room and fights off the tentacles around Elaine, and as he touches her stomach, she realizes it is the father of her child. Jarrod-Clone hoists her in his arms, fighting off more of the tentacles and then running off into the depths of the craft as the film ends.

In a twist to *Independence Day* then, the virus here is human love which is configured as an almost parasitic life-form in its own right that hybridizes and resists the homogenizing effects of the hive mind of the aliens—there is much to be said elsewhere about the promotion of heteronormativity and the idealized "American Family" in relation to the inherent "queerness" of the alien invaders. Interestingly, this alien/vampire-human hybridity is more in line with the hybrid human/vampires in Richard Matheson's *I Am Legend,* where the new "species" that will take over the Earth once the remaining humans and vampires are dead. *Skyline,* however, conveniently stops before having to resolve this development and uses it only to signal the imminent demise of the invaders.[33] The *Edge of Tomorrow* seems a very different film but it also uses the idea of human-alien hybridity as a weapon to stop the successful invasion of the Earth by vampiric aliens.

Edge of Tomorrow begins mid-alien invasion, but unlike many other alien invasion narratives that follow in the tradition of *War of the Worlds,* the sky is not full of extraterrestrial spacecraft as the invaders arrived via a large asteroid that landed in mainland Europe. In fact, the invaders seem to possess little by way of technology and represent a biologically, or organically, advanced species that has evolved to overrun any planet on which they land. As with the aliens in *Skyline,* they appear to organize themselves on the insect hive mind principle with a central master-alien that directs the rest—in this respect, the film clearly owes a debt to *Starship Troopers* (Verhoeven, 1997), an adaptation of Robert A. Heinlein's 1959 novel of the same name—though unlike the earlier films, here they seem to have no relation to a vision of human evolution but rather reflect the fragility of our position within the wider universe (a point at the center of Wells' novel).

33. There has since been a sequel released, *Beyond Skyline* (O'Donnell, 2017) which shows a similar story occurring, seemingly, simultaneously with that seen in the first film, with an L.A. detective (Frank Grillo) similarly trying to find and release his son from an alien ship with a similar ending of more widespread revolution inspired by red-eyed alien clones.

Edge of Tomorrow[34] opens with an exposition that recounts the irresistible spread of the aliens, called Mimics, across mainland Europe, all but one stand-out defeat at Verdun in France, largely due to the exploits of one Sgt. Rita Vrataski (Emily Blunt) who is subsequently named the "Angel of Verdun." This has given the combined forces of Europe and America enough confidence to launch an all-out surprise attack on the French coast to regain a foothold in mainland Europe and begin an assault to destroy the Mimics.[35] In a curious contrast to Wells' story, it is the Earthlings who have superior technology in the form of mechanized battle "jackets" that form a kind of weaponized exoskeleton around the wearer so that even untrained soldiers are deadly in action. Much of the early part of the alien invasion was shown as a series of news clips, in part relaying it as a conflict taking place on television rather than in actuality—in fact Jean Baudrillard's idea of Simulacra in relation to modern warfare finds much ground in this film (See Baudrillard: 1981 and 1991) with the continual cutting and reworking of the same material sees the narrative appear to be an ongoing editing process to produce the final "news story" at the film's end—and one of the prominent talking-heads in the program clips belongs to Major William Cage (Tom Cruise) acting as the main spokesperson and PR specialist for the military resistance. However, when called upon to actually take part in the French landings as a field reporter, Cage panics and ends up court martialed and sojourned to a ragtag unit that is part of the invasion squad.

Sometime later Cage is loaded onto an invasion plane and flown over France with the rest of the troops, only to discover that the Mimics are prepared and waiting for them. As the carnage unfolds Cage sees his squad killed and even Vrataski falling to the never-ending wave of Mimics on the beach. Cage finds himself in a blast hole as a particularly large Mimic emerges from the sand. He reaches for an explosive device abandoned in the sand near him and pulls it to his chest just as the alien turns and attacks him. The explosion is directed straight at the alien and covers Cage in a gush of bright blue blood that seems to burn and dissolve his skin.[36] He suddenly wakes up to find himself perfectly well again but on the pile of kit bags where he woke the previous day, and the events of the day unfold once again in the exact same order. Back on the beach again, Cage tries to do things differently to survive but fails and each time wakes up again on the pile of kit bags until in one re-run of events he has the chance to talk to Vrataski. She tells him to find her next time he wakes up, which he does,

34. The story is based on the Japanese light novel (intended for high-school students) *All You Need Is Kill* (2004) by Hiroshi Sakurazaka.
35. There is much in the story that correlates to World War I and World War II through various locations used from the beach landings to the use of war rooms in Whitehall.
36. The Mimic drones bear some similarity to the "sentinels" in *The Matrix* (The Wachowski's, 1999) that are part insect, part octopus, but all mechanical.

and discovers that the same thing happened to her, and that that was how she survived Verdun. She takes him to meet Dr. Carter (Noah Taylor), a discredited researcher who is a mechanic on the base, who explains his theory about the Mimics. He believes that there are three types of Mimics, the drones, the Alphas and one Omega; the Omega controls all the others but when an Alpha is killed it triggers the master Mimic to cycle back time so that the creatures can adapt and ultimately win every battle they take part in. When Cage killed the Alpha its blood infected him so that he too is now considered an Alpha and so when he dies a time loop is created—Vrataski had the same advantage until she got wounded and was given a blood transfusion which cured the infection passed on to her by the Alpha. Dr. Carter further explains that the Alpha blood creates a unique connection between Cage and the Omega which will eventually allow him to see where the creature is allowing them to find and kill it. There is, of course, a strong resonance with *Groundhog Day* (Ramis: 1993) and indeed the male protagonists from each film need to go through a process of self-improvement to escape the never-ending time loop they seem trapped in.

The vampiric nature of the Mimics is revealed in this premise. They do not seem to require blood or human flesh as a source of sustenance as Wells' Martians did—it is never made clear exactly what they eat—but they do seem to exhibit many other vampire tropes, particularly those of Count Dracula. The Omega, who is effectively the King Vampire, is connected to all its "creations" as is Dracula; consuming the vampire's blood, which Cage and Vrataski have done, via the Alpha, turns them into a vampire as well, or rather a vampire-human hybrid as were Lucy and Mina in Stoker's novel; this then directly connects the vampire-human hybrid to the master which allows for a psychic connection between the two, which recalls the connection between Mina and Dracula where she can see where he is as he speeds back to Transylvania at the end of the story. Finally, as in Stoker's story, blood transfusions provide the only restorative to the vampiric infection, seeing both Cage and Vrataski "cured" once they are given such a treatment.

Cage has a vision of where the Omega is hidden and he and Vrataski enlist the help of his squad to kill it. Just after the vision, Cage undergoes a transfusion and is therefore no longer in a time-loop and can die as easily as anyone else. He proceeds with the mission nevertheless.[37] The military team—a rather ragtag version of Stoker's Crew of Light—travel to a now ruined Paris and to the Louvre Museum where the Omega is hiding in its flooded underground basement—there is a sense here that as a repository

---

37. In a curious way Cage's personal narrative in the story is very similar that of Phil Connors (Bill Murray) in the seminal time loop story *Groundhog Day* (Ramis, 1993) who starts in the story as a self-centered obnoxious character who is only allowed to leave the eternally repeating day once he has learned to care about others than himself.

of European, Imperial history the Omega represents the curse of human history repeating itself until we learn from it, as Cage seemingly has done.

Cage manages to dive into the water filled chambers and drop a large number of explosives downward toward the King Vampire. As the charges explode, killing the creature, Cage can no longer hold his breath and is on the point of dying, but the blood of the alien smothers his body as he drifts in the water. Outside, all the Mimics die as they are no longer energized by their connection to their Master, not unlike some vampire narratives where the bloodline dies when their sire is destroyed (*The Originals* [Plec, 2013–18] makes much of this genre trope), and the war is declared over before the planned beach invasion has even begun. Cage wakes up in a helicopter, the same as he did before being court martialed and sent to take part in the invasion. However, this time the war is actually over. No one knows exactly what has happened but a power surge in Paris seems to have signaled the total demise of the invaders. Still a Major, Cage goes to the training camp to see Vrataski, who obviously has no recollection of what happened or even who Cage is. It would appear that the blood of the Omega has similar effects to that of the Alphas, being able to reverse time in some measure, but why Cage went back to that moment which was considerably before the previous starting point of his time loop is never explained. It does, though, suggest that he possesses even more profound powers than before and is still some kind of human-vampire/alien hybrid—oddly it is never suggested that this might allow him to control Mimics himself though it would seem a natural extension of his new powers. Consequently, as the movie ends the

Figure 2. Cage (Tom Cruise) swimming towards the alien Vampire King. *Edge of Tomorrow*, directed by Doug Liman (Warner Bros.: 2014).

invasion of the Mimics might have been repelled, but their undead presence is still there, a doorway to another world that is tantalizingly still ajar. The next pairing continues this idea of human-vampire hybrids but more closely follows Garrett Serviss' plot of a reverse invasion perpetrated by the humans causing the alien world's immune system to react accordingly.

Avatar, James Cameron, 2009/*Ghosts of Mars*, John Carpenter, 2001

James Cameron's *Avatar* reverses the plot of *The War of the Worlds* in the sense that it is the Earthlings who are greedily eyeing other worlds in order to harvest their natural resources, albeit these resources are minerals rather than blood. The film is set in an specified far future in which human technology has rapidly developed, furnishing humanity with spacecrafts that can travel huge distances across space and machines that can clone alien bodies and transfer human consciousnesses into them (though the film presents this process more as a neural link between the bodies of the human and the genetically engineered host). The world that humanity has been eyeing greedily is Pandora, a moon of a larger world that is 4.3 light years away from Earth and which contains rich sources of "unobtainium," a highly valuable mineral that would solve humanity's energy problems. The indigenous inhabitants of Pandora have no use for technology and enjoy a more symbiotic relationship with their environment with few needs other than their daily sustenance. Indeed, it is a rather idyllic, utopian (ectopian) view of an ecosystem at balance, which is disrupted by the arrival of the aliens, now human Earthlings rather than Martians but with much the same aspirations toward conquest and pillaging. Not unlike the Martians in *The War of the Worlds*, the all-too-human invaders require exoskeletons to protect them from the atmosphere. Indeed, Pandora's atmosphere is not breathable for humans, who therefore require an artificial source of oxygen in order to survive upon it, from oxygen masks to full robotic suits and insulated crafts of various kinds. While the humans construct these augmentations as a form of technological (evolutionary) superiority, they actually distance humanity even further from the planet's ecosystem, a distancing that is reinforced throughout the film and is articulated by the head of humanity's military operations in Pandora, Colonel Quaritch (Stephen Lang) who states that "Out there beyond that fence every living thing that crawls, flies, or squats in the mud wants to kill you and eat your eyes for jujubes" (Cameron, 2009).

The invasion is overseen by the Resources Development Administration (RDA) which seems to act as something of an East India Company for Earth's expansion into space—the East India Company being cited as the first Multinational Corporation that exploited trade in East, Southeast Asia, and India at the behest of the British Crown.[38] Their operations on the planet seem to be divided into three parts: the mining operation, a research department, and military security and enforcement, with the last seeming to have the most sway in the early, unsuccessful, interactions with Pandora's indigenous people, the Na'vi. In contrast, the research department, led by Dr. Grace Augustine (Sigourney Weaver),[39] has been trying to interact with the Na'vi in order to learn more about their culture and better understand their connection to the planet, ostensibly to allow for easier extraction of the unobtainium. To this end, the research department has developed a process of growing a cloned body (Avatar) made of a combination of Na'vi and human DNA, which allows for a neural connection to be established between the avatar and a human being whose genetic material was used in the cloning procedure. The human remains in stasis while their consciousness is uploaded into the avatar so that it can move, talk, and interact with the Na'vi. Yet the head of the RDA on Pandora, Parker Selfridge (Giovanni Ribisi), is dissatisfied with the pace of this process and therefore begins more invasive operations.

The protagonist of the film is Jake Sully (Sam Worthington), the paraplegic brother of a member of the research team who died on duty. Sully is invited to become part of the Avatar program. Although Quaritch tries to co-opt him as an informer for the military, he quickly becomes enamored with the Na'vi and their lifestyle and fights to save them from the human invaders—as part of the human community he will only ever be seen as a cripple, whereas with the Na'vi he is literally, because of his Avatar, whole again. Part of the Na'vi's appeal, for Sully, derives from their connection to the ecosystem and the energy forces of the planet—Cameron's film is very aware of the ecological issues at play here—and which is primarily depicted through the biological "connectors" they have that protrude from their heads and join them to a variety of fauna. These connectors take the form of a kind of pony-tail, or "queues," which the Na'vi can "connect" to similar appendages on bird-like and horse-like animals, allowing them to be "as one" with them. This creates an ecological/biological equivalent to human technology that forms a larger connection to a complete ecotopian society, which equates transcendental spirituality with environmental balance, along with problematic inferences toward Native American and other Indigenous people's relationship to their "homelands." The set-up

---

38. For more detail on the East India Company as the first global corporation see Ruggari: 2016.
39. The presence of Sigourney Weaver in the film rather strengthens the idea that the RDA is a similar outfit to The Weyland Corporation from the *Alien* franchise, suggesting that they too have nefarious plans afoot.

culminates in the revelation that the ecosystem is fueled by an organic jouissance that emanates from the 1,000-foot-tall "Home Tree." It is hardly surprising that beneath the tree is a large deposit of unobtainium and one which RDA are desperate to obtain. Although Sully claims he can persuade the "tribe" that he has joined to leave the site of the tree peacefully, the military under the leadership of Quaritch attack and destroy the tree, killing many of the Na'vi around it in the process.

The destruction of the tree marks a cathartic moment in *Avatar*, not unlike the destruction of the church in Haskin's film adaptation of *The War of the Worlds*. did, and which sees the ecological "god" of Pandora rise up against the invaders. This is not immediate, but it marks a distinct turn toward the narrative's conclusion. Sully is expelled from the Na'vi tribe that had sheltered him because of his involvement in the attack. Spurred by a desire to redeem himself, he then endeavors to fulfill the Na'vi prophecy of "Toruk Mato" (Rider of the Last Shadow), whereby a warrior able to ride the toruk—the largest predatory bird/flying reptile on Pandora—will unite the five tribes of the planet. *Avatar* thus differs from *The War of the Worlds* and many of its adaptations insofar as, rather than trying to develop weapons/technology comparable to that of the alien invaders, the indigenous people explicitly turn toward their past and the bond they have forged with their home world—this is above and beyond the rather spurious "white savior" angle that Cameron inserts into the plot that sees the people of color (in this case blue) being saved by the white man's (Sully's) self-sacrifice.[40] It also highlights the differing ways in which a planet's resources, mineral or otherwise, can be "mined" by those that live there. The Na'vi directly appeal to their ecosystem's defense systems, Eywa, to assist them in their efforts—Sully notes that humans killed their own Earth "mother"—so that in the final battle it is not just bacteria coming to the rescue, as in *War of the Worlds*, but the entire planet. This also contrasts with Wells' and Haskins' tales where humanity becomes increasingly divided in their panic—Haskins' adaptation in particular features a scene where scientists, who have developed a possible solution to the invaders, are swept away in a wave of panicking townspeople.

While the Na'vi are metaphorically and literally linked to their environment, via their queues, the humans are completely separate from it, blinded by their greed and overwhelming desire to "consume" the world around them. This separation reinforces the vampirism of the human

---

40. *I Am Legend* adaptations are particular prone to this with the central figure, Robert Neville, working to save humanity with his own blood. *The Omega Man* (Sagal: 1973) with Charlton Heston in the lead role is portrayed as an almost Christ-like figure as he dies, pierced by a spear with arms spread as if crucified. Aptly, or ironically, the Francis Lawrence version from 2005 sees Will Smith as Neville, similarly giving his blood to save humanity.

invaders, both as cyborgs with the cyborg/robotic augmentations they use to "protect" themselves from the world around them and in their insatiable desire to "suck" Pandora dry of its life blood/organic jouissance. When Quaritch and Selfridge realize the Na'vi are amassing they launch an all-out attack, intent on destroying the Tree of Souls, the last point of direct contact between the Na'vi and Eywa. Expressing the violent and deadly nature of consumerism (total consumerism) that views possession and profit as its only goals.

The battle begins in the air with military craft closing in on the Tree of Souls but Sully, finding his toruk, manages to derail the aerial assault, forcing the conflict to continue on the ground. On the ground, the ecosystem become more fully involved, with nearly all the species of predatory fauna on the planet attacking the human invaders. The denouement comes in the fight to the death between Sully and Quaritch with the military man defeated once he is finally exposed to the environment—he begins the fight in an aircraft, then in a robotic exoskeleton, and finally wears only breathing apparatus which makes him increasing vulnerable to the ecosystem of Pandora. At the end of the battle, the humans are not all killed but only exiled from the planet, suggesting that they might try and exploit other worlds. The RDA researchers, however, are allowed to stay, and Sully, with the aid of Eywa, has his consciousness permanently transferred to his Na'vi avatar so that he can fully integrate into Pandora's ecosystem. This creates a conclusion that is at once neatly resolved and more complicated and open-ended than first appears, with the story wrapped in a rather obvious eco-message around embracing the environment, whereas the deeper themes posit a non-resolvable antipathy between consumerism and ecology, demanding the mutual exclusion of the two; humanity is deadly to the universe and can only exist as disembodied consciousness, not unlike in *The Host* mentioned above. Even hybridity offers no resolution as it only allows for greater integration into the world one has already chosen, but it does nothing to bring the two worlds closer together. This situation becomes even more extreme in *Ghosts of Mars*.

Not unlike *Avatar*, Carpenter's *Ghosts of Mars* is also premised on humanity's journey to another planet, albeit one much closer to home than Pandora, with the purpose of both colonizing it and mining it for minerals. Indeed, at the beginning of the film, *Ghosts of Mars* seems more in keeping with Serviss' idea of galactic colonialism, reversing Wells' fears of a Martian invasion. In the film, set in the year 2176, 84 percent of Mars has been terraformed and it now has an Earth-like atmosphere with 640,000 colonists living there. The planet is governed by Earth Law, enforced by the Mars Police, and it is a Matriarchal society—this last is an interesting point that will be returned to later. As with the RDA in Cameron's film, Mars is governed by a high-tech aggregate processing company who have set up mining communities across the planet to take advantage of any mineral deposits they might find. And it is these explorations that activate the planet's natural defenses, though unlike Pandora, Mars is no lush ecotopia but a dried-out dust bowl. Those familiar with the *Alien* franchise would find much that is familiar in the opening scenes of the film and indeed it is quickly confirmed when cut-shots of news reports declare that parts of the planet have been blacked out to radio contact under mysterious circumstances. Lieutenant Melanie Ballard (Natasha Henstridge) is sent with her team to collect a prisoner, Desolation Williams (Ice Cube), from a mining community with which the company has lost contact. Once there she finds the town deserted except for those locked up in the local jail. Unsurprisingly, things begin to quickly go wrong and dismembered bodies are found and humans begin to turn into mindless savages. Ballard discovers that one of the men in the jail is not a prisoner but rather hiding out from the carnage occurring outside. On questioning she discovers that the stranger is called Whitlock (Joanna Cassidy) who was in charge of a mining project when they came across a buried chamber/doorway that was obviously constructed by one of the ancient civilizations from Mars—the planet appears to have no surviving indigenous lifeforms upon it at the moment. Whitlock tried to find some kind of lock or handle on the uncovered doorway but as she touched it, it disintegrated, releasing some kind of red smoke that swirled into the excavation and out into the world infecting all those it came into contact with.

It seems that Whitlock has unwittingly opened some kind of Pandora's box left behind by the last civilization on Mars, which now turns all those it touches into psychopathic lunatics. The red dust released from the cave seems to be some kind of spiritual, ghostly entity (hence the film's title *Ghosts of Mars*) and the film never reveals whether it is a trap left by the last inhabitants of the planet (as often appears in *The Mummy* films), the essence of the last inhabitants themselves (suggesting that the uncontrollable cannibalistic nature of those infected was the very reason the last population died out), or some kind of essence of Mars itself which has a similar effect on all organic life forms—an eco-immune not unlike that seen in *Avatar*. There is something here in line with Tanith Lee's *Sabella, or, The Bloodstone* (1980) where a young girl living on Nova Mars, a colony of Earth, becomes "infected" by the spirit of the indigenous population that used to live there but died out, becoming increasing sexualized and vampiric.

Lee's story is meant more as a feminist coming of age tale, but it shares something of the same impetus as *Ghosts of Mars*; there is a strong sense of a past race being reborn through the symbiotic connection between an environment and its inhabitants across the ages. Unlike the bacteria in *War of the Worlds*, the dust does not kill all the invaders but infects them with its spirit, producing a kind of hybridity that "kills" the new arrivals while resuscitating/resurrecting the former inhabitants—this creates the idea of a kind of undead indigeniety, a traumatic memory of the passing of the past people's that can never die. While Nova Mars in Lee's story is not depicted as any less patriarchal than Earth, the rise of female agency finds form in Carpenters's film with the designation of the planet at the start of the film as being Matriarchal in nature and the release of the "Ghosts" coming from the underground womb-like cave that is explicitly referred to as Pandora's box in the film. Both Lee and Carpenter see the forces released as vampiric, expressing a biological jouissance that is centered on blood; in *Ghosts of Mars* this sees human bodies literally deconstructed (dismembered) as an expression of the return of the old Martian bodies. This return of the repressed is further emphasized by the heavy mutilation and piercings that accompanies the change from human to Martian in the film. The newly released ghosts are thus an undead memory, or essence of, the former people, rather than a biological trap/weapon, and which also resonates with *Avatar*, as does the sense of planetary feminine agency.

Cameron's film is set on Pandora, and while this goes against the idea of it being a "box" that is opened, the awakening and release of a planetary defense system suggests otherwise. Indeed, the feminization of the Na'vi—the main protagonist we see is Neytiri, and the spiritual leader is Mo'at (CCH Pounder)—and of the planet itself, Eywa is identified as the "All-Mother" who takes into herself the "souls" of all the dead. Consequently, the power released upon the "opening" of Pandora's box is one which is directed specifically at "mankind" (corporate humanity), and which recurs in *Ghosts of Mars*. Although the planet is designated matriarchal, penetrative mining operations and colonial exploitation are historically more patriarchal endeavors. In each film the "box" is opened by a feminine body, much like Pandora's box; in *Ghosts of Mars* it is Whitlock, and in *Avatar* it is Sully, who is constructed as feminine (disabled, helpless and emotional) in contrast to the hypermasculinity of Quaritch (muscled, scarred, and physically threatening). This sees the indigenous peoples as a kind of feminized undead memory that, through the spilling of transgressive blood (which can equally be correlated to menstrual blood) resists and dispels the patriarchal (corporate) invaders that have come to exploit and "rape" the environment.

The indigenous people in *Avatar* and *Ghosts of Mars* are both constructed to resemble Native American cultures and societies in ways that are not unproblematic. In *Avatar* the resemblances are obvious, as the Na'vi are portrayed with social structures similar to those of certain Native American societies, their daily lives built around hunting and horse-riding and greater respect for the animals they kill to eat and the environment in general, and often centered around spiritual leaders such as Shaman. *Ghosts of Mars* relates to more cinematic depictions of Native Americans from the Western genre that stereotype various forms of body decoration and savagery seeing it as something of an ironic take on White American expansionism where the Martians turn the colonists into part of the indigenous population, a point made further by the white face paint worn by many of the reincarnated Martians.[41]

In *The Ghosts of Mars*, the workers from a nearby mining facility have all been transformed into reincarnated Martians who have stormed the nearest town, killing all its inhabitants. As Ballard and her team discover, when the infected are killed, the red dust, or ghost, leaves the dead body and tries to find a new host. Carpenter's use of the camera as embodying the cloud of mist makes it explicit that the dust forms the mind/essence of a single entity. The undead memories/identities of the former species are thus virtually immortal, a point further emphasized at the film's end. Ballard and Williams manage to escape on a freight train going back to the main city, but not before planting and setting off a nuclear device at the mining facility to destroy all the reincarnated Martians. As he is still a wanted criminal, Williams escapes, leaving Ballard on the train by herself. Once back in the city, an inquiry is held to discover what occurred on the base and once her testimony is over, Ballard goes back to her room to sleep, but is rudely awoken by noises outside. Suddenly Williams bursts into her room fully armed, declaring that the Martians are still alive and have invaded the city, suggesting that for all their bravado, the planet will not allow any humans to survive upon it. If these two films highlighted the idea of indigeneity and its symbiotic relationship to an environment, the last pairing in this chapter begins to question the very nature of this relationship, and subsequently the commodification of humanity itself.

Prometheus, Ridley Scott, 2012/*Jupiter Ascending*, The Wachowskis, 2015

The *Alien* series of films is not obviously connected to *War of the Worlds* or even vampires but *Prometheus*, which forms a prequel to the *Alien* films, has much about it to link it to Wells's paradigms of alien invasion and colonialism.

The film is set in the not too distant future of 2089 and follows

---

41. *The Omega Man* plays on a similar idea in relation to the African American community where all those turned into vampires have excessively white faces and hair.

archeologist Elizabeth Shaw (Naomi Rapace) as she discovers a star map in a cave on the Isle of Skye. This correlates to other such maps found in connection to other ancient cultures across the globe—a similar premise was used in the crossover feature of *AVP [Alien versus Predator]* (Anderson, 2004). This is interpreted as an invitation of some kind from an unknown extraterrestrial race that appears to have visited Earth at the earliest stages of human history. Shaw attracts the attention of Peter Weyland (Guy Pierce), the hugely wealthy and aging CEO of the Weyland Corporation (this corporation features throughout the *Alien* film series, usually as the face of vampiric consumerism) who then funds an expedition into space to try and find the alien race who he believes created humanity and might be able to grant him immortality.

Four years later the expedition's spaceship, *Prometheus*, arrives in the orbit of planet LV-223. The crew are awoken from their hibernation and told they are on a mission to discover the "Engineers," the alien race believed responsible for the star maps found on Earth—they are human in appearance, but very pale, hairless, and about 3 m tall. Shaw and her team land on the planet and begin to investigate the inside of a large pyramid-like structure. As they explore the tunnel system they discover a large metal door and, while finding a way to open it, activate a holographic recording that replays the final moments of the Engineers' time on the planet, including one of their number being decapitated by the metal door in front of them. They find the head and Shaw returns with it to the spaceship. The exposure to the outside atmosphere has had severe effects upon the severed head, but Shaw manages to extract a DNA sample before it disintegrates. She discovers that it has the same DNA as humans, which strongly suggests that humans are genetically derived from the Engineers. Closely upon this discovery, the team's plans go awry, largely due to the machinations of an android, David (Michael Fassbender), who while pretending to help the crew is on a secret mission for Weyland.[42] David infects Shaw's partner with a viscous black fluid taken from one of the hundreds of black cylinders stored in the pyramid, which causes the human body to break down. Furthermore, he infects Shaw with another substance that impregnates her despite her previously established sterility—in this respect, the excessive life in the dark fluid (biological jouissance) has transfigured Shaw into another Pandora-figure who carries a plague within her that will ravage humanity, and which is quickly on the verge of erupting from the "box" of her body.

Meanwhile, back in the pyramid, two crew members are attacked and seemingly killed by a snake-like creature that exhibits many of the physical characteristics of the xenomorphs that feature in the main *Alien* series

---

42. A recurring theme in the *Alien* series is the duplicitous and emotionless nature of androids that work for Weyland.

(*Alien* to *Alien Resurrection* [Jeunet: 1997]). The creature inside Shaw grows exponentially and she manages to access a robotic Medicare unit to remove it. Once outside of her the creature is seen to be a squid-like monstrosity that then tries to kill her, but she manages to escape. This sequence of events, together with the fate of the two presumably "dead" crewmen, suggest that contact with any of the creatures or substances found in the pyramid triggers mutations in human beings at an increased rate. The film gradually reveals that a huge spaceship is kept inside the pyramid and David has found the control room where an Engineer is kept alive and in stasis. David awakens Weyland, who was secretly traveling on the *Prometheus*, to meet the Engineer. However, the humanoid alien is less than happy once awoken and rips off David's head, kills Weyland and prepares to take off in the ship, destroying the pyramid above it. Shaw has been spying on these events and retrieves David's head and escapes from the ship. She reactivates David's head which tells her that the Engineer intends to take the cylinders full of the toxic black fluid to Earth and use them to destroy humanity. The remaining crew on the *Prometheus* crashes their ship into the alien spacecraft as it takes off, killing themselves but forcing the Engineer back down to the surface of the planet. The Engineer manages to escape and tracks Shaw to an escape pod. Fortunately, she manages to trap both the proto-xenomorph she had aborted earlier—which is now huge—and the Engineer onboard the pod, while she escapes. David then tells Shaw that there are other Engineer ships on the planet, upon which she hijacks an Engineer ship and embarks on a journey to the alien's home world, together with the android's head, on a quest to discover why the Engineers created humanity in the first place and why they now seek to destroy it.

The film exhibits in an intertwined network of connections to vampires and *The War of the Worlds*. In the film's prologue, the camera pans across a vast primordial landscape that recalls the paintings of early 19th century German Romantics, as well as scenes from Werner Herzog's *Nosferatu the Vampyre* (1979). Herzog's film charts the journey of the young traveler Jonathan Harker, marking his progress from modernity back to the beginnings of time in the vampire's lair across a landscape where humans are not only absent but positively unwelcome. Harker's journey sees him ascending across rocky outcrops and scaling waterfalls, intimating a spatial and temporal regression back in time, to eventually light upon the castle of the vampire towering above him. The camera in *Prometheus* creates a similar effect by panning across the mountains and waterfalls until it eventually settles on the towering home of the vampire, namely a spacecraft hovering just above the surface, which is the lair of humanity's oldest ancestor. This begins to map out the vampiric tropes that amass around the Engineers.

The extraterrestrials have not come to Earth to plunder its resources

Figure 3. Vampiric transcendence in a sublime landscape. *Prometheus*. Directed by Ridley Scott (20th Century–Fox: 2012).

but rather to create them, wanting to turn a barren planet into a fecund ecosystem—there is no sign of even the most basic kinds of flora and fauna present. One of the Engineers descends to the planet's surface and consumes a black liquid while he stands on the edge of a waterfall—we do not know if it is the same black liquid in the canisters seen in the pyramid. As the oily liquid begins to work the body of the humanoid alien begins to dissolve and break apart, down to the very DNA of its cells. As it is washed away by the water, its vampiric mutability comes to the fore and the genetic strands begin to reconstruct themselves using matter from this new world, creating life in its own image; the new cyborg selves of the alien that forms the spark from which all subsequent life on Earth is created.

Consequently, the film posits that the Engineers, and indeed the black liquid that was consumed by it, are integral to the development of all life on our planet—it is further suggested that the Earth is not the only planet that they might have seeded to create life. In this sense they become representative of the creation of life and oppositional to human consumerism as embodied by the Weyland Corporation—Weyland features throughout the *Alien* franchise (including the Alien-Predator crossover film *AVP* [Anderson: 2004]), though it is renamed United Systems Military in *Alien Resurrection* (Jeunet, 1997). Within the franchise then Weyland is represented as the face of human greed above and beyond all life, willing to sacrifice any amount of humans in its effort to accumulate wealth—as seen in the crews of the various ships they send to investigate locations where the xenomorphs might be present as in *Alien* (Scott: 1979), the sacrificing of the terraforming community in *Aliens* (Cameron: 1986), the prison community in *Alien3* (Fincher: 1993), and the horrific cloning experiments to create a xenomorph in *Alien Resurrection*. In part Peter Weyland himself is something of vampire, not just as the driving force behind the continual, undying, accumulation and consumption of his company, but in his own quest for immortality. This expresses something of the immortality of consumption which "eats" itself into eternity and is also a familiar trope within the vampire genre of aging billionaires trying to enlist the services of the undead to live forever, the group of industrialists around Dracula in *The Satanic Rites of Dracula* (Gibson: 1973), De La Guardia (Claudio Brook) in *Cronos* (del Toro: 1993), and Eldritch Palmer (Jonathan Hyde) in *The Strain* (del Toro and Hogan: 2014–17) being the most obvious examples. In *Prometheus*, Weyland is shown to be over 100 years old and a man that has fed off the energies of others in a frantic attempt to extend his own life. Indeed, in a speech not dissimilar to that given by Count Dracula where he positions himself as the embodiment of the history of his land, Weyland sees himself as the totality of humanity:

> 100,000 BC: stone tools. 4,000 BC: the wheel. 900 AD: gunpowder—bit of a game changer, that one. 19th century: eureka, the lightbulb! 20th century: the automobile, television, nuclear weapons, spacecrafts, Internet. 21st century: biotech, nanotech, fusion and fission and M theory—and THAT, was just the first decade! We are now three months into the year of our Lord, 2023. At this moment of our civilization, we can create cybernetic individuals, who in just a few short years will be completely indistinguishable from us. Which leads to an obvious conclusion: WE are the gods now [Scott: 2012].

The inference is obvious that he means himself, just as Dracula did before him. The eventual irony of course, as with many Renfield-esque (vampire-wannabe) figures, is that Weyland is summarily dispatched by the Engineer—his imagined Vampire King—as being inconsequential and his wealth as insignificant in relation to the biological powers that create life.

Alongside this there is much here that sees the Weyland Corporation, and the human consumerism it represents, as being the future of humanity as embodied by the Martians in Wells' story. This would see the Engineers as embodying a planetary defense system, at least in their desire to reset life on Earth by destroying humanity. Interestingly they are not planning on doing that themselves but with the black liquid stored in the large cylinders mentioned above which, in relation to *War of the Worlds*, represents the bacteria, the biological weapon, that kills the future humans (the Martians). The cylinders utilize a kind of organic jouissance to grow and recreate itself at exponential rates—in the course of the film we have seen it grow from a snake-like creature, to the squid-like entity that is extracted from Shaw's body and into a more familiar xenomorph at the end when it erupts out of the Engineer trapped in the escape craft (each stage requires gestation in a new host). In many ways, as will be discussed in more depth later, the xenomorph is a vampiric creature—its various life-cycles and growth spurts draw on human and/or biological energy and its mutations depend on the augmentation of its DNA with new genetic material—but also whose purpose is to cleanse the Earth, and indeed the galaxy, of humanity. This sees the xenomorphs as a kind of inter-galactic auto-immune system created to protect itself from the vampiric human-species, as manifested by the Weyland Corporation, that only wants to exploit and consume it.

Humanity in general seems to have no role in this scenario other than a plaything for the gods with its relation to the Earth more akin to that between the ant and the ant farm created for it for a science project—in fact, Wells makes such a comparison in *War of the Worlds* when the artillery man says "That's what we are now—just ants ... eatable ants" (Wells: 2018, 96). Shaw's righteous indignation at the end of *Prometheus* is seemingly nothing more than an inconvenience for her creators, the Engineers, though as seen in the sequel, *Alien: Covenant* (Scott: 2017), even ants can bring a house down if they dig in the right places. *Jupiter Ascending* takes up this idea of humanity as created by an alien race, one more explicitly marked out as vampires.

Jupiter Ascending explicitly refers to its aliens as vampires, though not the kind that drink blood but rather a species with an inordinately long lifespan that retains its youth by replacing the dead cells in their body with those found in an elixir made of the life force of humanoid species—a milky substance that is extracted by processing humans (we are never shown exactly what this process involves other than a brief scene of a naked body tested before it is dropped into a larger machine). This fluid rejuvenates the humanoid vampires and de-ages them. It is often explained in mystical terms whereby it bestows "time" on those who consume it. As explained by one of the vampires, who is hundreds of years old, Kalique Abrasax (Tuppence Middleton) as she steps out of her rejuvenating bath, in an obvious nod to the mythology around Elizabeth Báthory,[43] and looks no more than twenty:

> Each of us has a code for our optimal physical condition. The problem is our genes have an expiration date which is transferred to our cells. A long time ago, someone figured out how to replace deteriorating cells with new ones. Today, it's as easy as changing a light bulb [The Wachowskis: 2015].

---

43. Countess Elizabeth Báthory de Ecsed was a Hungarian noblewoman who lived between 1560 and 1614. Potentially the world's most prolific female murderer, she may have been responsible for the deaths of up to 650 people, though it has equally been argued she was a victim of political intrigue at the time. It was after her death that mythologies around her being a vampire that bathed in the blood of virgins began to circulate.

And then further observes:

> In your [human] world, people are used to fighting for resources … like oil, or minerals, or land. But when you have access to the vastness of space, you realize there's only one resource worth fighting over … even killing for: More time. Time is the single most precious commodity in the universe [The Wachowskis: 2015].

In this way the film literally declares that "time is money" and consequently the elixir is worth a lot of money, and money and time alike are commodities of which the space vampires have a limitless supply. The vampires are described as an ancient dynasty, but no species name is given to them other than their family name, The House of Abrasax. No other vampire dynasty, race, or family is mentioned in the film and the Abrasax family only consists of a Matriarch (who was over ninety-one millennia old when she was murdered but might have been reincarnated), two brothers, Balem (Eddie Redmayne) and Titus (Douglas Booth), and a sister, Kalique (Tuppence Middleton).

Various planets across the galaxy are owned by the family and are subsequently "seeded" by the Abrasax and "harvested" once the population has reached the point of overcrowding. Seeding consists of either creating or genetically modifying humanoid species on a planet, who are then left to develop on their own—unlike the Engineers, the Abrasax are never accorded a God-like status, but are represented only as hyper- or super-consumers. Once the human population has reached a certain point of evolution—it is never explained what this is but appears to be related to technological development and population size—it is harvested. Humanoids are thus rounded up and sent to a processing plant somewhere in outer space. Clones cannot substitute for live humans because, as explained by Kalique, they "lack genetic plasticity" and further, "Several million years ago, a gene plague caused by cloning nearly annihilated the entire human race."[44] The Abrasax are thus motivated by the desire to maximize the profits of their work, in this instance the work of creating the human race. Accordingly, all the varying galactic races that work for the Abrasax, or who serve them in some capacity, are genetically altered in order to strengthen certain characteristics that are seen by the Abrasax as useful, in a process of optimization. Thus, the bounty hunters who are sent to capture Jupiter (Mila Kunis) have many biological and technological augmentations, often involving data feeds and vision enhancers. They are likewise gene-spliced with other species, affording them enhancements such as wolves' sense

---

44. As I have noted elsewhere "This resonates with other vampire texts where humans are 'farmed' to provide a steady supply for the vampiric overlords, as seen in *Daybreakers*, *Matrix*, and *The Strain*, though as mentioned it is not so much as a food source in *Jupiter Ascending* as an elixir or power-smoothie to revitalize themselves" (Bacon: 2020, 220).

of smell that assists in tracking and cloned wings attached to their shoulders. Or in the case of Stinger (Sean Bean) spliced with bees, which have been altered themselves to identify Royalty and exhibit extreme loyalty to its members. This configures all life as a commodity to be maximized for greater value and usefulness.

At the start of the film, the camera scans across a very modern but deserted city. The ground is littered with bags, toys, etc., as though the inhabitants were whisked away at a moment's notice—not unlike images of the evacuation of Pripyat at the time of the Chernobyl disaster. The camera stops at the only humanoid figures in the scene, those of Balem, Titus, and Kalique. As they stand surveying the scene, Titus and Kalique touch upon the process that has just taken place:

> KALIQUE: I've heard they feel no pain. It's all quite humane, from what I've been told.
> TITUS: Well ... there are marshals and administrators to make sure everything is done according to code ... but still ... it can be rather ... affecting [Wachowskis: 2015].

This telling moment reveals the emotional distance of the Abrasax family from the objects of their harvest, even those with whom they share their DNA.

Like the Engineers in *Prometheus*, the Abrasax are shown to have the same genetic make-up as the human race. The human protagonist of the film, Jupiter Jones, who is believed to be the reincarnation of the Matriarch, is given a DNA test to prove that she is the rightful heir to the murdered vampires' estate, upon which the genetic makeup of the Abrasax is shown as identical to humans.' Recalling *The War of the Worlds*, where the Martians are the evolutionary future of the human race, both the Engineers and the Abrasax are simultaneously the past and the future of humanity. Hence the need to cull or harvest humanity once it evolves to a certain point. The Engineers and the Abrasax thus emerge as vampires, indeed cannibalistic vampires, as they quite literally consume their own genetic material, parts of themselves, to stay young forever. Unlike the Martians in *The War of the Worlds*, the Abrasax are not repelled by the Earth's auto-immune system because they do not destroy the planet as the Martians had done with their red weed. Rather, they restrict their intervention to harvesting the people on it, thereby allowing the ecosystem to continue without the problematic human factor.

In the Wachowkis' film this would all seem to be going to plan until Jupiter shows up. The daughter of a Russian immigrant family living in Chicago she has been pinpointed by the Abrasax as the receptacle of their mother's essence—this is never explained that well in the film as if the Matriarch was reincarnated in the body of the human at birth, then why has it taken

20 or so years for the vampires to locate her, and if it is just a mind transfer how come Jupiter's DNA matches the dead woman's? Each sibling sends their own respective bounty hunters to bring Jupiter to them because if she is their Mother then she has the rights to the Earth, which is a very valuable property for harvesting. After much to-ing and fro-ing Jupiter ends up with Balem on his mining facility—a huge, seemingly planet-wide structure that is possibly for the sole purpose of processing humanoid life-forms into elixir—who it transpires was the one that killed his Mother. He claims that she asked him to do it as she had grown tired of life after so many millennia alive, though it is equally probable that he did it for his inheritance as oldest child. In a final struggle Balem and Jupiter fight and the vampire falls to his death leaving the human as undisputed owner of the Earth.

Jupiter decides to return to Earth and go back to her job as a maid for the family business rather than take charge of a galactic empire. It is assumed that although she has the exact same DNA as the dead Matriarch, she is not connected to her in any way, or that the vampire spirit is not dormant inside her somewhere. This is interesting in terms of what Balem told Jupiter about his mother wanting to die as she had become bored of life, as she might be quite happy existing within the human girl as a passenger and experiencing a life she would not normally have access to—similar scenarios have occurred in other vampire films such as *Daughters of Darkness* (Kümel, 1971), *The Devil's Plaything* (Sarno, 1973), *Nadja* (Almereyder, 1994), and *The Last Sect* (Dueck, 2006) where the consciousness of the Matriarch vampire inhabits/shares the body of another woman, though not always in a dominant manner. This constructs Jupiter as a hybrid entity, part herself and part vampire, or current and evolved human selves, and liable to change at any moment making for an uneasy ending to the film. As with many of the narratives here hybridity is not always an uncomplicated solution to the human or vampire conundrum and usually has the potential to take the present in unexpected, unthought of directions. In this sense while this chapter began more closely aligned to *The War of the Worlds* it has finished up nearer *Dracula* with the feeling that although the action might have finished the story has not and the characters have all changed in some way, and in the case of Mina in ways that are not fully understood or realized. In this sense the ghost of the vampire world is haunting the human one with the hybrid body becoming a portal between the two. This is an idea explored more thoroughly in the next chapter where vampires inhabit the human world through inhabiting the human body.

2

Planet of the Vampires

This chapter follows the thread of Mario Bava's *Planet of the Vampires* (1965), which hinges on the premise that an alien life form inhabits the body of a humanoid host. This paradigm resonates more with Stoker's *Dracula* than with Wells' *The War of the Worlds*, notwithstanding that the alien's purpose is often to take control of another world, usually the Earth. This paradigm correlates in particular with Count Dracula's ability to influence his victims from a great distance. While at sea on his way to Whitby the vampire was able to communicate with Renfield in his cell— though the inmate's mental state made him especially susceptible to this influence.[45] He was able to influence Mina to a greater degree after they had joined and shared fluids, a form of mutually assured infection, which allowed them to virtually share minds and see through each other's eyes. The Count may even have some measure of control over Mina's body. Bava's film takes this influence still further, as the vampire's spirit (soul) re-energizes a dead human body, transforming it into a fleshy exoskeleton and human escape-pod. The vampires in this film mirror Wells' Martians, insofar as they hail from a world that is exhausted of all resources and life; a dried-out ghost world plagued by the memories of the undead. This chapter thus charts the journey of these space vampires from their own world to ours with each pairing of films marking their nearer proximity, until they reach their destination and start conquering humanity, hidden from the Earth's defenses in their human body-suits. This chapter thus examines cultural anxieties over identity, particularly around those who have gone away (into space) and returned but are different from their former selves. A similar premise actually formed the basis of the vampire panic in the early 17th century, albeit for travelers or soldiers closer to home, who had returned and begun behaving strangely, a change that the locals attributed

---

45. This can be read as Renfield being an Empath that can reach out and sense such "vampiric" entities, something which is seen in the film *Species* (Donaldson: 1995) discussed below.

to vampirism.[46] In a more contemporary milieu, such a narrative model reflects contemporary fears since the War on Terror, Al Qaeda, and ISIS, where our neighbors might not be who they seem. Rather aptly, given that the previous chapter ended on a pair of films of which one was *Prometheus*, this section opens with *Alien* in its first pairing and follows the vampires from another world as they forge an escape from their planet.

It: The Terror from Beyond Space, Edward L. Cahn, 1958/*Alien,* Ridley Scott, 1979

Edward L. Cahn's *It: The Terror from Beyond Space* (1958) and Ridley Scott's *Alien* (1979) both begin on alien worlds on which unknown entities try to escape this planet to find new sources of food, which appear to be predominantly human. These malevolent creatures thus target Earth—while they might be generally planet-hopping, the films always show them specifically threatening humanity's home world—and so human space explorers struggle against these malevolent aliens who threaten their home. These aliens do not fully inhabit their victims, though the xenomorph in *Alien* uses the human body as a vital stage in its development and a vessel by which it enters the human spaceship undetected.

It: The Terror from Beyond Space recalls Serviss' riposte to *War of the Worlds*, opening with the first spaceship from Earth landing on Mars. *It* plays out on a smaller scale than *Ghosts of Mars* or *Avatar*, focusing on the first expeditionary landing on Mars in the near future (relative to the time of release) of 1973. When communications with the ship are lost, a rescue mission is undertaken—a not-uncommon strategy for vampiric entities to entice their unsuspecting victims into their lair, which recurs in *Alien*. Once the crew of the new ship locate the wreckage of the expedition, they discover only one survivor, Colonel Edward Carruthers (Marshal Thompson), who explains that his colleagues were not killed in the crash, but were murdered by a mysterious and unseen entity on the planet. The new arrivals do not believe him, suspecting he killed the crew to save himself from starvation. They receive instructions to return him to Earth to face a court martial. This motif, whereby only the victim knows of the vampire's existence on account of the particular bond between them, recurs frequently in the genre of the vampire story—see *Fright Night* (Holland: 1985), *Vampires Kiss* (Bierman: 1988), *Rise* (Gutierrez: 2007), and *Let Me In* (Reeves: 2010)—and emerges more starkly in the *Alien* franchise in the relationship between Ellen Ripley and the xenomorph.

---

46. See the case of Arnold Paole, Ruickbie: 2013.

Mars itself is shown as a dry, barren planet with rocky outcroppings, seemingly inhospitable to all lifeforms, as if the terrain itself has been sucked dry. As the rescue ship prepares to depart, an unknown creature materializes out of the shadows and steals onto the ship through an unguarded airlock. Indeed, in the early stages of the film, the creature appears to be made up entirely of shadows. Its depiction is reminiscent of Count Orlok in *Nosferatu* (Murnau, 1922), who seems to exist as a shadow as much as he does a material body. In *Nosferatu*, the vampire's shadow acts independently of its caster, seeking out victims and haunting their waking dreams.[47] The entity from Mars similarly emerges as a ghostly presence on the lower decks of the space craft. This does posit an interesting link to *The War of the Worlds* where this version of Mars is the one that Wells' Martian had sucked dry causing their attack on Earth. If so then this creature that seems to almost "haunt" the surface of the planet is all that remains of humanity's future—as Wells' Martians have been described as representing. This would then see the monster, possibly the sole survivor of the former interplanetary invaders, as representing a warning to the Earthlings that land on its planet that we too might become ghosts on our own home world.

Once the rescue craft has begun its return journey to Earth, the crew hear a noise from the lower decks—effectively a bump in the night—and one of their number, Kleinholz (Thom Carney), investigates the scene only to be abducted by the creature who emerges from out of the darkness. Another crewman, Finelli (Richard Hervey), discovers Kleinholz's body stuffed in an air duct, upon which he too is attacked by the creature. When the surviving crew examine Kleinholz's body, they discover that it has been drained of blood and all other bodily fluids, leaving it as a dry husk. The monster materializes into its complete physical form upon this discovery of its vampiric nature. This materialization renders the earlier scenes more ethereal, lending a mystery to the creature's spinning of shadows. It also brings the creature closer to Count Dracula himself, who could dematerialize into mist at will. Likewise recalling Count Dracula, the creature cannot be killed with conventional weapons. Thus, as the remaining crew try and kill it with bullets, gas grenades, and finally the ship's atomic reactor, he remains untouched.

At this point Carruthers realizes that the oxygen levels on the ship are much lower than they should be, suggesting that the creature also consumes the oxygen in the space craft—Carruthers surmises it is due to its larger lung capacity because of the thin atmosphere on Mars. Consequently, they devise a plan where they will put on space suits and then evacuate the air

---

47. Something similar is seen in the film *Beast from Haunted Cave* (Hellman: 1959) though here the vampire is specifically shown to be from the Earth's past.

from the upper decks while the creature is trapped there. This they do and the monster does indeed eventually die. In part it confirms the physicality of the entity in the latter part of the film, the side of the creature that exists and lives in the same universe as humans—in Stoker's *Dracula* this would relate to the fatal throat wound inflicted on the vampire.[48] The otherworldly part, though, is still present, even though the creature is no longer an entity of the shadows. In fact in many ways it is this inhuman aspect of the creature that needs to consume human energy to survive, as seen in the earlier victims being killed as the monster materializes out of the darkness. Consequently, it is the other world, the supernatural one, consuming this one that provides sustenance for the creature, hence the parched-out terrain of Mars and its desire to return to Earth on the spaceship. Once onboard the creature begins to absorb all the elements of life it can to remain alive, both the energies of the crew members but also the oxygen on the craft—the film identifying this as the basic stuff of life. Indeed, it seems the creature has only remained alive on Mars because it has some minimal, if thin, atmosphere—potentially it might mean that this single creature has drained an entire planet of its energy for life. Following on from this, the way to extinguish the entity is obviously to separate it from all forms of life, and this the film identifies as the vacuum of space. As such, the only way to annihilate this otherworldly creature is to suffocate it from the life and breath, the oxygen, of this world.

This effectively breaks the link between the two worlds, one that seems to have been established on the surface of Mars. We never discover whether more than one entity was on the planet, though the film ends rather ominously, stating that the Red planet must he avoided "because another word for Mars is death" (Cahn: 1958). This film continues the idea of the innately dangerous nature of outer space and its antagonism to human life. More so, the ongoing sense that the planets encountered by the astronauts are in some way, as with Wells' Martians, future visions of the Earth once human consumerism has vampirized it, makes space travel a constant warning for mankind to mend its ways. There is a sense, then, that the ghostly presence of the Martian, as mentioned above, describes outer space as more like an insatiable and inescapable hungry ghost, a specter of humanity's future, that can only be destroyed by allowing it to consume our present. Much of this idea informs the next film where the vampire from another world seems to be a physical manifestation of outer space itself and its unquenchable desire to consume humanity.

48. The death of the vampire in *Dracula* is rather curious. Although the text tries to explain that certain knives are fatal to the undead, that means of death does not really relate to the supernatural aspects in the same way as a stake through the heart, beheading or other methods. Indeed, it suggests more that the physical presence might have been curtailed in some way, but his supernatural nature is still alive ... and hence the unease at story's end.

Alien is a far more sophisticated film, though one cannot help thinking that Ridley Scott must have seen *It: The Terror from Beyond Space*. *Alien* was followed by three sequels and then two prequels—*Prometheus*, mentioned in the previous chapter, is the first of the latter—making six films in the *Alien* series so far, though if we include the two Predator crossover films, *AVP* (Anderson: 2005) and *AVPR* (The Brothers Strause: 2007), the tally rises to eight. The universe that has expanded from the original film is thus incredibly varied, particularly if one includes the directors' cuts of all the films and promotional short films, various novels and games as well, so much that one might find it difficult to consider *Alien* as a standalone text. As part of the larger narrative, the action in *Alien* takes place on a world that is possibly the same one seen in *Prometheus*, though even if this is not the case, the creatures discovered in *Prometheus* are still part of the same mission to destroy humanity that was first uncovered in the prequel.

Alien opens on a commercial spaceship, the *Nostromo*, towing a refinery loaded with twenty million tons of mineral ore, an opening that anticipates *Avatar* insofar as it suggests an Earth that is happily exploiting the world and galaxy around it. Also, like *Avatar*, this opening frames the ensuing events in *Alien* as the environment ridding itself of the "human" consumerist contagion as mentioned in the previous chapter in relation to *Prometheus*. The central computer onboard the *Nostromo*, "MOTHER," intercepts a transmission from a nearby planet and consequently awakens the seven crew members that have been kept in hyper-sleep. Once fully awake, they realize they are nowhere near Earth, as they expected, but in an outlying system still a long way from home called Zeta II Reticuli. The signal, which repeats every 12 seconds, is coming from a small planetoid which appears to be a moon of a much larger ringed world. The crew are not keen to go down to the planet but are reminded that it is company policy that "all signals by unknown intelligent life must be investigated or all payment and crew bonuses are forfeited" (Scott: 1979). Individual and corporate greed are underlying vampiric motifs throughout the film, and indeed the entire series.

Once near their target, the *Nostromo* separates from the refinery and descends to the surface of the planet, though it suffers some damage on landing due to a raging storm on the surface. Two of the crew, Dallas (Tom Skerrit) and Kane (John Hurt), leave the ship to find the source of the signal that should be two thousand meters away. As they approach its source, they discover a huge spaceship—identical to the one in *Prometheus* though not buried under a pyramid of earth as it is in the later film—seemingly abandoned voluntarily, as there is no crash damage visible. They enter the vessel, which is an enormous, almost womb-like, Gothic construction oddly reminiscent of the Romantic, other worldly landscape seen in Murnau's *Nosferatu*, and even more so in the remake, *Nosferatu the Vampyre* by Werner Herzog (1979), where the innocent traveler—Jonathan Harker—has been summoned to the lair of the vampire. Here it is Dallas and Kane who travel into the home of the vampire, sharing the role of the innocent that goes to the "land beyond the forest" (Stoker: 1997, 259) and returns with unwanted baggage. The two men find a huge fossilized, humanoid alien sitting in a large pilot chair with a hole in its chest caused by something exploding out of it. Below the chair is a large gap in the floor, through which Kane is lowered into the vampire's real lair. The crewman finds himself in a huge, yet oddly claustrophobic, chamber lit with almost supernatural lighting that contains pools of mist harboring hundreds of large leathery eggs—the swirling mist is very reminiscent of the surface of the planet in *Planet of the Vampires* that also features floating points of light. Kane slips into the mist and disturbs one of the eggs. As the alien egg opens, Kane places his face over the top to have a closer look and suddenly he is "kissed" by the vampire—the vampiric nature of the creature will be discussed shortly. The "face hugger" wraps him in an embrace that he cannot escape from in a transgressively sexual act of deep throat penetration, not unlike the penetrative, illicit kisses that Dracula bestowed upon the innocent Harker. Thus, penetrated and emasculated, neither Kane nor Harker are the same men ever again.

After Kane has been taken back on board the *Nostromo*, and has seemingly returned to his normal self, the newly created vampire erupts from his chest and scuttles off before the rest of the crew can react. The plot unfolds henceforth in beats that resonate with *It: The Terror from Beyond Space* as the vampire/alien becomes a creature of the shadows that materializes out

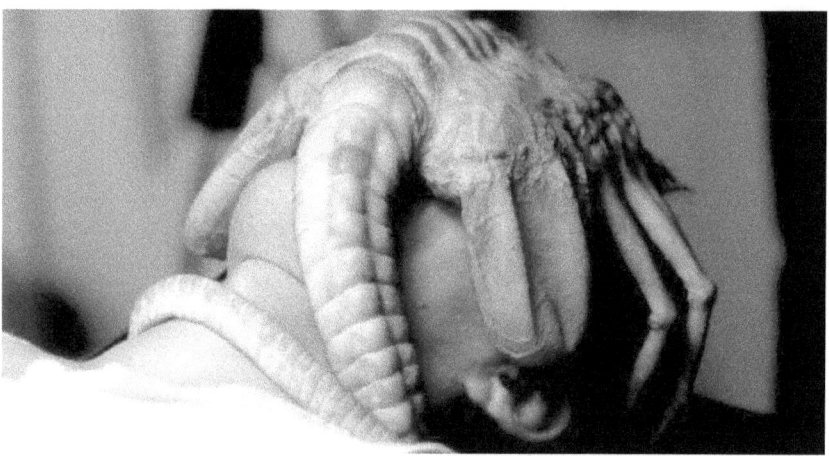

Figure 4. Kane (John Hurt) suffers the deathly "kiss" of the vampire. *Alien*. Directed by Ridley Scott (20th Century–Fox: 1979).

of darkness and returns to it at will. The crew decide to try and find the creature and begin searching the ship in two groups. The interior of the *Nostromo* appears as Gothic as the alien spaceship on the surface, with the lower decks and machine areas almost cave-like in their shadowy dankness and even the high-tech control rooms oddly cluttered with random pools of darkness. In one of the lower decks Brett (Harry Dean Stanton) gets separated from the others, as he searches for the ship's cat, when suddenly the alien appears behind him. No longer the rat-sized creature that burst out of Kane's chest, it is now a huge man-sized monster with a double mouth that is simultaneously a toothed vagina and a penis, thereby manifesting the transgressive sexuality of all vampires. The crew find no trace of Brett and thus begin a series of frantic attempts to kill the alien invader, not unlike the similar sequence in *It: The Terror from Beyond Space*, as the monster haunts the ship and manifests and dematerializes as it works its way through the surviving crew members.

The eponymous alien manifests the inherently spectral nature of Orlok as a creature made as much of shadow and darkness as of solid materiality. Indeed, even more than Orlok, the alien absorbs people into itself to both "consume" them and reproduce—the alien creates a "nest" from its saliva or bodily excretions to entomb its victims so that they can be impregnated with new embryonic vampires—though this is not explicitly seen until the next film in the series, *Aliens* (Cameron: 1986).[49] The only vampire quality it does not manifest is a dependence on blood, but even this quality is strongly suggested. As noted previously in relation to *Prometheus*, the alien needs to absorb some form of nutrients to fuel its growth and to produce its fluid and saliva. In *Alien*, more than in its sequels, the alien's growth is explained in pseudo-scientific terms. The remaining crew gather together after Brett's death and discuss the dramatic change in size of the creature and Ash (Ian Holm)—who has been closely studying the entity since it came onboard—declares that its new manifestation is "Kane's sum," intimating that its growth is due to what it sucked, or absorbed, from its birthing from the host/victim, Kane.[50] Not unlike Sil in *Species* or the proto-xenomorph that is taken out of Shaw in *Prometheus*, this alien is a vampire from another world who uses its brief, violent exchanges with human bodies to absorb nutrients and energize itself.

49. As told to me by Andrew M. Boylan, "In a deleted scene to *Alien*, which was re-added into the director's cut, Ripley finds Brett and Dallas cocooned, but Brett is further gone and appears to be morphing into an egg, meaning a drone can reproduce by turning a victim into an egg until a Queen is birthed to create them en masse. This morphing would fit with the polymorphic nature shown in *Prometheus*."
50. This is a point that has caused much Internet discussion, which I'd like to thank Dr. Neil Jackson for pointing me toward, as it is also interpreted as being "Kane's son" with the more obvious biblical connections if Kane is read as Cain.

This originating moment of vampiric birth marks the opening of a doorway between worlds, where the human body becomes a portal through which the universe of the vampire alien enters the human realm. This is a feature of many of the films discussed throughout this study, where it is the human body that stands between the human and vampiric otherworld. The victim's body thus becomes the "abhuman," Gothic body described by Kelly Hurley, a "body on the cusp" that is "a not-quite-human subject, characterized by its morphic variability, continually in danger of becoming not-itself, becoming other" (2004, 3). The victim's body is thus placed in constant tension between the homely and the unhomely, the familiar (itself) and the unfamiliar (the "monstrous" self). Kane in the film fits this model perfectly, as his sudden return to health and the seeming death of the alien "face-hugger" signal that his body is on the edge of transformation, no longer homely and safe but dramatically unhomely and dangerous. Similarly, another crew member named Dallas is discovered by Ripley (Sigourney Weaver), still alive but, unlike Kane, fully aware that his is now an abhuman body, one on the verge of mutation. He consequently begs Ripley to kill him and thereby try and shut the door to the monstrous world that is about to pass through him and into our own.

Upon realizing that she is the sole survivor on the *Nostromo* (together with Jones the cat), Ripley sets the ship to self destruct and prepares to depart in the escape craft. Throughout the film, Ripley takes on multiple protective roles, working as the ship's security chief, checking repairs, and trying to enforce quarantine procedures when the alien entity is allowed onboard ship. Her wide skillset and leadership, which become more pronounced from one film to the next in the *Alien* series, make her a perfect fit for the character of Van Helsing, the natural born nemesis of the vampire. In *Alien*, not unlike the crew in *It: The Terror from Beyond Space*, she attempts to kill the alien by depriving it of oxygen and blasts it out into space to finally defeat it, but as with Van Helsing, it would seem that no matter how many times she kills the alien vampire, it is reborn at the beginning of the next installment. Indeed, with each installment she increasingly becomes the sole source of esoteric knowledge about the vampire, its past and the ways in which it can be killed.

In the final scenes of the film, the vampire materializes out of the shadows of the escape craft's cabin, slowly approaching Ripley. She dons a spacesuit, and once again echoing *It: The Terror from Beyond Space*, she opens the airlock doors, which instantly sucks out anything not nailed to the craft. The alien finally departs but is only fully detached from the craft by thrusters when it attempts to re-enter the ship. Believing she has finally killed the vampire, Ripley sets course for the frontier and returns to a hyper-sleep pod to remain in stasis, in the hope that she will be picked up by the network in about six weeks' time. And yet, the film ends on an uneasy note that the struggle is far from over, that the shadows still harbor secrets, as does the darkness of space itself, secrets that seek to consume humanity. The implied danger of outer space is developed in the next two films that feature vampiric aliens trying to bring their world down to Earth.

Planet of the Vampires, Mario Bava, 1965/ *Life* Daniel Espinosa 2017

Bava's *Planet of the Vampires* marks out the next step in the journey of the vampiric alien on its way to Earth. *Planet of the Vampires* follows two spaceships, the *Argos* and the *Galliott*, on an expedition into deep space, as they receive a distress signal from an uncharted planet called Aura. As they approach the planet, their respective crews begin to behave erratically, becoming increasingly agitated until they finally attack each other. Captain Markary (Barry Sullivan) on the *Argos* manages to resist the unknown influence and to land his crew safely, but the *Galliott* has no such luck and the ship crashes into the planet's surface.

Once everyone has returned to their senses, Markary leads a team to search for survivors on the *Galliott*, as the *Argos* cannot establish radio contact with the *Galliott* and the Captain's younger brother is onboard. The planet's surface is barren except for a strange swirling mist that appears to have flashing lights in it—a not uncommon trope for planets that have vampiric, ghostly presences on them. Once at the crashed ship, the team quickly discover that the crew are all dead, though they are unable to break into the ship's control room and can only see the carnage within through a window. After burying some of the dead, Markary makes a round trip to the *Argos* to retrieve tools to break into the sealed control room, but when he returns to *Galliott*, its door is open and all signs of violence have disappeared except for a pool of blood in the middle of the floor. The crew returns to the *Argos* once more, but it is not long before their ship is plagued by mysterious occurrences, not least of which are sightings of some of the presumed dead from the *Galliott*, walking around as though alive. Markary becomes convinced that a life form stalks the planet, not just on account of the distress signal that drew them to it in the first place, but the spectral presences that seem to haunt the environment. As highlighted in his discussion with the ship's doctor, Dr. Karan (Fernando Villena):

> **MARKARY:** One entire crew lost; two of our own crew gone. Bert dead, Eldon disappeared. And this unknown enemy keeps getting closer!
> **KARAN:** The enemy is also becoming visible.

MARKARY: What do you mean by that?
KARAN: Well, you saw something. Something not quite identifiable out of the corner of your eye.
MARKARY: Ah, yes. As if it were composed of little globes of light, something fleeting, nothing definite. And the minute I looked at the things directly, they were gone [Bava 1965].

Not unlike the reaction of the crew in *It: The Terror Beyond Space*, the planet itself is seen as inherently dangerous, so that any life form that can exist on it must be evil as well—oddly reinterpreting the human-Earth symbiosis in *War of the Worlds*. Markary thus decides that "if there 'are' any intelligent creatures on this planet ... they're our enemies" (Bava: 1965), a conviction that is vindicated when crew members begin to disappear. Unable to leave the planet until repairs to the *Argos* are completed, one of Markary's crew discovers there is another ship on the planet. They send a team to investigate and discover that all its crew are long dead, largely calcified skeletons are all that remains of them, and they were most likely drawn to the planet by the same signal that drew the *Argos*.

At this stage in the narrative, *Planet of the Vampires* is very much a ghost story, not unlike *Alien* and the earlier stage of *It: The Terror Beyond Space*, as there is no physical manifestation of the alien life force, only moving shadows, swirling mists, and something hovering just outside the field of vision. In fact, at this juncture, the entity could be as much the manifestation of a disordered psychology as a physical creature, given the emotional state of its victims. However, the alien begins to take on physical form when two supposed survivors of the *Galliott* appear at the *Argos* but behave erratically. They are definitely alive but have no memory of events before the crash. The remaining crew respond to the newcomers by investigating the graves of the dead crew members of the *Galliott*. None of the graves contain bodies any longer, harboring naught but the plastic shrouds that once wrapped the dead. Shortly thereafter, Markary catches one of the men in the act of stealing the meteor deflector from the *Argos*, and on questioning him, catches a glimpse of rotten flesh beneath the man's spacesuit. Realizing that he has been caught, the alien explains that his race is dying much like the sun of their planet, and that they must leave their world or face extinction. To this end, they have inhabited the dead bodies of the astronauts, revitalizing them by their parasitic presence if not regenerating the bodies themselves. The full-fleshed appearance of the alien lifeforms is never shown, beyond the ethereal presences that accompany the flashing lights in the mist. Nor does the film disclose whether this ethereal form is the result of the catastrophic events that occurred on the planet or if it is the aliens' natural form. A similar ambiguity surrounds the aliens' desire to reach a new world—the film never clarifies whether they will remain in the same humanoid decomposing bodies, migrate to new hosts, or revert to their true form (if they have one). The alien further informs Markary that they will inevitably take control of the ship and crew and escape the planet, but the captain informs him that the remaining, unchanged crew would rather die than allow this to happen. Taken aback, the alien departs from the body it inhabited, prompting Markary's realization that the alien's subterfuge and concealment are an existential threat—a reference to the Soviet Union and the paranoia attending the Cold War. The Captain instructs the few remaining crew members to help load a large number of explosives on the *Galliott*, whereupon they are attacked by re-animated astronauts, and only Markary and Sanya (Norma Bengell) make it back to the *Argos*. The *Argos* departs the planet just as the *Galliott* explodes, and one of the three survivors, Wes (Ángel Aranda) realizes that both Markary and Sanya are acting oddly. Just before they kill him, Wes manages to destroy the newly re-installed meteor deflector, knowing that there is no way the aliens could survive the long trip through space to his home world without it. The aliens consequently alter their course to the nearest inhabitable world, a small and rather backward planet called Earth. This twist reveals that the humanoid race we assumed were earthlings were actually a distant, more advanced alien race that looks just like us—an idea not uncommon in science fiction and often tied to the idea that we were either created by the more advanced race or they acted as gods in our world, as in the *Alien* and *Stargate* (Emmerich, 1994) franchises respectively. This twist also marks a departure from the central tropes of *The War of the Worlds* where the "greedy" alien race comes specifically to the Earth to plunder its long coveted reserves, or from the *Avatar* trope where the greedy alien race are the Earthlings. In this variation on the theme, Earth is merely an insignificant backwater, and pure chance brings the vampiric parasites to our home world, though we never see the results of this encounter, as the story ends with the vampire aliens still in space and a shared sneer over their intentions once they have reached their destination. The idea of parasitic, vampiric life forms in outer space is not uncommon and is reinforced in the next film where, once again, the first life form humanity encounters in outer space just happens to be one that seems intent on consuming all life in its vicinity and is equally intent on conquering Earth.

Life combines many elements of films discussed already, and draws particularly on *Alien*, though the film returns to Mars—arguably the planet most consistently depicted as a source of anti-human malignancy, possibly because it has long thought to be the home to intelligent life, with Sir William Herschel writing in 1784 about Martians enjoying a "similar situation to our own" (Pappas: 2012). *Life* opens with a probe returning to Earth's orbit after completing its mission of collecting soil samples from Mars. The probe is retrieved by the six-person crew of the International Space Station in order to safely examine the samples before sending their findings and possibly the material itself back to the control center on Earth. One of their number, Hugh Derry (Ariyon Bakeri), who is an exobiologist, meticulously examines the samples until he finds a dormant, frozen cell in a scene that recalls *The Thing from Another World* (Nubu: 1951) and its remake *The Thing* (Carpenter: 1982), both of which feature the resuscitation of a dormant life form from its frozen state with its associated theme of bringing the distant past into the present.

As it thaws out, the cell becomes active and grows into a multi-cellular organism. Unlike human cells, these cells seem to be multi-functional and can become muscle, neuron, or photo-sensory as required, recalling *The Thing from Another World* (see above) and *Splinter* (Wilkins, 2008) where parts of the vampire act autonomously. An accident occurs in the lab and the organism—named Calvin by school children back on Earth—stops responding. Hugh tries to "shock" the organism back into life but is taken surprise by a sudden and violent response from Calvin, who has grown big enough to grab the scientist's hand in its limbs. Not unlike the "face-hugger" in *Alien*, any attempt to detach the organism only increases its grip until the scientist's fingers break and he collapses. The creature then uses the tool that Hugh had been holding to escape the specimen tank in which it was kept. Calvin reveals its vampiric qualities by consuming a lab rat kept in a nearby container and absorbing it into itself, subsequently growing in size—again in a similar manner to the xenomorph in *Alien*.

Another crewman, Rory (Ryan Reynolds), rushes into the quarantined room to try and retrieve the unconscious Hugh. After a struggle, the creature penetrates Rory's mouth and consumes him from the inside, emerging from his body a much larger entity. In this respect, this creature resembles the xenomorph in *Alien* insofar as both use a human body as a source of fuel to energize its propulsion between the human and the otherworld. The crew of the space station finally realize the danger posed by Calvin but find themselves unable to warn the center on Earth as communication system has gone down. A member of the crew, Ekaterina Golovkina (Olga Dychovichnaya), goes outside the spacecraft to try and repair the communications antenna but discovers that Calvin, in trying to leave the laboratory and enter the main part of the ship, has gotten into the cooling system and has emerged outside of the craft. The creature latches onto Ekaterina, causing the coolant on her backpack to leak into her space suit. She tries to return to the craft, but the rest of the crew refuse her entry because they fear that Calvin will follow her inside, and so she drowns in the fluid filling her suit. Calvin then tries to reenter the craft via the thrusters,[51] and in their attempt to expel it the crew consumes too much fuel and begins to fall to Earth. The pilot, Sho Murakami (Hiroyuki Sanandaj), tells the other crew members that their only chance is to use the remaining fuel to return to a safe orbit, allowing Calvin back into the craft. Once the creature is inside, they would then evacuate all the oxygen from the ship—not unlike *It: The Terror from Beyond Space*—to make Calvin dormant again.

However, while they are preparing to enact this plan, they discover that Calvin is already in the ship and has been feeding on the unconscious Hugh. In a rather frantic denouement Sho races to receive a Russian spacecraft sent from Earth to rescue them, but Calvin intercepts him, killing many crew members in the process and destroying the docking bays. The two remaining crew members, Miranda North (Rebecca Ferguson) and David Jordan (Jake Gyllenhaal), then get into separate pods to escape the plummeting station and try and lure the creature off with them. David manages to attract Calvin toward him and into his pod and intends to blast into deep space with it, leaving Miranda to return to Earth safely. But in the chaos of debris from the station Miranda is blasted out into space and David, enveloped by the now huge Calvin, lands on Earth. The film ends with the pod found by two Vietnamese fishermen who unsuspectingly open the door of the pod, allowing Calvin to escape.

Calvin, like the creature from *It: The Terror from Beyond Space,* seems driven to consume all life forms in its vicinity. Yet Calvin would appear to be a species more suited to outer space or water than earthbound life, as in its stages of evolution it changes from a slug-like creature into something similar to a rubbery jellyfish and finally a huge, translucent starfish with wings/petals on its back and something of an opening flower blossom as a head. This otherworldly feel to Calvin is emphasized by its almost angel-like appearance, particularly when it is depicted with light shining from behind it and luminescing through its petals/wings. The Christian imagery that clusters around it suggests the involvement of a higher power, as if Calvin were sent by some other being in the vein of the *Alien* franchise. Yet Calvin emerges as more ethereal and fluid than the xenomorphs, which are harder, spikier, and more shockingly penetrative. Calvin's appearance connects more directly to the Demagorgon in *Stranger Things* (Duffer Brothers, 2016–present) and the plant-based monsters in *The Day of the Triffids* (Wyndham: 1951). Together they connect the Calvin creature to the kind of biological jouissance seen in *Annihilation*

---

51. This scene mirrors an earlier one from *Alien*, though there the thrusters blast the xenomorph away from the ship and into space.

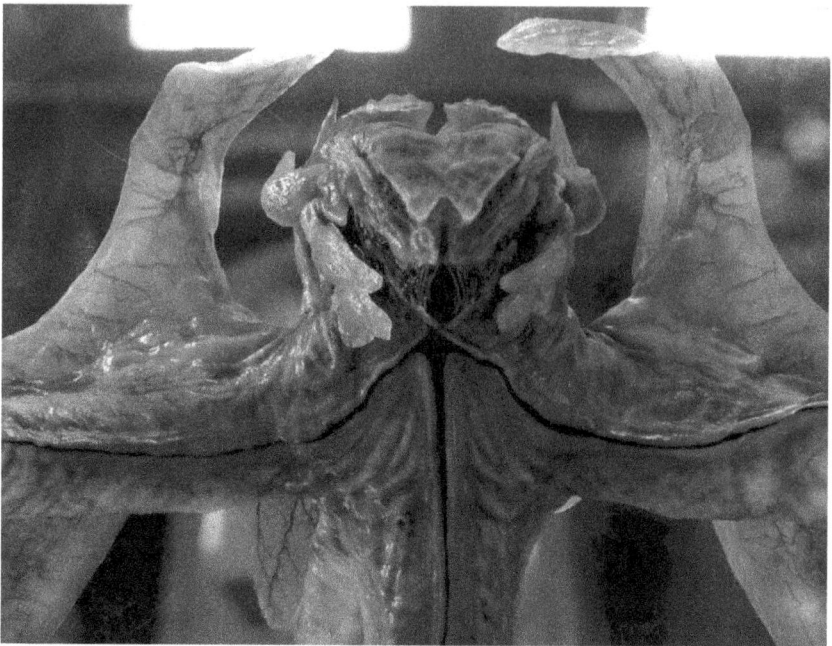

Figure 5. Superorganic organism. *Life.* **Directed by Daniel Espinosa (Sony Pictures Releasing: 2017).**

(Garland, 2018), taken from Jeff VanderMeer's 2014 novel of the same name, where an organism from outer space aggressively attacks all organic life on Earth. The Calvin creature can be seen to be doing something not unlike this but internalizes all the released energy and hybridized matter. This sees it as a hugely efficient energy vampire and something of an expression of a dark ecology that reverses the expected universal expansion into a great concentration of bioenergy.

Calvin seems to have no need to reproduce itself in order to establish its world within the heart of the human one, but rather takes everything into itself—each new energy source fueling its own growth onto another stage of maturation (curiously like *Species*)—making it a perfect example of vampiric consumption and accumulation. We do not see anything beyond the moment the rescuing fishermen open the door of the craft as it bobs around in the ocean. It might not cope with the greater gravity on Earth or it might succumb to any of the myriad bacteria that fill our atmosphere, but one suspects it might be more resilient than Wells' Martians. The next films take this process a step further, envisioning the implications of when aliens successfully make it down to the surface of the Earth and begin to lay the groundwork for an alien world to be established here.

The First Man into Space, Robert Fay, 1959/ *The Astronaut's Wife*, Rand Ravich, 1999

Unlike the previous films discussed in this chapter, Robert Fay's *The First Man into Space* and Rand Ravich's *The Astronauts Wife* are set not in the distant future but in the present time, relative to their year of release, and they consequently depict the threat from outer space as a clear and present danger. Indeed, the vampiric aspects of outer space are brought to the fore in these films, where outer space is configured as a malevolent entity waiting for mankind to depart Earth in order to attack it and find a way down to the planet's surface. The alien threat in these films uses the human body as both a carrier (vehicle) and a doorway, in order to protect itself from the Earth's natural defenses and to attack humanity at will. In *The First Man into Space*, a human spacecraft is attacked moments after it clears Earth's atmosphere, suggesting that the manifestation of the vampiric world awaited its approach.

The First Man into Space depicts an alien that lives on the surface of a human body. Analogously, the space flights that it depicts are small-scale and remain close to the surface of the Earth. The film focuses on the brilliant but maverick pilot Lieutenant Dan Prescott (Bill Edwards) who is flying a test aircraft, the Y-13, with orders to take it up to a height of 600,000 feet, level off, and then descend again. However, Prescott does not follow orders and continues ascending to 1,320,000 feet before encountering a shower of meteor dust that forces him to eject the safety pod from the craft in order to return safely to the ground. Central command loses contact with Prescott in the process and they quickly gather a search team, led by his brother Commander Charles "Chuck" Prescott (Marshal Thompson). The team follows intel from a report of a craft and parachute falling near Alvarado, whereupon it finds wreckage that indicates no human could have survived the crash. The team further investigates a peculiar crust-like substance that coats the spacecraft, discovering that it is resistant to x-rays, infrared and ultraviolet rays.

A preternaturally strong creature breaks into a nearby blood bank the same night, consuming large amounts of the blood reserves and killing two nurses before escaping. Chuck arrives at the scene and discovers small shiny specks in the jagged wounds across the throats of the nurses and around the scene of the stolen blood supplies. He is called into another site out of town, where some cows were killed, and finds a piece of tubing on the ground near the bodies of the cows, which resembles debris from the Y-13. He sends the splinter, along with the silver specks, to the government laboratory for testing. The laboratory informs him the next day that the silver specks are meteor dust that matches those found in the pieces of crust on the aircraft. The meteor dust apparently formed a protective layer over pieces of the craft to which it attached itself, shielding the craft from the high temperatures of Earth's atmosphere. After some consideration, Chuck theorizes that this dust might constitute a form of "cosmic protection" akin to the protective skin developed by primeval creatures when they first emerged from the water onto the earth and into the sunlight. This conceit reinforces the theme of outer space as a cohesive world onto itself that attempts to penetrate into the inner world of the Earth. This positions the dust as akin to the exoskeletons worn by the humans in *Avatar*—a more bacteria resistant form of the tripods used by Wells' Martians—that protects foreign bodies from the anti-immune system of the alien world. Yet unlike *Avatar*, in *The First Man into Space* this "cosmic protection" only seems to work on non-human entities, like the space craft, and is possibly lethal to human life, as seen in the later parts of the film.[52]

Chuck follows a trail of new deaths, surmising that Dan must have been coated in the meteorite dust when his aircraft's canopy was destroyed. The dust would have protected him on the descent back to Earth and forced large amounts of nitrogen into his body, enabling him to breath in space. This process would have triggered a dramatic change in Dan's metabolism,

Figure 6. Mankind trapped within the horrors of space—anonymous State Trooper being attacked by the space monster (Bill Edwards). *First Man Into Space*. Directed by Robert Day (Metro-Goldwyn-Mayer: 1959).

---

52. *The Quatermas Experiment* (Guest: 1955) shows a similar idea of an alien entity entering the Earths atmosphere via an astronaut, though here it's more internal than external.

limiting his ability to absorb nutrients to the consumption of blood. This conceit harks back to Stoker's *Dracula* and the refrain of "blood is the life" (Stoker: 1997, 158), so often repeated by Renfield in its adaptations. If blood is symbolic of life (humanity) itself, then Count Dracula must consume it due to his non-human status, as do the non-human alien vampires.

Chuck's theories are proven correct when Dan's encrusted helmet is found at the site of the latest victim, confirming that the marauding alien is none other than his brother. In the test center, Chucks hears screaming and a crashing sound and discovers that a transformed Dan has entered the building. Realizing that Dan is having trouble breathing, Chuck tries to replicate high-altitude air, effectively putting the space creature back into outer space while still on Earth. This procedure calms Dan sufficiently to allow him to recount his fleeting memories. He recalls blacking out, a feeling of suffocation and a need to return to the test center. The protective layer over his body loosens its grip on him and Dan apologizes for his actions while, in part, blaming them on his desire to be the first man in space. He then falls and dies, bringing the film to a close, apart from a final thought from Chuck that space travel will happen as "there will always be men willing to take the risk" (Fay: 1957).

As an alien-human hybrid, Dan manifests multiple anxieties around the figure of the vampire: dangerous outsider; violence; miscegenation. The last in particular is worth considering as the film treats the idea of hybridity as a dire threat. Given the time period of this film's first release during the Cold War, the premise whereby Dan is instantly attacked by the environment and becomes a portal into the human atmosphere configures humanity as American and outer space as the Soviet Union. Dan is thus exiled from humanity and life as punishment for venturing into the space of the other, i.e., outer space that is also the USSR, triggering an uncontrollable desire to reconnect and consume "life," as he is effectively no longer "alive." The film thereby warns of the inherent dangers of leaving the earth's atmosphere This gives rise to two connected readings. First, that space is an existentially dangerous place for humanity, and second, that anyone who ventures into it will instantly become unhomely, a stranger to their home world. Astronauts thus become instantly abhuman once they are no longer on Earth, exampling a body that is potentialized, othered, and on the cusp of changing into something that is dangerous to humanity as we currently know it. In a sense then the space crust around Dan does not connect worlds like a doorway, but rather disconnects him, never allowing him to find home on Earth again. The next film, *The Astronaut's Wife*, while taking up much of the anxiety around abhuman bodies returning from space, sees the hybrid human/alien vampire as most definitely a doorway into our own world.

Ravich's *The Astronaut's Wife* is also non-futuristic, and is very much part of late 1990s America. In many ways it picks up the general sense of anxiety over outer space which also permeates films such as *Solar Crisis* (Smithee: 1990), *Species* (Donaldson: 1995), *Event Horizon* (Anderson: 1997), *Contact* (Zemeckis: 1997), *Armageddon* (Bay: 1998), *Virus* (Bruno: 1999), where extraterrestrial beings and even space itself seem intent on causing death and destruction on Earth. *Species*, mentioned in the previous chapter, is of particular importance in this context as it shares many narrative similarities with *The Astronaut's Wife*. In some respects, *Species* and *The Astronaut's Wife* offer competing views of feminine and masculine monstrosity, the former hyper-sexualized, emotional, and "gooey" and the latter violent, rational, and controlling.

The Astronaut's Wife focuses on an American space mission where two astronauts, Spencer Armacost (Johnny Depp) and Alex Streck (Nick Cassavetes), leave the safety of their craft to perform some repairs on its exterior. An explosion occurs while they are outside, and they lose communications with Earth. They manage to return to Earth but seemingly have no recollection of recent events. Their respective wives are overjoyed to see them, but slowly realize that their husbands have changed. Spencer decides to leave the space program and finds a civilian job in New York, but at his farewell party his wife Jillian (Charlize Theron) learns from Natalie Streck (Donna Murphy) that her husband Alex is also acting differently. This is borne out by his unusually violent behavior at the party before he falls to the floor dead. In short order, Natalie electrocutes herself in the bath. Spencer then has aggressive sex with Jillian, which is very unusual and seemingly sparked by these recent events, and she later discovers she is pregnant with twins.

Meanwhile, an ex-NASA employee, Sherman Reese (Joe Morton), believes he has proof that something untoward occurred in space and that the seeming explosion outside the space craft was actually a signal from outer space that had struck the astronauts. He further believes that this signal contained an alien life form seeking to reach the Earth and then to produce twins to pilot a sophisticated aircraft that is currently developed by the company for which Spenser now works. This aircraft can disable certain weapons that would leave the planet defenseless in the face of an extraterrestrial attack. Reese arranges to meet Jillian briefly and rely these facts to her, further informing her that Natalie was pregnant with twins when she killed herself. Jillian tries to get rid of the unborn twins, but Spencer intercedes, displaying a psychic connection to the children, almost as if they are all part of the same entity. In a final desperate act, she barricades herself in a room and then fills it with water from an overflowing sink and threatens to kill herself with bared wires when Spencer breaks in. He tries to calm her, but she exclaims that she has no idea who he is now, to which he replies:

> No? Well I'll tell you what. There was a time I remember when you didn't want me to go up there [space]. And you begged me not to. Remember how scared you were? And I told you then, that I was going to bring back with me a little piece of heaven. And you cried. You remember that? Well fuckin' A! I did it! What do you think is inside you? I gave you heaven [Ravich: 1999].

This is an interesting reply, as it suggests that the entity is on some level equated to the other world of space itself and that the astronauts' bodies have become its doorway into the human realm. Further, the only way for it to bring more of the other world into this one is by replicating itself through biological reproduction. This part echoes a similar impetus in *Species*, whereby the "alien" is shown in a "desirable" human body—young, physical and film star attractive—as though designed to lure unsuspecting humans to their doom. With Sil, the alien DNA is a physical reality within her, literally part of her genetic makeup, and as her emotions rise it causes physiological transformations in her body. For Spencer, the alien seems to have no physical form and its ability to travel as a kind of electromagnetic wave through space suggests that it haunts or possesses his body more like an other worldly spirit.[53] Unsurprisingly then, Spencer acts more like he is possessed by a demon or a vampiric parasite—although he has great strength there are no external signs of his changed nature. The story then unfolds much like *Rosemary's Baby* (Polanski: 1968) with Spencer as both the Satanic group influencing Jillian and the Devil himself impregnating a host to allow the forces of Hell into the world. In this sense, the human body acts equally as a doorway between worlds and as an exoskeleton of sorts for the vampiric entity protecting it from its new environment—indeed it seems that even via reproduction the entity still requires a human body to protect it and is still linked to the "parent" from which it emerged.

The only way to permanently close this doorway appears to be by killing the human body, and more specifically by using electricity. Notwithstanding that Spencer's fellow astronaut Alex keeled over and died from an unspecified cause (it is only called a stroke as it appears to involve similar symptoms and no postmortem is undertaken), his wife Natalie uses electricity to kill herself and the unborn babies inside her. Jillian opts for the same approach, first trying to electrocute herself and the unborn twins, but when Spencer stops her and threatens physical violence to her own

---

53. The film *Night of the Big Heat* [aka Night of the Burning Damned] (Fisher, 1967) similarly shows aliens that are able to travel as electromagnetic waves but manifest as amorphous energy vampires that are rather too easily disposed of by rainwater.

family—her sister is a frequent guest at the household—she then throws an electric appliance into a pool of water she has made on the apartment floor while Spencer is standing in it. This kills Spencer, but curiously not the entity within him that then transfers to Jillian, ensuring the survival of the twins. While this does not make a lot of sense in terms of the "lore" established earlier in the film—though there is never any mention of esoteric knowledge confirming that electricity would kill such an entity—it is something that is not uncommon within vampire mythology. Dracula himself was an ethereal entity able to exert influence and enter the minds of others from a great distance. Other films such as *Planet of the Vampires*, *Daughters of Darkness* (Kümel, 1971), *The Devil's Plaything* (Sarno, 1973), *Nadja* (Almereyder, 1994), and *The Host* (see below) also feature vampiric "souls" that are able to move from one host to another when the physical body has died. Consequently, this helps to affirm the alien entity's vampiric credentials as well as their reliance, at least while on Earth, on humans to survive.

At the end of the film, a possessed Jillian has now remarried and is seeing off her twin sons as they get on the school bus, and the boys and their mum exchange knowing glances as they leave. Again this nods to demon or Devil possession films and *The Omen* (Donner: 1976) in particular where the son of Satan shares just such a glance with the audience at the film's close to ensure that we are in on the story and its inevitable conclusion. Similarly, the children are doing their father's (now mother's) bidding so that one day they will allow the other world into this one. Much of this is seen in the next two films where we more clearly see the effects of the vampiric other world once it has found a way to enter the human one.

The Andromeda Strain, Robert Wise, 1971/ *The Invasion of the Body Snatchers*, Philip Kaufman, 1978

The Andromeda Strain takes place on Earth and in present day (relative to the time of release) 1971. It opens with a satellite crashing to Earth near a small hamlet of sixty-eight souls called Piedmont in New Mexico. The troubles begin when the local doctor retrieves the object and carries it to his offices to investigate it. By opening this extraterrestrial Pandora's box, he releases a deadly alien disease that decimates the small town's population. The film thereby picks up where *Life* left off, with an aggressive alien entity introduced into the human world.

The film begins in pseudo-documentary fashion, creating the impression of a series of events that have already taken place, an impression reinforced by the flashback construction of the ensuing narrative. The opening flashback follows a team of government specialists, Dr. Jeremy Stone (Arthur Hill) and Dr. Mark Hall (James Olson), who are sent in to Piedmont to investigate the satellite and ascertain whether it has brought back some kind of alien organism. They are dropped into the town by helicopter, wearing full hazmat-style protective clothing, and make their way to the doctor's offices. Once there they find the doctor's body and begin to examine it, discovering that all the blood in his body has been crystallized into powder. This deadly symptom points to the vampiric nature of the organism that draws energy from its victim's blood, consuming the blood and processing it into a desiccated or petrified substance. Indeed, to all intents and purposes the vampire from another world is invisible inside the human body and undetectable to the naked eye. It only becomes apparent when the veins of the victims are opened and shown to be full of crystallized blood. The team realize the danger that this organism poses and headquarters decides the area needs to be "cauterized" to prevent any spreading of the infection, not least by carrion birds that have picked at the bodies. As the scientists continue their examination, they find the same crystallized powder in everybody they come across except for a young baby and an elderly alcoholic that are the only survivors of the event. From here the scientists and the two survivors are taken to a top-secret government facility in Nevada and their research assumes the code name of "Wildfire." The facility itself looks like an old building belonging to the Department of Agriculture but extends deep underground. Its five descending levels are so deep that a full day is needed to descend from the highest to the lowest. As an extra level of security, the entire facility is built above a nuclear device that would evaporate the entire construction and anything within it should any leaks occur.

Jeremy and Mark join a team that has already assembled on site and they begin to examine the detritus of the satellite. On it they discover a greenish, pulsating life form that is extremely aggressive and able to instantly kill all human life—birds are seemingly unaffected. Events above ground reveal the extent of the organism's reach and the further dangers it might pose as a military jet flying over Piedmont falls out of the sky as all the rubber seals are dissolved by the alien entity. This resonates with a later text with a more virulent version of the Andromeda organism, *The Day the Earth Stood Still* (Derrickson, 2008). In the later film, an alien intelligence that acts as a universal eco-police force sends a huge robot constructed of nanobots to remove humanity from the planet before they destroy the Earth. The nanobots act like an all-consuming cloud that break down (consume) all the matter with which they come into contact in order to replicate themselves. The Andromeda organism can be seen to anticipate this later threat, as it could potentially replicate something of this specifically targeting humanity to return the planet to a far greener, and potentially more balanced, ecosystem.

The scientists continue to conduct experiments on animals in the laboratory, but these only increase the mystery surrounding the survival of the baby and the aged alcoholic. Dr. Hall seemingly cracks the puzzle, deducing that the baby, which is always crying, would have an extremely alkali blood while the alcoholic would have a very acidic one, intimating that the organism can only survive within the human bloodstream in a very narrow range of PH values. Although this points to a potential weakness in the organism—it can only affect the average human—the scientists are still no closer to discovering a way to kill it. Indeed, while conducting their tests they discover that the Andromeda strain consumes energy—very much like the alien entity in *Night of the Big Heat* (Fisher: 1967)—and that trying to destroy it using nuclear weapons as planned (and the facility itself is built on such a device as mentioned previously) would only give it an unlimited power source, allowing it to grow at an astronomical rate—the organism exists as a crystal that converts energy to nourishment.

The earlier report of the military jet crashing over the infection site is brought back into focus as the scientists realize that the entity is mutating. In this new form it no longer kills humans but attacks certain kinds of rubber/plastics, turning them to dust (as it once did blood). The new kind of plastic it "consumes" is a synthetic Polycron which resembles human skin and, when crystallized, looks like bone shards. However, the specialists at Wildfire do not realize that the Andromeda strain is mutating until it eats through the seals around the laboratory doors, setting off the quarantine alarms that begin a countdown to a nuclear explosion to purge the facility. Dr. Hall thus embarks on a superhuman mission to reach the third floor to switch off the detonating system, which he does with eight seconds to spare. The scientists now realize that they can cause the organism to mutate to a "friendly" form and neutralize the cloud of material that has drifted away from the original site by seeding clouds so that the subsequent rain triggers the appropriate chemical reaction. The film closes with Dr. Stone explaining to a faceless committee that although danger was averted this time it might not always be so. The closing scene of the organism dissolving into the ocean fades into a computer simulation of the evolution of the organism forming into the numbers "601" which the computers at Wildfire used to designate the influx of too much information.

This ominous ending suggests that the organism might continue to mutate, suggesting that this is probably an ongoing process that may well result in harmful, potentially deadly, consequences for humanity. Indeed, the fact that this present mutation attacks a substance that resembles human skin does not bode well for humanity. This marks another instance of the well-known vampire trope of an end that is not final and the suggestion that time is on the "monster's" side. *The Andromeda Strain* promulgates a very human-centric vision, as do nearly all the films mentioned in this book, where outer space is a world that is specifically anti-human and more so a vampiric manifestation that needs to consume mankind. The next film follows in this vein. It ostensibly features an organism that drifts through space and randomly seems to alight on the Earth, not unlike *Planet of the Vampires*, but its actions upon arrival intimate that Earth was its destination from the beginning.

Invasion of the Body Snatchers is a more extreme version of the trope of the vampire from another world using the human body to disguise itself. Kaufman's film is a remake of Don Siegel's 1956 film and inevitably contains an element of Cold War paranoia from that era, of an "alien" ideology changing one's friends and family into dangerous strangers.[54] Kaufman's film transmutes this theme into a more general paranoia and fear of difference in the Watergate era[55]; in the latter the vampire virus releases a kind of sexual, emotional chaos but the former sees an increasing repression and suppression of such human emotions. *Invasion of the Body Snatchers* opens on a distant world that resonates with both *Planet of the Vampires* and *Solaris* (to be discussed later) as it is a barren environment apart from mists swirling across its surface. There are no lights flashing in the luminescence but slowly we see the formation of translucent pods—reminiscent of the body of Calvin in *Life*—not unlike frog's spawn or even human sperm at various points in the scene. These eventually become concentrated enough to detach from the mists and rise into the atmosphere and leave the orbit of the planet—again we are not sure if this is their home world (though a speech later suggests it might be) or just the next in a chain of migrations—and drift into space. By the time it reaches Earth it has morphed into an organism that drops from the sky in rain (not unlike the seeded clouds in *The Andromeda Strain*). This combination of organism and rain may be read as a symbolic merging with the eco-system of the Earth to enlist its cooperation in ridding itself of the human pestilence. The organism thus falls on vegetation and makes this its first point of mutation on the surface of the Earth itself. Indeed, this natural attraction, or point of least resistance on the planet, points to the inherently plant-like nature of the alien entity, which recalls the original *The Thing from Another World* (Nyby, 1951)

---

54. Interestingly the novel *The Body Snatchers* (1955) by Jack Finney from which all the film versions derive, is far more like The War of the Worlds and its commentary on colonialism with the aliens only having a life cycle of five years which would doom the Earth to inevitably become a dead planet. One of the invaders even claims this is exactly what humans do: using up resources, killing indigenous peoples, and destroying ecosystems.

55. It should be noted that Cronenberg's film was more directly related to political events in Canada than any kind of comment on American politics or wider Cold War anxiety.

and *Queen of Blood* (Harrington, 1966). This is a major theme throughout the film, with constant references to plants and vegetation, culminating in a mud-sauna which is often lit with green lights glowing through billowing white cubicle curtains as if it were a huge hot-house complete with gestating alien pods.

The alien life form flows in water down trees and bushes and collects on leaves as a coagulated jelly, stretching its veins out across its new host and vampirizing it by drawing into itself the life essence (new DNA material) from it and creating a small pod-like growth which eventually produces a small flower.

The flower seems to emit a scent as it is picked by Elizabeth Driscoll (Brooke Adams) who inhales it deeply and then takes it back to her home and puts it in a glass of water. Not noticing that the pod has grown roots in the water, Elizabeth and her boyfriend Geoffrey (Art Hindle) go to bed—the glass is nearest Geoffrey. But when she awakens, the glass has disappeared and Geoffrey, unusually, is fully awake, smartly dressed and tidying some unidentified mess which he hides away in a garbage truck parked outside their house—the city suddenly seems full of garbage trucks disposing of the detritus of the alien pods. Geoffrey behaves still more strangely the next night, not responding to any of Elizabeth's advances and seemingly, and suddenly, devoid of all emotions. Elizabeth in turn consults her friend and colleague Matthew (Donald Sutherland), telling him that "her Geoffrey" is no longer Geoffrey. Matthew does not quite believe her, but the following day he hears a similar story from the owner of a launderette, which

Figure 7. The parasitic vampires that live in the darkness of the human mind. *The Host*. Directed by Andrew Niccol (Open Road Films: 2013).

he then repeats to Elizabeth. Upon Elizabeth's urging, Matthew decides to take her to a renowned psychologist of his acquaintance, David Kibner (Leonard Nimoy), but they encounter a stranger (Kevin McCarthy from the original film) on their way, who throws himself on the bonnet of their car and screams that "They're coming! Something terrible! You're in danger!" (Kaufman: 1978). The stranger tries to escape on foot but is knocked down and killed by another car, while the bystanders are all emotionlessly staring down at the inert body on the ground. This is a key feature in the story from its beginning where random people in the background will just stop and stare at the main protagonists. The most unnerving incident occurs during the first rain shower, when a priest (Robert Duvall) on a children's swing in a playground stares with a fixed expression at the camera (us) while swinging.[56] This resonates with the "possession" theme mentioned earlier in relation to *The Astronaut's Wife*, whereby alien entities increasingly possess the planet—everyone being filled with a "little bit of heaven." *Invasion of the Body Snatchers* differs from *The Astronaut's Wife*, however, insofar as the aliens do not possess human bodies, but rather create human avatars for their consciousness, more in the vein of *Avatar*.

Matthew and Elizabeth meet Kibner at a book signing where a hysterical woman confronts him about her changed husband. Many in the room just stand and stare, but Elizabeth is fascinated with the woman's story. Kibner calms the woman, and later tells Matthew and Elizabeth that he is seeing more and more of this type of hysteria over the past few days, though he blames it on the problems of relationships in the modern world[57]—the 1970s had seen the introduction of laws increasing women's rights and control over their own bodies with the effect that dating and relationships were no longer solely the precursor to marriage (see Mavis: 2017). A poet friend of Matthews, Jack (Jeff Goldblum) leaves the book party and goes to see his wife Nancy (Veronica Cartwright) who works in a mud baths (the scene described above). A stranger brings a peculiar plant into the baths and when Jack falls asleep in the steamy atmosphere a huge pod, produced by the plant, begins to take on his form. Nancy discovers this and calls Matthew who suddenly realizes he has no idea if Elizabeth is all right and goes to her house. There he finds the same thing happening to her and grabs her off the bed where she is sleeping and runs out of the house with her. Back

---

56. This scene begins an odd sexual undercurrent that flows throughout the film; male priests in children's playgrounds; Elizabeth fondling Geoffrey's genitals; only naked men in the mud showers; a scene on the streets in the sex district of San Francisco; the repressed sexual tension between Matthew and Elizabeth throughout; and finally a naked alien Elizabeth running amongst the pod factory workers and no one noticing.

57. There is a sense that this comment is aimed at the hangover of 1960s liberalism, the hippie movement and free love, though the film equally takes aim at political/ideological conformity.

at the baths they call Kibner to come and see the evidence they have, but by the time he arrives the half-formed pods are no longer there. Kibner tries to calm them down and rationalize what they "think" they have discovered, but when he departs, he gets in a car with Geoffrey and another pod-person.

The infection escalates until San Francisco seems to consist of more avatars than real humans, with crowds of them emerging at night to clear away evidence of their creation, sweeping away the remains of the pods and rounding up any humans who have remained unchanged. The aliens' routines mark out their vampiric nature, as signaled by their preference for the dark. Not unlike Dracula, their nutritional requirements demand closeness, if not intimacy, with their victims. As in the failed attempts to clone Elizabeth and Jack, the plant needs to be close to the body of its victim so that it can send out tiny fibrous roots/feelers to connect to it. Once joined to the skin, the roots begin to draw out the human's life energy, which lends the pod its form, followed by the victim's mind and memories. Thus, if the victim is awoken before this final stage, they can still survive, while the pod collapses and dies. The victim's memories would seem rather superfluous to this process, but Geoffrey's interactions with Elizabeth make clear that he is aware of their past relationship. The end result of this process is dramatically revealed at the film's end, when Elizabeth falls asleep in a field and a pod connects to her. By the time Matthew finds her the process is too far gone and as he holds her in his arms, she crumples like an empty paper bag, only her dried-out skin remaining while everything else becomes part of the alien pod. The resultant pod-avatar is a naked version of Elizabeth that seems to rise up out of the ground and wails at Matthew to call attention to the other pod-avatars nearby.

Like the aliens in *Planet of the Vampires*, the aliens in *Invasion of the Body Snatchers* seek absolute control over Earth and are not content to leave any "real" humans alive. The film comes to an end with the unstoppable spread of the pod-avatars and the world of conformity and uniformity holding sway over that of emotion and individuality. The aliens might not suck the Earth dry and then move on to another planet, and indeed, their arrival could be seen as an intergalactic blessing on the ecosystem and its continued survival, not least as the volatile humans are no longer a threat to the planet. What the pod-avatars might require as sustenance once they have assumed human form is never made clear. In this sense, if we compare *Invasion of the Body Snatchers* to *War of the Worlds*, the ending paints a bleak picture for humanity, with no intimation of how we might change now to prevent such an occurrence in the future, nor any suggestion of a human resistance that might save the last remnants of humanity. However, the final two films examined in this chapter are a little more hopeful of the prospect of closing the doorway between worlds and repelling the alien invaders.

The Host, Andrew Niccol, 2013/
Get Out, Jordan Peele, 2017

Andrew Niccol's *The Host* and Jordan Peele's *Get Out* take up the idea of the human body as part receptacle or part avatar and part doorway for alien entities to travel from their world to ours, thereby continuing Wells' evolutionary link between humanity and the Earth. Neither film is obviously about vampires though both feature vampiric parasites, in the same mold as *Planet of the Vampires* and *The Astronaut's Wife*. They also examine the possibility of resistance despite the overwhelming odds stacked against humanity in the face of the vampires from another world.

The Host is an adaptation of the book of the same name by Stephenie Meyer from 2008 and is a follow-up to her extremely successful *Twilight Saga* of novels and their cinematic adaptation, with the first film adaptation, directed by Catherine Hardwicke, released the same year as the publication of the first book. And although ostensibly *The Host* is a separate tale from the *Twilight* saga, the shadow of the vampire looms large over it. *Twilight* and *The Host* both recount the trials and tribulations of an adolescent girl trapped in a mundane life and striving for more, dreaming of freedom and experiencing "life" at its fullest. A staple of these desires is that she must choose between two young men. In *Twilight*, the normal world was human and the special world was vampiric. In *The Host*, this dynamic is reversed with the Earth largely populated by "vampires" so that being human is the key to achieving her aspirations. The future world in which *The Host* is set is almost a vision of what the planet would be like once the pod-avatars in *Invasion of the Body Snatchers* had completed their plan. The world has become a rational, emotionless, ecologically friendly environment, as one character, Jeb (William Hurt) narrates: "There is no Hunger. There is no violence. The environment has healed. Our planet has never been more at peace. Only, it's not our planet anymore" (Niccol: 2013). His remarks bring to the fore the idea of ownership and the suggestion that humanity might not be the best steward of the Earth.

The vampiric aliens are called "Souls" and are small, luminous parasitic entities, effectively energy vampires, that live in a hosts body and take control over it by suppressing its consciousness.[58] After the vampiric

---

58. There was an earlier version of such an idea in the television series *The Tomorrow People* (Price: 1973–9). In the episode "The Living Skins" (Season 7, episode 3, November 1978) the Earth is invaded by Bubble-aliens—effectively inflated balloons of skin—that take over their victims by encasing them in skin (which looks like a tight fitting cat-suit). The aliens aim to digest all living matter but one of the victims realizes he is immune as he has a cold—an obvious nod to *The War of the Worlds*. The authorities then manufacture enough cold virus to infect the world to save humanity.

parasite has infected its human host, it leaves few visible traces of itself apart from silver rings in the hosts eyes and their calm and emotionless demeanor. Unlike in The *Invasion of the Body Snatchers*, the alien vampiric parasites in *Host* specifically chose the Earth because its inhabitants were too violent and on the verge of doing irreparable damage to its ecosystem. They thus arrive on Earth almost as an intergalactic police force to save the planet, in much the same way that Klaatu and Gort are sent in *The Day the Earth Stood Still*.

The vampiric parasite's penetration of the human body usually "kills" the human consciousness in the body, leaving it as a fleshy exoskeleton that enables the vampiric parasite to survive the environment of its new world. The cause and origins of this process are never explained, but by the beginning of the story the majority of humans have been colonized and groups of "Seekers" are tasked with searching out the remaining survivors so that they too can become hosts—a not uncommon trope in vampire apocalypse films where the human "resistance" is hunted down by specialized vampire forces (see *The Matrix*, and *Daybreakers* [Spierig Brothers: 2009] for example). The Souls appear to be transported through space in small silver egg shaped containers that are then "beamed" through space—quite literally as they appear to travel through beams of light—to be "caught" in a docking station. The docking station's equipment appears to be extremely specialized, calling into question how the parasitic vampires landed on the Earth in the first place. Once implanted into a host, these parasites are extremely difficult to remove, not least due to their fragile, almost ethereal form, and the fact they directly connect to the brain. The few examples

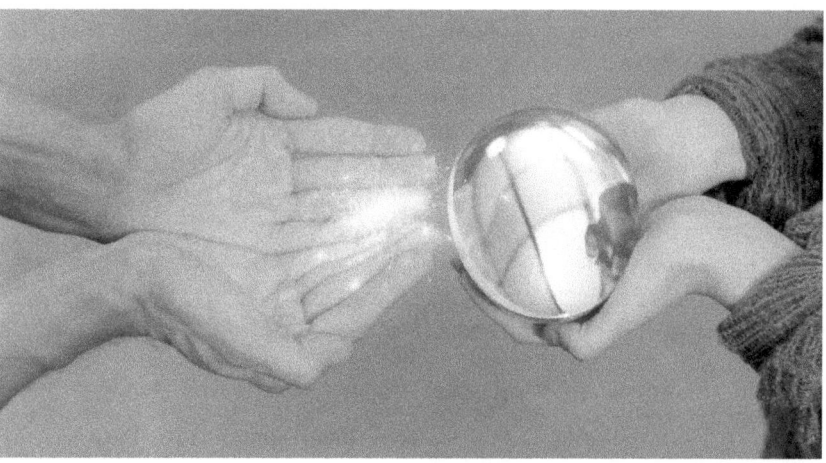

Figure 8. Alien vampire sucking life out of its new host. *Invasion of the Body Snatchers.* Directed by Philip Kaufman (United Artists: 1978)

shown of human bodies that have undergone such a procedure for removal depict the human left in an almost vegetative state. As such, the conversion of Earth from a human world into an alien one seems almost complete until "Wanderer"—the individual Souls have names and are seemingly gendered with the Wanderer identifying as female—is implanted in Melanie (Saoirse Ronan).

When humans are assimilated the Seekers often interrogate the newly "bodied" Soul for information on the host's former life to discern where resistance groups might be hiding out—the parasites can also read their host's memories—but this process seems to awaken, rather than subdue, Melanie's consciousness, so that the two entities are living and aware of each other in the same body. This is highly unusual, and curiously Wanderer and Melanie quickly strike up a friendship. Thus, when the Seeker (Diane Kruger) in charge of questioning Wanderer demands to be implanted in Melanie's body to look at the host's memory directly, Melanie assists the Soul to escape from the facility where they are being kept. Melanie is trying to get in touch with her younger brother who is staying in a hidden human community run by her uncle Jeb (mentioned above). Unfortunately, the Seeker had managed to glean some clues of her plans by questioning Wanderer, and therefore has some idea of possible locations in which to capture them as she sets out to find the escapee.

The Seeker she/it seems to belie the supposed emotionless state of the rest of the Souls. Even before Wanderer and Melanie escape, there seems to be a personal dimension to the Seeker's interrogation to discover the hideout of the human resistance. In this sense she is actually very similar to the vampire James (Cam Gigandet) in *Twilight,* who is called a "tracker" in the film, denoting a vampire that becomes "locked" on its prey once they have its scent and will pursue them until they are dead. The Seeker, upon realizing that Melanie is not suppressed, becomes positively obsessed with tracking them down, so much so that even other Seekers seem perturbed by her actions.[59] Indeed, the relentless, almost sadistic nature of the pursuit resonates with the ending of *Planet of the Vampires* with their shared sneer as they head toward an unsuspecting Earth, as well as the inevitability seen at the end of *Invasion of the Body Snatchers.* Even when the central authority decides to stop the operation to find Wanderer, Seeker persists, driving out into the wilderness to continue the search.

In the meantime, Wanderer has been accepted into the human community run by Melanie's Uncle Jeb. The community realizes that Wanderer

---

59. The world of the Souls is shown as hyper-modern, clean lined, and efficient in comparison to the human world which seems to have reverted back to the Wild West (a not uncommon trope of post-apocalyptic films) seeing the vampiric parasites as a presage of a technological future sucking the life out of the human past.

and Melanie are two entities in the same body. They have attempted on various previous occasions to remove the vampiric parasites but always with bad results for both the vampire and the human. Wanderer eventually tells them how to perform the removal procedure properly, on the condition that they save Melanie but let her die. Wanderer has grown tired of continually watching those she loves dying—the various hosts' bodies are not immortal and thus the Souls must move on before the host dies or risk dying together with their host.[60] Wanderer's disclosure coincides with Seeker's discovery of the community's hideout. The community manage to incapacitate her long enough to remove her parasite and send it via the launching pad to a distant planet, ensuring they will all be dead by the time Seeker manages to find its way back to Earth.

Wanderer is then removed from Melanie's body and implanted in a new host, who was left effectively braindead after an earlier unsuccessful de-coupling operation. Joined to this new human body, Wanderer can live a normal human lifespan and die—Meyer of course sets up a romantic scenario with one of Melanie's two suitors to make this seem like a desirable, human outcome. *The Host* marks two interesting divergences from the established trope of the vampiric parasite. First, they do not seem driven by survival as an end in itself, unlike the other films discussed in this chapter, and as the story ends Melanie's group of survivors encounter another Soul that has defected to the side of the resistance. Second, humanity is not inevitably doomed in *Host*, and furthermore, the film suggests that the human condition makes the continued survival of humanity possible or even desirable (possibly because of its link to evolutionary imperatives). The next film also shows that the success of the vampiric parasites is not necessarily eternal, and that human resistance is possible, even when the vampires are from the alien world of white wealth and privilege.

Get Out is vampiric in the literal sense of a vampiric parasite from one world living within the body of those from the other, and in the metaphorical sense of the wealthy sucking the life out of the poor, specifically in terms of white wealth and black exploitation. The film centers on an up-and-coming African American photographer, Chris Washington (Daniel Kaluuya), who leaves New York city to visit the family of his white girlfriend, Rose Armitage (Allison Williams), in upstate New York. Her parents, Dean (Bradley Whitford) and Missy (Catherine Keener) are a neurosurgeon and a hypnotherapist respectively and they live in a large, white, mansion-style house on extensive grounds and appear to have hired

60. Although it is not explicitly stated in the film, the implanting process of the vampiric parasites will implicitly cause humanity to die out as they never seem to reproduce and so will only inhabit the Earth until the current human population runs its course.

only black people as their domestic help. Along with Rose's brother Jeremy (Caleb Landry), they all appear to make disconcerting remarks about African American people. Ill-at-ease, Chris notices both servants, Georgina (Betty Gabriel) and Walter (Marcus Henderson), behaving strangely and making odd remarks. One night, he is unknowingly put into a trance by Missy, supposedly to help him quit smoking. The unnerving tone of *Get Out* rises to a pitch at a large gathering at the house composed almost entirely of wealthy white people. The exception is Logan King (Lakeith Stanfield), an African American of roughly the same age as Chris but who acts like an elderly man. When Chris accidentally activates the flash on his camera when trying to secretly take a picture of Logan, he appears to have a seizure of some kind and rushes toward Chris, screaming for him to "Get out" (Peele: 2017). Chris decides he needs to leave immediately, with or without Rose, but before he can do so, Missy puts him into a trance and he awakens tied to a chair and about to be prepped for some kind of surgery. Realizing that Rose has betrayed him, Chris discovers that the impending operation will implant the consciousness of an elderly, blind, wealthy white gallery-owner into his brain, suppressing his own identity, so that the newly inserted consciousness will take possession of his body and thereby receive a new lease on life. This premise resembles that of *The Host*, where Wanderer was surgically implanted into Melanie's body and given full control of it. In *Get Out*, the two aforementioned "servants" have already been subjected to this process and implanted with Rose's grandparents. However, before the operation can be performed, Chris manages to escape and kills the entire Armitage family in the process, after which he is rescued in the nick of time by his friend, TSA agent Rod Williams (Lil Rel Howery).[61]

Get Out thereby constructs two worlds, the vampiric one of white wealth and privilege, based on ownership of land and property and a perceived "natural" superiority, which is a manifestation of the United States' long and painful history of racism and slavery. As a counterpoint to this portrait of rural Upstate New York, New York City emerges as a shared, if unequal, space where black and white Americans can uneasily coexist. In this respect, Chris' journey to the Armitage manor is not unlike Jonathan Harker's to Dracula's castle through the land beyond the forest, and the more he distances himself from civilization (the city), the more he approaches manifestations of a dark past—if Harker was given a warning by a superstitious old woman on his journey, Chris is similarly warned

---

61. The original ending was to have Chris killed by a member of the local police force, mirroring the ending to George Romero's *Night of the Living Dead* (1968) where the one African American character, Ben (Duane Jones), escapes the zombies only to be shot by the white police at film's end. The theatrical release has the more upbeat ending mentioned here.

when Rose's car hits a deer and a policeman demands to see his identification even though he is only a passenger, suggesting that the officer immediately assumes black skin to be a marker of guilt. That this is a trip to another world, the one beyond modernity, is further confirmed by the old woodlands that surround the Armitages' house, cutting them off from both their neighbors and the world beyond. This sense of isolation increases inside their house and on their land, where Chris can only contact his friend in the city via phone, not unlike an astronaut on a space ship communicating with Earth, with the signal similarly breaking up and going dead at the most important moments in their conversation.

The Armitages' manor is reminiscent of the planation house that was the heart of the wealth and violence of slavery. The similarity is noted by Sarah Juliet Lauro (2018) and immediately configures the African Americans there as zombies, soulless machines at the disposal of their white masters. The Armitages' house thus emerges as a modern-day incarnation of slavery and its legacy, newly risen from the dead like an undead monster. If the African Americans in this film are cast as mindless zombies—zombi in the pre–Romero, voodoo sense—then the Armitages and the wealthy white society of which they are a part are the vampires, literally living off the lifeblood of their slaves which are exclusively black[62]—it is suggested at one point that putting their consciousness into black bodies, as opposed to white ones, is a recent fad or fashionable accessory, which squares with the fact that the procedure, at least as Dean undertakes it, would seem to require quite recent technology. The reduction of African Americans into objects or animals that may be handled as one pleases takes further point in a large gathering at the Armitage house, which is actually a glorified slave market with Chris the unknowing "lot" up for auction, which is confirmed later on as we see them bidding for a picture of Chris with Dean as the auctioneer.

The world of vampires in *Get Out* is centered on the Armitage house, even though it expands its tendrils to the wealthy areas of countryside beyond their house. The "vampires" of this world gather annually at the big white house to choose the next host for one of their number who wishes to implant their consciousness in a black man. In this vein, all the members of this group are white and old, reinforcing the stereotype of rich, old white men as vampires who promulgate the vampiric ideologies of late capitalism and new-liberalism where money can buy anything

---

62. The connection between slavery and vampires, and particularly with the American South, is one that occasionally appears in vampire narratives with *Abraham Lincoln: Vampire Hunter* (Bekmambetov: 2012) being one of the most obvious examples. Though the first vampire story to feature slavery is *The Black Vampyre: A Legend of St. Domingo* (1819) by Uriah Derick D'Arcy.

and everything can be owned. As noted by another old white man, Karl Marx, "Capital is dead labour, that, vampire-like, only lives by sucking living labour, and lives the more, the more labour it sucks. The time during which the labourer works, is the time during which the capitalist consumes the labour-power he has purchased of him" (Marx: 2007, 257). As mentioned before the film intimates that this is an ages-old tradition that has been carried on for generations[63]; as declared by Dean at one point, "we are the gods trapped in cocoons" (Peele: 2017) and which is to some extent confirmed when Chris finds Rose's photo album, hidden in a small cupboard in her bedroom. Rose has always told Chris that he was her only Black boyfriend, but the album shows images of her in romantic embraces with many Black men and women, two of which are Georgina and Walter. However, once Chris is tied to a chair being readied for the operation, he is forced to watch a video of what is going to happen to him. This describes a secret society called the Coagula, a White supremacist organization dedicated to retaining their wealth and power through immortality, which is achieved by transplanting their consciousness into new, younger bodies. It becomes obvious that Rose actually goes into the city to choose and bring back victims for her father to sell to the highest bidder and, as seen in the opening scene of the film, that Jeremy does something similar but he mugs unsuspecting lone Black people on the street and bundles them in his car to bring home.

The operation itself seems to involve opening the top of the skull of the host and the man whose consciousness is being transferred and implanting the white man's brain into the brain of the black man, as Dean is heard to describe to Chris:

> The piece of your brain connected to your nervous system needs to stay put to keep those intricate connections intact. So you won't be gone, not completely; a sliver of you will still be in there somewhere. Limited consciousness. You'll be able to see and hear, but what your body is doing—your existence—will be as a passenger [Peele: 2017].

As a preliminary to this procedure, Missy must hypnotize the victim and send their consciousness to the "sunken place," which appears to be akin to the unconscious or repressed parts of one's memory—a point emphasized by the fact that she uses Chris' most traumatic memory, his mother's death, to cast him into this psychological purgatory.

Yet Chris refuses to be victimized and manages to escape, killing Dean

---

63. This is something of a contradictory point in the film which simultaneously suggests that the process has been going on for generations, and yet also says the process was only perfected by Dean Armitage. There is no indication of how the procedure would have been possible before that point.

Figure 9. Chris (Daniel Kaluuya) falling into the sunken place inside his own head. *Get Out*. Directed by Jordan Peele (Universal Pictures: 2017).

with the antlers of a mounted stag's head, thereby staking him in an appropriate and necessary destruction of the King Vampire.[64] Chris knocks over some candles in the process, igniting a fire in the operating room, and as he runs away he likewise kills Missy, Jeremy, and accidentally, Georgina. Chris goes back for Georgina after hitting her with his car, but she attacks him, because her body is inhabited and controlled by Rose's grandmother, leading to Chris crashing the car and killing Georgina, thereby resolving his trauma around his mother's death and his failure to help her. Rose holds a gun on Chris while Walter, inhabited and controlled by her grandfather, restrains him, but Chris sets off his camera flash in Walter's face, allowing Walter's true personality to resurface, upon which Walter snatches Rose's gun, shoots her, and kills himself. A TSA vehicle arrives[65] and Rose, who is still alive despite her stomach wound, calls for help from what she believes will be a white law enforcement officer. However, the Armitage house is now in flames behind her and the doorway it represents to the other world of vampiric white influence and power is now closed, and so the figure that steps out of the car is not a white officer of that world but a black one of Chris's world, specifically Chris's friend, a TSA agent named Rod. Now that

64. In a discussion with Andrew M. Boylan, he identifies strong ties between *Get Out* and *The Lost Boys* (Schumacher: 1987) seeing a correlation between the character involved in each where "Rose is the lure (Star in *Lost Boys*), Dean is the one who is to change him (David in *Lost Boys*)... but Roman (Walter in *Lost Boys*) is arguably the King Vampire (he created Coagula).... The killing of Dean mirrors the killing of David in *The Lost Boys*. The next Jordan Peele film, *Us* (2019), also has a *Lost Boys* connection [a coastal location and the centrality of the boardwalk to the plot]."
65. There is a running gag throughout the film that Chris' friend Rod acts as though he is a policeman when he actually works for the Transport Security Administration.

the pull of the old world has been broken, Chris is safe to leave and return to his modern life, leaving Rose dying on the ground.

Just as with Stoker's Dracula, this is an open-ended conclusion, as Rose has not died by the end, much as vampires are particularly resistant to death, and thus, while the doorway to that other world is closed, it is not irrevocably locked and sealed. And of course, there are still many, many vampires left alive in the vampiric realm of white privilege, hoping to find a way to cross over into this world. This imperative to get to the Earth, whether literal or embodied in the black man, motivates many of the vampires in the next chapter as well, though the next chapter will focus more on the types of "food" they require once they arrive.

3

Lifeforce

This chapter continues to examine/explore the theme of parallel worlds, but it focuses on the diverse nutritional requirements of the vampire aliens from other worlds. Blood appears surprisingly low on the list of their nutritional needs, which range over many varieties of life-essences. Tobe Hooper's *Lifeforce* (1985), which also provides the title to this chapter, provides a very obvious version of this idea where aliens from space are "rescued" and brought to Earth where they proceed to suck the life energy out of the humans they encounter, leaving just a dried-out husk. The aliens in *Lifeforce* are exhaustive if rather indiscriminate in their energy requirements—though there is a suggestion that life force on some level equates with the human soul. Other vampires are rather more specific in the kinds of energy that they require, often sustaining themselves on energy of the emotional variety. The emotional states that sustain them are often uniquely human, and indeed, define the human condition as such. These alien vampires thus attack the very nature of our humanity, confirming our uniqueness even as it ensures our ultimate demise.

Citadel, Ciarán Foy, 2012/*NOS4A2*, Jamie O'Brien, 2019–present

Citadel takes place on a council estate in Scotland called Edenstown. The estate takes on a markedly post-apocalyptic appearance, with burned out cars and rubbish blowing across the abandoned streets. Ironically, the sign for the estate lists it as a site of "regeneration" correlating to many inner city regeneration projects that have become shanty towns for the poor and dispossessed.[66] At the heart of the estate are some tower blocks which appear empty, together with the housing units around them,

---

66. For issues involved around inner-city regeneration see Weaver: 2001.

as they dominate and glower over the surrounding environment not unlike Dracula's Castle over the Carpathians. *Citadel* opens with Tommy (Aneurin Barnard) leaving his apartment in one of the tower blocks and saying goodbye to his pregnant wife Joanne (Amy Shiels). He enters the lift at the end of the corridor and waves to Joanne as the doors close, but just as they do so, a gang of youths wearing hoodies attack his wife—the character of the gang of hoodie-wearing youths is kept purposefully ambiguous during much of the film, as they shift from seemingly innocuous to feral and almost demonic in a short space of time. Frantically trying to get the doors to reopen, Tommy is unable to help his wife, and by the time he reaches her, the gang has run off and Joanne is seriously injured, with a syringe plunged into her stomach, as though they were specifically trying to infect the unborn baby. Joanne is hurried to the hospital, Tommy is traumatized by the events and, although his daughter Elsa is born safely, he is left suffering from crippling agoraphobia.

Some months after the attack, Tommy is now living in a mid-terrace house on the estate with Elsa, while Joanne is still on life-support at the hospital. His house appears to be the only one with lit lights, making it seem that only he and the feral children inhabit the area, as if it were cut off from civilization. The council estate thus appears unreal, as though it exists solely in the mind of the protagonist. This impression is reinforced when Tommy returns home by bus only to be forcibly expelled from the vehicle by the driver, who refuses to enter the estate. Granted, this sequence correlates to real life situations on council estates in Britain, where communal housing, poor services, and budget cuts exacerbate declining infrastructure, poor hygiene, crime, and ghettoization, turning them into lawless, desolate areas to live into which bus drivers dare not venture (see Taylor: 2014). Scotland thus emerges as a world divided between the wealthy and the disadvantaged, where those on the side of despair and fear are caught in a downward spiral of economic, moral and urban decay they can never escape. In this respect, the bus driver literally refuses to pass from one world to the other. The gang (pack) of feral children thereby become a manifestation of the uncontrollable despair of the estate that to which the weak and disadvantaged succumb.

Joanne's life-support is finally turned off at the hospice—St. Anthony's the patron saint of lost souls—and Tommy takes Elsa to the funeral, accompanied by a nurse, Marie (Wunmi Mosaku). He runs into a priest (James Cosmo) at the funeral, who asks why he has not yet left the estate. Tommy wonders at his words and the Priest, who is accompanied by a small boy, explains that the gang are after Tommy's daughter, Elsa. Sometime later the Priest offers to take Tommy, and only him, to the children's hideout. Tommy leaves Elsa with Marie and accompanies the Priest in his car, together with the little boy, Danny (Jake Wilson), to the tower block where Tommy once lived. The Priest explains that the children/gang thrive on fear and are drawn to it, further noting "They *see* you Tommy." He elaborates as the children approach, "we need to get rid of them before the fucks spread somewhere else.... I don't see kids ... do they look like kids to you?" (Foy: 2012). Quickly returning to the car, they head back to Marie and Elsa. Tommy tells Marie about his exchange with the Priest, but Marie replies that it's "so easy to demonize children ... people like that man want to lock them up in a building and burn it to the ground" (Foy: 2012), which does indeed describe the Priest's plans.

As the story gathers pace, Marie's words return to haunt her when she accompanies Tommy and Elsa to a bus stop near her home. Reassuring Tommy there is no need to be afraid, she approaches the group of children who are now hanging around the subway entrance, upon which they viciously attack her and leave her for dead. The gang then turn toward Tommy, sensing his fear, screeching like animals as they approach. Tommy bolts out of the subway in terror, nearly crossing into the path of a bus. The bus stops in time and Tommy alights with Elsa, but just as it begins to move, the children waylay it and attack the driver. They knock Tommy down, rip Elsa from his arms and leave him unconscious on the floor.

The attack near Marie's house demonstrates the extent of the feral children's influence. Their constant feeding on fear seems to remove hope from a wider and wider area around them, which also gives credence to the Priest's warning about the children expanding their area of influence, suggesting that they operate rather like a contagion. Their influence now seems to have extended to the hospital where Tommy awakes after the attack. He finds himself in a hospital bed with no one else around him, as though the desolation from the estate has followed him to the building. When he eventually finds some patients, they are all sitting in a darkened room watching television, ignoring the world around them and fixated on their own entertainment, almost as if Tommy does not really exist. Tommy suddenly hears a noise behind him and turns to see the Priest there. The Priest reassures him that his daughter is still alive because the feral children remake other children in their own image. The Priest agrees to lead Tommy to the children, provided that Tommy helps him destroy the tower block in which they live. The Priest warns him that he will have to stay close to Danny to try and mask the fear that flows off him. He further explains that Danny was taken by the children and kept captive by them for a while but managed to escape. Consequently, Danny can see fear much like the feral children, and he is able negate the aura of fear of those close to him, thereby making it invisible to the feral children. Danny describes fear as being red, while Tommy's is "scarlet," drawing a connection between fear and blood and positioning the feeding habits of the children "feeding" as more clearly vampiric in nature.

The Priest discloses his knowledge of the children's nature and history as they prepare for their attack. In the early 1970s, the Priest knew of a junkie girl who lived in the tower block. The girl was pregnant, but abandoned by friends and family, and lived (survived) in the basement where she gave birth.[67] Local rumor suggests that she gave birth to multiple children that subsequently interbred creating the "dog children" that plague the estate. Equally it seems the despair and abandonment in which they were raised has turned them into creatures that simultaneously consume and cause those same emotional states/conditions that have festered in the environment around them.

Tommy discovers snatched children in the tower block, chained up in windowless rooms or locked in cages until they go blind and become dark, feral creatures that exist on the fear they inspire in others. Tommy, Danny and the Priest set explosives and begin descending to the basement of the block until they find Elsa in the company of the feral children, who are licking a dark fungus that grows up the walls of the building. The fungus seems to embody a kind of structural cancer, coalescing the hopelessness and dissolution of the estate into a malignant growth that provides something of a link between the original block and its spawn.

Indeed, the idea of cancer as a rot from within slowly spreading across the entire body underpins the film. The cancer of poverty and despair creates the vampiric children and the vampiric, alien, world they live in, which in turn spreads the disease ever further across the town, and the ideological system that engenders it. Furthermore, the Priest himself is dying from cancer and, as he reveals, was the father of the first monstrous children who abandoned them to their fate. The Priest thus embodies the failure of church and state to care for the most vulnerable elements of society, suggesting that both institutions are economically and spiritually bankrupt. In this respect, it is church and state who emerges as soulless demons that are predicated on the despair of the vulnerable.[68] Within the cancerous environment of the building, the Priest's own deadly disease erupts with renewed virulence, causing him to cough up blood and igniting fear within him. This instantly causes the feral children to "see" him, enacting the spread of a cancer that sees those born of the body (the father) attack

---

67. Curiously the girl was said to have died of an "unknown infection," which was the same cause of death attributed to Tommy's wife Joanna. One of the occasional coincidences, oddities, that occur throughout the film that suggest that the action all takes place inside Tommy's head.

68. The construction of the children as demonic in some way links it to films like *Heartless* (Ridley: 2009) where hoody-wearing demons roam the streets of London.

and consume it. The Priest then draws the feral children toward him, allowing Tommy and Danny to safely complete their journey to the basement, but as they enter the lift to descend, the same one from the beginning of the story, a feral child grabs Danny. Tommy manages to escape the lift this time around and fights off the feral child, eventually killing it and revealing it as an eyeless, ashen-skinned creature that crumbles to dust when it dies. Tommy seems instantly cured of his agoraphobia, suggesting that much of the film is about Tommy overcoming the trauma of losing his wife, a waking nightmare from which he must escape to regain his life. Suddenly it is Tommy who has become invisible to the children and it is now Danny, feeling vulnerable after the altercation, who needs calming down. Tommy leads the way and he quickly locates Elsa and prepares to make an escape from the building. However, by now it is morning and the majority of the children that were out scavenging for scraps of fear in the night are returning home to the block and entering it through the same tunnel that Tommy, Elsa and Danny are leaving it by. Tommy, with his newfound bravery, becomes the rock that protects Danny and Elsa as the vampire children flow around them and back into the basement from whence they came. Returning to the car, Tommy takes the detonator for the explosives in his hand and destroys the building and the children along with it. While this signals a new dawn for a land now safe from the vampires from another world, the estate behind the car is still apocalyptic and cold and lifeless due to the layer of snow covering it; Tommy might have awoken from his nightmare but it is unclear whether the world beyond him ever will. It should be noted that the denouement of the film is not without its problems, for if the feral children and their vampiric world are indeed the product of systematic neglect and abandonment, destroying them via explosives without addressing the underlaying issues will just allow the cancer to spread and grow again. In fact, the next narrative, *NOS4A2*, suggests such an outcome. This world is far more dream-like or nightmarish and more in the domain of another dimension that requires human emotional energies to traverse between the two.

NOS4A2[69] also features an alien world of vampiric children, though they are not in a real-world environment in the vein of *Citadel*'s housing estate, but an imaginary "dream" space named Christmasland. This world is in another dimension that can only be reached by a vampire named Charlie Manx (Zachary Quinto). Arguably it is only Manx's Rolls-Royce Wraith—its vanity plate bears the inscription NOS4A2—that can make the journey, taking with it whoever is sitting inside, which usually means

69. It is worth noting that this study is about the television series and it only focuses on the first season and the development of the story thus far.

Manx and the latest child he has abducted. It seems that Manx himself created Christmasland—we discover he is an especially gifted "creative," or one of a group of people who can construct imaginary places with their minds—which appears to be taken from adverts from American newspapers of the 1950s and '60s, but is a place where it is permanently Christmas and indeed looks like a romanticized postcard of where Santa Claus lives. It seems that Manx has created this specifically for young children, seeing it as a place of never-ending joy and happiness. For whatever reason, and one can only assume it is born of his own childhood, Manx collects children that he thinks are being abused by their parents—killing the parents and kidnapping the children[70]—and drives them in the Wraith to this other world. However, the children are always put in the back seat, which seems to be a separate world in itself—you cannot pass from the back seat to the front seat while inside the car. However, as the car gets closer to Christmasland the child "loses its soul"—which is signified by them growing large, razor-sharp teeth—and Manx gets younger, suggesting some form of vampiric activity. Indeed, when we first see Manx, he looks extremely old but quickly returns to the appearance of a man in his 30s after transporting his first victim to Christmasland. This partially corresponds to the children in *Citadel*, where if one reads them as demons, then it is their soulless nature that causes them to consume the souls of other children—making them like themselves—and also to *Lifeforce* where it is strongly intimidated that it is the "soul" which the alien vampires feed on. Once at the house in the middle of Christmasland—a cross between a gingerbread house and a Christmas lights wonderland—the new recruit, soulless child, is met by the other children there who all have similarly huge teeth, clawed hands and partially luminous eyes. The children all seem to treat Manx as their father, and in an interesting reversal of Dracula and his Brides, rather than bringing babies for the adult vampires to eat, he brings adults for the baby vampires to consume.

That said, Manx is not a direct correlation to Dracula as the vampiric entity in the series is more accurately called Manx-Wraith, that is the cyborg entity of Charlie Manx and his Rolls-Royce. As the story unfolds it becomes clear that Manx and the car are linked in some way. The exact nature of their symbiosis is never quite made clear, but we do see that if the Rolls-Royce runs out of fuel Manx visibly withers and ages. The Wraith itself is jet black and seems to haunt the series, manifesting a shadowy presence, that is almost spectral in its ability to pass between worlds. In this sense it very much reflects the qualities of another vampiric car, Christine,

---

70. "Child" seems a vague definition here which also partially extends to anyone who is still a virgin.

created by Stephen King—the father of *NOS4A2*'s writer Joe Hill.⁷¹ Christine, from the eponymous novel and film from 1983, is not shown as possessed or demonic in any way, but is inherently created as evil on the factory production line. Even there, when an interior finisher on the line drops ash on the car's front seats, Christine kills him. After leaving the factory Christine seems to choose her owners—while the car obviously has no gender it is sexualized in the film—always going for a certain kind of man that can be manipulated and controlled. Christine inevitably kills any women, wives, girlfriends, that vie for her owner's affections and also attacks anyone that threatens either herself or her driver. Blood seems central to the earlier film and while her driver/owner, Arnie, is merely human, Christine seems immortal through the imbibing/absorbing of blood. *NOS4A2* is vastly different and blood seems unnecessary for either the Wraith or Charlie Manx, although the children in Christmasland seem rather fond of it. However, the Wraith seems to have always been with Manx. We are told that Manx is 135 years old and that the car was built in 1938, making it extremely possible he has had the vehicle from new, and from what we find out later it is highly likely that he has made the car what it is. As mentioned above Manx is a "creative," someone that can make imaginary worlds with their mind, but needs the right artifact, a car, a motorbike, or anything—categorized as a "knife" that can cut through the skin separating dimensions⁷²—to travel there and back.

Manx, as already intimated, is not a traditional vampire and the series does not explicitly equate "creative" with "a vampire." Indeed, we see at least three other creatives in the series that do not exhibit such vampiric proclivities. One suspects though it is Manx's designation as "special" even amongst creatives and the energy it takes to support Christmasland and his constant traveling between worlds—we are shown that traveling beyond reality and back is mentally draining—that has brought out his vampiric characteristics. This supposition seems borne out as Manx appears to get old very quickly and has to regularly find children to take to the other world. Interestingly, as noted above, aging also occurs when the Wraith is low on fuel, suggesting that it is not Manx who consumes the children's souls but the car, with the intimate connection between the automobile and its driver allowing for the distribution of rejuvenating energy for both of them. We see this graphically in two scenes in the first series, when someone trapped in the Wraith's trunk manages to damage the fuel tank and as gasoline drips out, Manx gets older. A similar effect is seen when Manx's

---

71. Andrew M. Boylan pointed out that there is a purposeful connection between Manx and the True Knot, the group of energy vampires in King's book *Doctor Sleep* (2013).

72. A similar idea is used in Philip Pullman's *His Dark Materials* trilogy (1005–2000) where Lyra can cut through space to different locations/worlds using a "Subtle Knife."

nemesis Vic McQueen (Ashleigh Cummings), sets fire to the car and similarly he ages tremendously quickly as the vehicle erupts in flame.

If Manx/Wraith is the Dracula figure in the story, then Vic McQueen is the Van Helsing. Vic discovers by accident that she is gifted. Her parents are often quarrelling, and her father is an alcoholic, and one day she storms out of the house, sits on her motorbike and rides off. She arrives at an old wooden covered bridge, but when she rides out of the other side of it, she does not emerge into the woods that extend from that end of the bridge, but finds herself in the location she had envisaged in her mind. She begins to realize that when she is in a heightened emotional state, she can go anywhere by riding her bike across the bridge, which functions as a portal that is accessed by the motorbike that opens it like a dimensional "knife." This quickly puts her in opposition to Manx as he kidnaps a young girl who is her friend. She determines to discover where Manx has taken her, and then subsequently release all the children in Christmasland. Manx realizes that Vic is more than the average creative and decides he wants to make her his wife to look after the soulless children in his parallel world—not unlike Max in *The Lost Boys* (Schumacher: 1987)—however, she vows to destroy both Manx and the Wraith.

Vic still seems convinced that the children can be saved, as though by killing Manx their "souls" might be released back into their bodies. However, all the encounters with them in the real world suggest they will never be able to return to their bodies and their former identities, as they are as tied to Manx as he is to the Wraith. As the first series comes to a close, Manx is hospitalized in a coma and the Wraith is a burned-out husk in a junkyard. Unlike Christine, the Wraith seems incapable of rejuvenating itself, but a car enthusiast sees the wreckage of the Rolls-Royce and decides to begin working on it. The moment he begins working on the car, Manx awakens from his coma in the hospital, once again opening the bridge between worlds. While fear or strong emotion do not seem to be of much interest to Manx, the children in Christmasland certainly seem to delight in them in those they are about to consume. Such emotions come more to the fore again in the next pairing and both of them feature worlds that have opened up doorways into our world, but more than in *NOS4A2*, they do require the collusion of an unsuspecting victim in our world to invite them in.

Stay Alive, William Brent Bell, 2006/ *Slender Man* (White: 2018)

Stay Alive crafts an urban legend by linking it into a wider network of real-world examples. The film centers on Elizabeth Bathory, a vampiric and sadistic governess of a girls' home in a former plantation house. This would seem an odd transposition, moving a 16th century European Countess to the Deep South of America, but it does follow the footsteps of the first cinematic vampire entering the USA in 1943 in *Son of Dracula* (Siodmak).[73] There, toward the end of World War II, a young heiress, Catherine "Kay" Caldwell (Louise Allbritton), invites Count Dracula (Lon Chaney, Jr.) to visit her on a plantation just outside New Orleans. She then schemes to become a vampire, kill the Count, and live forever with her fiancé. While this plan goes awry, it left a vampiric imprint in that part of America, not least by its connection to slavery as often symbolized by the plantation house (see previous chapter). While neither *Son of Dracula* nor *Stay Alive* features slaves, and the latter film no black characters at all, both films carry the memory of this in the plantation house as a place of cruelty, violence, and vampirism. In *Stay Alive*, Bathory, mirroring her European counterpart, was convicted of killing the young girls in her charge in an attempt to stay young and subsequently breaking all the mirrors in the plantation house to hide the fact it was not working. Buried alive, it seemed the curse of her existence was over and only a thing of memory, rumor, and local legend—it is unclear of when this occurred though it is suggestive of the late 19th, early 20th century. As the story starts, however, none of this is known, and like many horror films it focuses on a group of self-obsessed young adults, though not teenagers this time. Rather it is a group of friends brought together by their love of video games. One of their number, Loomis (Milo Ventimiglia), dies in mysterious circumstances along with his housemate and his girlfriend, while they were testing a video game. Hutch (Jon Foster), who was close friends with Loomis, goes to his friend's funeral and is given a box of Loomis' possessions. He also meets a friend of the murdered housemate's girlfriend, Abigail (Samaire Armstrong). Accompanied by Abigail, he takes the box back to his friends and they find the game that Loomis was playing, called *Stay Alive*, and decide to play it together. Once on, the game seems to have no way to begin it, with the opening scene hanging on the screen with the following block of text on the right-hand side:

> Come to me, clouds. May you rise as an evil storm born to rip them open. Let the cover of night bear witness and destroy those who resist so they shall harm me not. Let the blood of many cleanse me, preserving beauty eternal, I pray you [Bell: 2006].

However, as they begin to read it, the text disappears, and the game begins. As with *Slender Man* below, this acts as a summons to the vampire from another world and once the invitation has been accepted your fate is sealed.

---

73. The same trip was also made by Carmilla but just before the American Civil War in Gabrielle Beaumont's tv film *Carmilla* (1989).

The game centers on the figure of Countess Bathory and the inscription on the opening scene of the game is interesting as it highlights the Countess's need for blood, yet as the narrative develops it becomes far more about her need to cause and feed upon the fear and belief she induces in others. Once the friends are all playing the game it is not long before the character of one of their number, Miller (Adam Goldberg), is stabbed and killed by the Countess using a large pair of scissors. Disconcerted by this they decide to stop the game and the friends go their separate ways. Later that night Miller is at his office when the Countess materializes and stabs him with a large pair of scissors just as she stabbed his character in the game—the in-game avatars look exactly like the people who are playing. Thus, once the player has recited the imprecation a psychic link is formed between them and the virtual, vampiric world of the game. It is this link that creates the avatar which has similar qualities to a voodoo doll so that what happens to one of them has physical repercussions on the other. The correlation between the real world and its virtual equivalent is conferred significant meaning by the limitations of the quality of gaming graphics in 2006, which look quite basic compared to those available in 2021. As such it shifts the mirror like representation of one world by the other into the purely symbolic, so that while the vampire world can control our own, the real world has little effect the other way; it can feed on our world but that energy cannot be given back, a point that will become important later.

The surviving friends now realize the power of the game and the gateway they seemed to have opened between the virtual and real worlds, which is allowing the vampire to move freely between both. Indeed, their belief and fear in the reality of the other world is such that another of their number, Phinneus (Jimmy Simpson), is killed by the Countess even though his character survived in the game. Hutch, Abigail, and one of the other surviving friends, October (Sophia Bush), begin investigating the Countess and the Gerouge Plantation where the game takes place. While they find few established facts about her, they unearth many rumors and urban legends, suggesting that Countess Bathory used the blood of young girls to try and stay young. They also discover that she was subsequently locked in a tower on the Plantation until she died. However, before death took her, she vowed to return and take revenge on the (real) world. It further transpires that the makers and distributors of the game are listed at the address of the Plantation and thus even the material creation of the game becomes supernatural and virtual. The friends decide that the only way to save themselves is to go to the Plantation and try to kill the Countess in the real world. October, who has an occult sensibility, discovers that spirits cannot cross rose bushes and therefore to kill the Countess they must drive nails into various parts of her body to "trap her evil soul" inside a rose bush and then set fire to it. But before they can embark on this endeavor October is killed by the Countess on a construction site. The remaining friends arrive at the Plantation in a heightened emotional state, empowering the Countess with increased strength and enabling her to cross between worlds. They leave Swink (Frankie Muniz) outside of the house at the center of the plantation to distract the Countess by playing the game, hoping it will keep the vampire in her virtual world, while Hutch and Abigail enter the house and try to find the Countess' body and kill her. Their plan goes awry as the Countess, in her energized state, locks Swink out of the car in which he was playing the game and then runs him over in her carriage, but fails to kill him as he dives into a rose bush. Meanwhile, Abigail and Hutch have found the tower but get separated. The Countess appears in front of Abigail and begins to torture her, but Hutch finds her physical body and begins the ritual of driving nails into her body. Just as he drives one into her forehead, her spectral self leaves Abigail and reenters her body, reanimating it and attacking Hutch. In the ensuing struggle an oil lamp is knocked over but before the Countess can escape, Hutch remembers her abhorrence of mirrors and uses one to hold her in the room long enough to be engulfed by the flames.

The three survivors leave the Plantation with the tower in flames, seemingly victorious and closing the doorway between the worlds. Yet, as suggested earlier, the ending is not so straightforward, and although they may have disposed of the Countess in this world, they have not eliminated her in the virtual one, and the film ends on a shot of boxes of *Stay Alive* arriving at a gaming store and arranged on the shelves. It seems that while Hutch, Abigail and Swink may have severed the link between themselves and the Countess, there are many more invitations to be given and accepted, and fear to be generated and fed upon. Proving once again that once the vampire from another world has been invited in, it can rarely be revoked.

Slender Man, not unlike *Stay Alive,* taps into an already existing belief, but one that has far more recent real-world currency. As described by Alexandra Heller-Nicholas (2018), the character was born of the imagination of Joseph DeLage and Troy Wagner and their YouTube-based horror series called *Marble Hornets* (2009–14). It specifically cites popular youth culture and tales of the boogeyman, but for a technologically savvy generation. In *Marble Hornets*, the Slender Man, or The Operator as he is known, is a ghost in the machine, an entity of supernatural powers that haunts the world of reality. Those who believe he is real are drawn into a hallucinatory world where they are no longer in control of themselves until death finds them. A scenario of this kind allegedly took place in reality when, in 2015, two twelve-year-old girls from Wisconsin stabbed a classmate almost to death, supposedly under the direction of the Slender Man (Heller: 2018, 77). Probably the most well know of "creepy-pasta"—online urban legends—the Slender Man is blank, lacking a face, hair or any distinguishing features apart from his complete whiteness. He is thus a doppelgänger who is simultaneously a mirror and a void. Sylvain White's *Slender Man* taps into the real-world buzz still circulating about this entity from beyond our world. In this mythos, the Slender Man lives within the space created by a common lack of comprehension and understanding around modern technology. *Slender Man* plays on the audience's real-world semi-belief in the figure of the Slender Man as a "real world" urban legend, so that in a sense the movie itself feeds off the fear produced by thinking about the character.

As is common for the horror genre, *Slender Man* begins with a group of teenagers, four girlfriends at high school who, in an attempt to outdo some boys they know, decide to contact the Slender Man, known to them as a figure who abducts children.[74] Not unlike the Countess in *Stay Alive*, the Slender Man must be summoned, and appropriately for the context of this figure, this summoning is performed not by repeating a name in front of a mirror nor by using a ouija board, but by following the dubious advice of an online video. Modern technology and especially the internet thus becomes not just a malevolent entity in its own right, but a gateway or portal to the supernatural. The girls access the internet to find out how to summon the Slender Man and find a video that purports to do just that. They follow the instructions at the beginning of the video and then close their eyes, waiting to hear the sound of a tolling bell which will indicate they have attracted the attention of the vampire from the other world. They hear the bell, but nothing seems to happen, and they are left with a heightened sense of unease. A week later, the girls are on a field trip when one of their number, Katie (Annalise Basso), vanishes. Her disappearance in an outdoor setting suggests that woodlands and nature are linked to the Slender Man. Thus, at times he seems to be an ecological force rather than a technological one, and these two aspects of this figure play off one another. The disappearance of Katie increases the fear and paranoia of her remaining friends, which draws the Slender Man to them. The surviving girls, Wren (Joey King), Hallie (Julia Goldani Telles), and Chloe (Jaz Sinclair), then go to Katie's house to retrieve her laptop, on which they discover many videos made by others who have contacted the Slender Man and were subsequently abducted by him. Among them they find one video that claims to know how to get rid of this vampire from another world. Upon questioning the author of this claim, the girls discover that they must give the

---

74. There is something of the monster of choice of the early 21st century here, the paedophile, especially as it is the younger sister of the main character who starts the subsequent chain of events and which also resonates with *NOS4A2*.

Slender Man something they personally hold as precious. They go to the woods—again seeming to equate the Slender Man with the environment—with their offerings, but Wren tells the other two to put on blindfolds and under no circumstances remove them to protect themselves. Chloe panics and removes her blindfold, becoming vulnerable to the Slender Man, who can now "see" her—not unlike the children in *Citadel* who can see fear in their victims. She runs off and straight into his embrace, but when Wren and Hallie find her unharmed, she is unnaturally calm. The Slender Man appears to have possessed her, and it is not long before nowhere is safe from his presence, as Wren says to Chloe: "He gets in your head like a virus. … Like a computer virus that infects your hard drive, but instead of your hard drive, it's your brain!" (White: 2018). This begins to describe how the Slender Man is integral to the internet, a veritable vampire-in-the-machine that haunts the World Wide Web waiting to be invited in. Not long after this Chloe loses grip on reality and goes mad.

There is much here that shares the shadowy stalking methods of Nosferatu with a dark presence just on the edge of vision that haunts its victim in their homes, their schools and every aspect of their lives, indeed the only real difference being that the Slender Man, while preferring the shadows like Count Orlok, is not affected by sunlight. Consequently, the girls' lives are no longer their own as the Slender Man erupts into their waking world when and where he pleases, creating more and more fear for him to feed on.

In this sense *Slender Man* has much in common with films such as *Candyman* (Rose: 1992), *Bloody Mary* (Valentine: 2006), and *The Bye Bye Man* (Title: 2017) that all invoke either real or imaginary figures from urban legend that are given substance through human belief, gaining life through the fear they inspire once released into the real world—*The Boogeyman* series of films is particularly interesting in this respect (*Boogeyman* [Kay: 2005], *Boogeyman 2* [Betancourt: 2007], and *Boogeyman 3* [Jones: 2008]) as the energy vampire can only be killed by no one believing in it.[75] All of these films see their respective energy vampires existing in a kind of limbo world—the internet can be seen to serve this function with technology such as laptops and smart phones serving as thresholds between domains—waiting to be invited into our world, but always with some kind of summoning or verbal invitation. More than many the Slender Man captures the anonymity of the internet in general and social media in particular, seeing his blankness embodying the notions of being faceless and having a million faces; simultaneously no one and everyone.

75. Belief operates in a similar if mirrored way in *The Matrix*. To control the matrix, rather than believing the imaginary is real in the real world, the imaginary version of Neo must believe the imaginary world is imaginary and not real.

3. Lifeforce 97

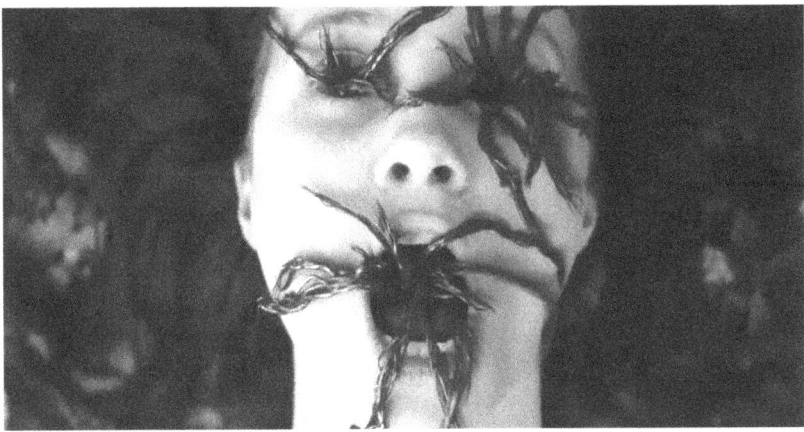

Figure 10. The organic excess of the Slender Man erupting in the real world through Hallie (Julia Goldani Telles). *Slender Man*. Directed by Sylvain White (Sony Pictures Releasing: 2018).

Unable to cope, Lizzie has a nervous breakdown and is hospitalized, constantly repeating "he has no face," referring to the Slender Man. Trying to find a solution in Lizzie's house, Hallie and Wren finally realize the only precious things Slender Man wants is in fact them, which is explosively confirmed as his tentacles—they seem more akin to tree or vegetative growths rather than belonging to a more animal-like creature—burst in through the window and pull Wren out. Hallie runs out of the house and follows him into the woods where she confronts him—"him" being only a nominal signifier here as the creature only seems to have moments of coalescing in a humanoid form from its otherwise vegetatively amorphous state. In this respect Slender Man is not unlike Count Dracula and Orlok in that they all exist in many states so that their human looking manifestation is merely a momentary face of a multivalent entity.

Wren seems to have disappeared already by this point, but Hallie offers herself to the creature in return for it leaving Lizzie alone. Seemingly agreeing to the deal, the Slender Man, now in a spider-like form, grabs her in his/its arms and pulls her into its body as it transforms into a tree-like form. In this shape Hallie becomes fused into its surface until she disappears from sight—in this final terrified form she is absorbed by the entity, becoming part of the Slender Man itself. As the film ends Lizzie awakes in the hospital screaming for Hallie, and although alive, as "promised" by the Slender Man, she is effectively part of him, acting as a means to increase the level of belief in him and lure more victims into inviting him in to their worlds—she becomes the Slender Man's familiar, facilitating his/its entry into our world by keeping belief in the urban legend very much alive. The next two films continue in this vein, seeing otherworldly vampires feeding on various kinds of emotional energies that emerge from human bodies.

Nothing Left to Fear, Anthony Leonardi III, 2013/ *Odd Thomas*, Stephen Sommers, 2013

Nothing Left to Fear explicitly suggests that the vampire's home world is Hell or variations thereof. *Citadel* constructs its vampire children as demonic and *NOS4A2*'s Christmasland is hellish for non-vampires. *Slender Man* utilizes the (urban) belief generated around its eponymous monster to maintain the power of the world beyond and its ability to cross from one world to the other. *Nothing Left to Fear* taps into a real-life urban legend that locates one of the seven gateways to Hell in the town of Stull in Kansas.[76] The film never mentions this legend explicitly but it casts the power of collective belief in its more traditional mold, that of religious conviction. The film centers on a small town in rural America, and consequently its legend is configured as rural rather than urban. Notwithstanding, its legend appears to represent the kind of extreme, fundamentalist evangelical faith that has a significant influence on certain sections of 21st century America. The film further makes use of fungal growth, or a kind of organic excess, that appears around the sites of crossover between worlds, so that as the vampiric entity bursts into our world, or draws things back through to its own, a kind of mold oozes out of the alien dimension. The mold in *Nothing Left to Fear* is reminiscent of the red weed in *War of the Worlds*, as neither of these fungal growths are vampiric in their own right but they appear to thrive in places where the vampires are or have been. The plant-based vampires from another world are thus tied to the intersection and crossing of worlds.

The story begins when a young pastor, Dan (James Tupper), moves to a small town named Stull in Kansas with his family. They experience strange events upon arrival, culminating in his eldest daughter Rebecca (Rebekah Brandes) witnessing a young man killing a sheep and collecting its blood. As they move into their new home, the previous resident, Pastor Kingsman (Clancy Brown), appears to welcome them, but although friendly he is also oddly controlling. The following day Kingsman brings a cake to the family that was supposedly baked by one of his congregation, but when the youngest daughter Mary (Jennifer Stone) takes a bite out of it, she almost chokes on a huge tooth hidden within it. It is not long before Mary starts feeling ill and Rebecca discovers, from a young man, Noah (Ethan Peck), whom she

---

76. See Turk: 2013.

has befriended, that because Mary found the tooth she is the chosen one, but for what he will not say. The town's preparations for its Summer Festival are now in full swing, with the new pastor and his family lending a helping hand, but once the festivities actually begin, Mary is drugged and taken away by Kingsman to a special shrine constructed inside a building in the middle of town. The shrine consists of a dried-up pool and Mary is tied to a stake in the middle of it, with Kingsman and the other townspeople arrayed around her. Kingsman explains that they release the Devil from Hell once a year and offer him a sacrifice among the newcomers to the town. The rationale for this ritual, as he further explains, lies in his disbelief in angels and a caring God: "there's only us" (Leonardi III: 2013). He thus cuts Mary with a sacrificial blade, allowing her blood to spill into the dry pool, thereby opening the "Gateway to Hell" and summoning the Devil, or another vampiric entity as it may be, from its own world into ours. The entity emerges and spreads like ivy from the hole in the pool and snakes its way to Mary, taking possession of her. Not unlike the other alien entities in this chapter, the vampire from another world seems incapable of surviving independently in our world and requires a human "exoskeleton" to survive the atmosphere.

Once the vampire from another world has fully possessed Mary, she is released from the stake and returned to her parents' home. Once she awakens, they tell her they found her very ill so they brought her home. Kingsman calls Dan to the church in town where he drugs him and ties him up. Back at the house, Mary awakes and begins to attack her own family. The two other children, Rebecca and her brother Christopher (Carter Carbassa), are sent to town to find their father, by their mother Wendy (Anne Heche), and they do so in the church. As they travel back to the house, they notice all the houses have a large "X" painted in blood on them—we assume the sheep's blood acts not unlike the blood on the doorposts during Passover, protecting the residents of the house. When the children return with their father, they find Wendy dead and crumbling to ash as she has had all the life drained out of her by the vampiric entity that has possessed Mary. Dan sends away Noah and his children and tries to save Mary by the power of his faith, but the entity inside his daughter infects him and similarly drains his life-essence. Noah and Rebecca argue in the car while Christopher leaves the car to take refuge in one of the houses, but no one will let him in as they know the cost of doing so. Mary catches Christopher by the leg on the street and drains the life out of him. Meanwhile, Noah has taken Rebecca to the building containing the portal to the other world, explaining that she is the only one who can stop the vampire. He then cuts Rebecca with the sacrificial blade, letting her blood drip into the pool. They thus draw the "Devil" out of Mary and send it back to its own world, sealing the gate. Noah reveals that the same had happened to his family and that now

Rebecca will be taking his place as leader of the preparations for the next Summer Festival.

The entity in *Nothing Left to Fear* does not conform to any traditional image of the Devil, and indeed Dan's faith has no effect upon it. Its organic nature points to a more biologically excessive monster, rather than a religious one, more in the manner of *Annihilation* (Garland: 2018) or *Venom* (discussed later). The entity in *Nothing Left to Fear* requires a host and takes possession of its form and changes it, as seen in the impossible movements, stretches, and contortions of Mary's body after she is possessed. Furthermore, the entity often acts like a virulent fungus that contaminates its victims, not unlike airborne spores. In many respects, Mary is not just a host for the entity but is configured as an extension of the gateway itself, facilitating the entity's ability to enter and inhabit this world and nourish itself and its homeworld. The ritual of possession that summons this entity has been in place for a long time, as suggested by its ancient-looking shrine. While not explicitly stated in the film there is the inference that left unfed, the vampire from another world makes its own arrangements around breaking through into our domain which causes far more damage and loss of human life than these controlled rituals. The film dramatizes a rural-urban divide that often features in horror films, where city dwellers often become victims of "the old ways" that only those in tune with their environment can understand. It thus becomes a meditation on the primeval forces that contemporary America fails to understand. The symbiosis between the inhabitants of Stull and their environment makes them more akin to Wells' humans, while the arrivals from the city—the new pastor and his family—are placed in the position of the Martians who will inevitably die due to their unsuitability to their environment. The vampire in this film thus comes to resemble Orlok in *Nosferatu*, a necessary if deadly part of the natural order of things. *Odd Thomas* similarly features vampiric entities that appear to be part of the natural order and harboring equally dark intentions.

In some ways *Odd Thomas* is indeed the odd one out in this chapter, as it seems a more out-and-out tale of the supernatural, or as one website described it, "a ghost whisperer for men."[77] The film begins with a very familiar format for ghost movies with those that have unresolved issues at the point of their death, or even about their death itself, remaining on Earth seeking some kind of reparation or justice before they can move on. The premise of the film is that Odd Thomas (Anton Yelchin) has a "gift" that allows him to see the recently deceased, particularly those who were killed in violent ways and/or murdered, enabling him to track down the culprit and report them to the police. The film opens with a young girl who

77. Hilton: 2014.

materializes before Thomas, unable to speak to him—none of the dead can speak—and leads him to the man that raped and killed her. Confronted, the murderer runs off and Thomas is in pursuit, catching him and knocking him unconscious until the police arrive. The stage is thus set for the appearance of the bodachs,[78] who are neither alive nor dead.

The bodachs are beings from another world who resemble creatures from the depths of the ocean that have evolved in the dark; almost translucent, the "flesh" of their bodies is like a firmer version of jellyfish matter with a wiry kind of skeleton beneath it. They appear simultaneously skeletal, insectile, reptilian and predatory—there is something of a passing resemblance to the mimics in *Edge of Tomorrow*.

However, the other worldly bodachs depend on humanity for sustenance. Unlike the deceased, they are not tied to the other world but can freely travel to the land of the living, drawing sustenance from the scene of someone's death. They are probably attracted to strong emotional distress, which also physically nourishes them. One imagines that this "harvesting" of emotional energy at the point of death must have been occurring for some considerable amount of time. Thomas is familiar with them and he knows they seek to conceal their presence from the world and if anyone makes it clear that they can see them, they kill them.

Figure 11. Stormy (Addison Timlin) unknowingly being caressed by a Bodach, a death-eater from another world. *Odd Thomas*. Directed by Stephen Sommers (Fusion Films: 2013).

78. A bodach is the name for a trickster or bogeyman in Gaelic folklore, though it seems to have little to do with what we see in *Odd Thomas*.

Normally, Thomas would steer clear of them, but they have appeared in unusual numbers in his hometown, all hovering around one man, Fungus Bob (Shuler Hensley), the new stranger in town who is named after the appearance of his hair. Odd has a vision involving a possible large-scale murder, the details of which are confirmed by the dreams of a gifted teenage girl of his acquaintance. Suspecting Fungus Bob, Thomas breaks into his house and uncovers information suggesting that he is planning a mass murder on August 15 with unknown accomplices. Upon receiving this information, the police chief (Willem Dafoe), who is aware of Thomas's gift, puts two new deputies on surveillance duty outside Bob's house. Thomas and his girlfriend Stormy (Addison Timlin) are accosted by Fungus Bob in church as other unusual and violent events erupt around town. These events culminate in the appearance of Bob's dead body in Thomas' bathtub, his advanced rigor mortis suggesting that it was his ghost who assailed him and Stormy at the church. Thomas returns to Bob's house and discovers evidence that the surviving killers have produced large amounts of homemade explosives and hired a removal van of some kind, and that they are connected to a Satanic group whose disciples bear the tattoo "POD" (Prince of Darkness). This tattoo appears on the arms of Bob and, more to the point, one of the new deputies of police. Thomas finds a room in Bob's house that appears to have fungus growing in it, spreading out from some kind of portal through which the bodachs are entering this world. Not unlike *Nothing Left to Fear*, or even the red weed from *The War of the Worlds*, the growth seems to thrive in our world, absorbing energy by just entering our environment. As Thomas begins to piece together the truth, his sixth sense draws him to the shopping mall in town, which he finds teeming with bodachs, suggesting that the mass murder is on the verge of taking place. Shooting breaks out in the mall with the inference that the barrier between the worlds has collapsed as the vampiric bodachs are swarming everywhere. Thomas eliminates two of the gunmen, the first with a baseball bat and the second with a gun taken from the first shooter. A ghost guides Thomas to the loading bay where the deputy policeman with "POD" tattooed on his arm has placed the truck full of explosives. Thomas enters the truck and drives off before the corrupt officer can respond. Desperate to secure their feeding frenzy, one of the bodachs possesses the policeman, who then shoots and wounds Thomas and jumps onto the truck as it is driven away. Thomas continues to drive the truck away from the mall toward a large gully outside of town. The possessed policeman attacks Thomas, who leaps out of the vehicle and leaves the policeman inside as the explosives detonate. The bodachs disperse as their feast is denied them, their fungal traces disappearing with them. The bodachs require a world full of humans to ensure their own survival. Thus, hybridity and assimilation hold no interest for the bodachs, nor for the next examples of vampires from another world, who would prefer the total extinction of the human race.

Terminator 3: Rise of the Machines, Jonathan Mostow, 2003/*Predators*, Nimród Antal, 2010

The *Terminator* franchise has become a temporal Gordian knot that not even the sharpest of swords could slice through. Its convoluted storyline is the corollary of a long running series of films (1984–2018?) that hinges on time-travel and insists on bringing back the main actor from the first film (Arnold Schwarzenegger) to later installments of the franchise. For the purposes of this book, the third installment, *Rise of the Machines*, will serve as a case study, because it features the most explicit vampirism in the series, but I will also refer to the two previous films in the series, *The Terminator* (Cameron: 1984) and *Terminator 2: Judgment Day* (Cameron: 1991) when helpful.

The Terminator series is all about machinery, robots and technological superiority. Yet even though the machines are clearly physically and mentally superior the humans manage to resist their attempts to wipe them out. Thus, in the year 2029, the machines, who have invented a time machine, send a cyborg assassin to 1984 to kill the mother of the future leader of the human resistance, John Connor, while the humans send one of their own back in time to save the targeted woman. The cyborg that is sent back, the T-800 (Arnold Schwarzenegger), is heavily muscular, extremely violent, and emotionless, embodying a connection between the machines and military and patriarchal ideologies—there are strong resonances here with Wells' Martians with their mechanical bodies and militaristic, colonial imperatives. The robot requires augmentations of living human flesh to travel through time, linking it with the other vampire from another world discussed herein. Rather than utilizing the body of a host, the robot is covered in a flesh exoskeleton—cloned flesh rather the flesh of a specific human. Unlike the other vampires discussed in this study, the cyborg wears human flesh to disguise itself in the human world rather than to survive differences in the atmosphere. Indeed, it is as if the future of humanity, the machines, must cloak itself in the past to become acceptable to the human present.

The T-800 from the first film in the series has few transformative capabilities, though various parts of it are able to exist separately from its main body. It is thus in the process of ongoing change, with the human appendages configured as a stage in its development toward non-normative expressions of the body and its relation to the environment around it. The

T-1000, from *Judgment Day*, is made of liquid metal that can transform into any human appearance, and even objects, though it does seem to have a "base" state, which in this film is played by Robert Patrick—and to be able to time-travel, it must be in this state. This imparts an individual character to each of the robots, and it is important that in the sequel, *Rise of the Machines*, the robot is configured as female.

This time the killer robot is sent back to 2004 to dispatch John Connor (Nick Stahl) and Kate Brewster (Clare Danes), his future wife. The robot is now a T-X (Kristanna Loken) which is similar to the T-1000 in its ability to transform but can also control/communicate with other machines—technological telepathy. This new incarnation of the vampire cyborg/robot from the future is heavily sexualized, a sexualization that draws on the association of the female robot with the figure of the vampire that harks back to the film *Metropolis* (Lang: 1927), where a robot is created by an alchemist/scientist to bewitch the son of the city's mastermind and bring the metropolis to its knees.[79] In this cinematic tradition, the T-X first appears naked in the window of a women's fashion shop and proceeds to take what she wants from whoever she wants, when she needs it. Her costume of choice is a tight leather jacket and trousers and she drives a sports car. In contrast when Arnold Schwarzenegger arrives from the future naked, he walks into a biker bar, and while it hints at a certain measure of homoeroticism, it becomes far more about hyper-masculinity as he beats them all up.

The sexualization of the T-X is important as it reinforces the vampiric nature of the robots from the future. In the first two films the male identification of the robot hunting its prey aligned the slasher horror films such as *Halloween* (Carpenter: 1978)—there is much similarity between the plots of the original *Halloween* and *The Terminator* films—whereas constructing the robot as female changes this interpretation into that of a sexually aggressive woman, or a vamp (see Dijkstra: 1988); this is seen in films as varied as *Vampire's Kiss* (Bierman: 1988), *Eve of Destruction* (Gibbins: 1991), and *Species* (Donaldson: 1995), where non-human females are highly sexualized and as intent on emasculating the males around them as on destroying the world. *Rise of the Machines* specifically plays into this, bringing out the T-X's vampishness in three particular ways; the first is only a passing scene but very telling and occurs when she is confronted by a male police officer while sitting in her car. To assist in getting her own way with the policeman she swells her bust so that more cleavage is revealed at the neckline of her jacket, suggesting she is

---

79. Interestingly there are strong parallels with the earlier *Species* film and the use of a highly sexualized blonde woman from another world who aggressively seeks out her man with the ultimate intention of eradicating humanity.

very aware of her appearance—as intimated above in the opening scene—and the power of female sexuality on male humans. While this can be seen as a machine taking advantage of human frailties it is still very much within the cultural construction of a "vamp" that optimizes their assets for personal advantage. Secondly, as with the T-1000 she also needs to "taste" her or vampirize her victims before becoming them—interestingly we never see her become an inanimate object as the earlier robot did—with the added twist that she is also able to identify the DNA of anyone she tastes. This in itself is not an inherently sexualized action, except to perform this test the TX is shown to have to put this viscous male fluid in her mouth, specifically by licking it off her fingers. Finally, in the closing scenes she engages in a fight to the death with the T-850, that is trying to save humanity, and when he eventually manages to trap her in a blast-door, that slowly crushes her, she changes form from a liquid metal Medusa into a skeletal vampress.[80]

Of note here is the changing symbolism of the two machines. In the original film, the Arnold Schwarzenegger robot was configured as the future technology that would destroy humanity—just like the tripods of Wells' Martians—but by *Rise of the Machines*, it is the technology that will save mankind. This is achieved in various ways, many of which accentuate the vampiric qualities of the new T-X robot. Much of

Figure 12. The vampiric essence of the robot. *Terminator 3: Rise of the Machines*. Directed by Jonathan Mostow (Warner Bros.: 2003).

80. A similar transformation happens to the "female" robot Alice (Isabel Lucas) in *Transformers: Revenge of the Fallen* (Bay: 2009).

this is constructed around the outdatedness of the T-850 in comparison to the super slick T-X that marks it out as being more human. The newer robot, in contrast, slithers when in liquid form and conceals itself under a wide range of guises. Even its slighter build, compared to the beefy Arnold Schwarzenegger, feeds into image as a deceptive, cunning serpentine creature. This is emphasized by the age of Schwarzenegger himself—he was in his late 50s in this installment of the franchise—making him seem an all too human cyborg in comparison to the human/nonhuman enemy played by the young nubile Kristanna Loken, who was only 24 at the time. The T-X is thus constructed as a soulless vampire from an almost alien future world that seeks to destroy the values and traditions of the past as inscribed on the body of the T-850. In her tight leather clothes and sports car, the T-X becomes a hyper-modern "Bloofer lady" from Stoker's *Dracula*.

The *Terminator* film series forecloses any possibility of the integration of the world of the present with the world of the future or vice versa. The robots, humanoid or otherwise, must not be allowed to survive in any form lest they make a nonhuman future inevitable; it is as though the vampiric world of the future will suck the energy of change and possibility (life) out of the present if allowed to exist. Yet the post-human future envisioned in the *Terminator* series is fueled by continual conflict with its human past— the vampiric robots from the future seem to feed on the violence of conflict—all images of them only ever show them in battle as though they are entities created in, and of, war—a point oddly reinforced by the immediate obsolescence of the robots saving humanity (the T-850) once the threat from the future has passed. A similar form of vampiric sustenance from war, conflict and battle informs the next film, *Predators*.

Predators is one installment in a long-running franchise featuring an alien species called the Predator. Like the *Terminator* series, it brings together many contradictory storylines and temporal loops and intersections, which have only increased with its occasional connections to the *Alien* franchise. As with *Rise of the Machines*, this chapter will use *Predators* as a focus of vampiric characteristics and features that recur throughout the franchise as well as its fascination with humanity as a preferred source of sustenance.

In the first film, *Predator* (John McTiernan, 1987), a predatory alien species travels across the universe in search of new ways to put its skills and bravery to the test. Drawn to the conflict in the jungle in Central America, the Predator lands near a guerrilla camp simultaneously with the arrival of a crack team of U.S. military. The Predator, which is humanoid in shape, is extremely muscular and seven to eight feet tall, and it possesses extremely sophisticated technology that can cloak its appearance, detect various heat and light emissions from its prey as well as provide a variety of weaponry. The film intimates that this is the Predator's first visit to Earth, but the locals attribute unexplained events in the area that have been ongoing for an appreciable amount of time to the same "monster." The alien is outsmarted at the film's denouement by the leader of the American soldiers, Dutch (Arnold Schwarzenegger), causing the Predator to set off explosive charges and thereby destroy itself and all evidence of its visit. Yet the emotional energy levels produced by the struggle, be they a sexualized energy or a psychic expression of hyper masculinity, make the Earth a magnet for other members of the alien species, prompting their return in *Predator 2* (Hopkins: 1990), *AVP* (Anderson: 2004), *AVPR* (Strause Brothers: 2007), *Predators* (2010), and *The Predator* (Black: 2018). Each of these installments features a different environment or "hunting ground" such as the city (Los Angeles), snow and ice, underground, or outer space.[81] *AVP* (*Alien Vs. Predator*) further establishes that the relationship between the Predators and the Earth is longer than first suggested, when an ancient structure that could have been once a fighting arena or a temple is found buried deep underneath the surface of Antarctica. The structure features motifs from many of Earth's ancient civilizations, particularly the Aztecs and Mayans, and its carvings imply that Predators have been coming to the Earth for thousands of years and were worshipped as gods. *AVP* highlights the vampiric propensities of the Aliens rather than the Predators— as central points of miscegenation and hybridity—but *Predators* returns to the central motivation and desire of the Predators, the hunt. This also marks a shift in this chapter as the vampire from another world no longer remains on Earth but takes humans away to its own domain. Framed in the logic of *The War of the Worlds*, this shift whisks humanity away from the present to a new world manifesting its future and from which there is no return.

Predators opens with nine humans dropped by parachute into a jungle with no knowledge of how they arrived nor of the identity of their companions. Royce (Adrien Brody), a mercenary and former Black Ops soldier; Isabelle (Alice Braga), an Israel Defense Forces sniper; Doctor Edwin (Topher Grace), who we later find out is a sexual predator, and five others who we later discover are violent criminals, mercenaries or guns for hire. The ninth is found dead hanging in a tree as his parachute did not open. As they try to make sense of their situation and to make each other's acquaintance, they discover a fort containing the dead body of a U.S. Special Forces soldier, intimating they are not the first to have

---

81. The various sequels similarly show this fascination with humanity to have a long historical precedent with *Predator 2* showing the creature with American Civil War relics, while in *AVP* it is suggested that ancient Aztec, Egyptian and Celtic civilizations knew of them.

undergone this process. Making their way to higher ground to get a better sense of their surroundings, they realize that the sky above them is not Earth's sky and consequently that they are no longer on Earth. They are then attacked by a strange pack of four-legged animals, prompting their supposition that they are on an alien game reserve, leading to their first encounter with the Predators. Barely managing to escape, they lose another one of their number and run into Noland (Laurence Fishburne) who has been in hiding on the planet for sometime and is rather a Renfield-type character who is centered on his own preservation and has lost his grip on reality due to his constant proximity to the vampiric Predators. Thus, his instinctive recourse on discovering the outsiders is to attempt to kill them so that his hideout remains secret. Yet his attempts to save himself and serve his "masters" end with his death at their hands, not unlike Renfield.

As the film heads to a close, Royce and Isabelle are involved in a battle to the death with the last remaining Predator on the planet, again an ideal situation to harvest hyper-masculine energies. The original plan was to help the smaller Predator defeat the larger one and then persuade it to take them back to Earth—the film brings in a peculiar plot twist of there being two kinds of Predator with the diminutive variety in rebellion against the bigger ones. This quickly goes awry with the smaller Predator killed and the larger one destroying the only spacecraft. Royce manages to kill the Predator with Isabelle's help, leaving them as the sole survivors but also stranded on the alien world and unable to return home. Upon registering more prey parachuted onto the planet, Royce intones "we must find another way off of this planet" (Antal: 2010). This would seem to suggest that the only option for humanity is to try and return to the world of the past, but there is another possible interpretation.

Humanity seems to share a special connection to the Predators. During the short time with Noland the surviving warriors learned that the planet is indeed a game park to which the Predators bring selected warriors in order to hunt them. Although Noland says that the purpose of this hunt is to hone the Predators' skills, the park also serves as a "fast-food" drive-in for the Predators where they can consume emotional energy (hyper-masculinity) as a stop-over, due to the planet's proximity to their home world. Indeed, the hyper-masculine aspect of hunting is brought to the fore in the film, with various set scenes of one-on-one battles/fights between Predators and humans. No explanation is given for the Predators' penchant for one-on-one combat other than the nutrients it must provide for them as energy vampires. It is worth noting that although Noland said that the Predators collect warriors and beasts from other worlds, the evidence points to the warriors being predominantly human, suggesting they are their "food" of choice.[82] This special bond with humanity is limited to humans who are armed, violent, or try to defend themselves. If they are harmless, they are of no interest to the Predators, suggesting that humanity does not need to return to its past (home) world but needs to embrace a peaceful present. It is worth noting that the most recent installment, *The Predator*, adds to the vampiric characteristics of the alien by explicitly showing them farming human DNA with which to modify themselves—hybridity was a large part of *AVPR* (*Alien Vs. Predator: Requiem*) where xenomorphs used Predators' DNA to evolve. Thus, the Predators not only prey on human emotion, but also conform to the transformative aspects of the vampire that mutates and modifies itself, creating a hybrid biological cyborg. The last two films in this chapter also feature alien worlds to which humans have been transported by vampires from another world, though the respective outcomes are not necessarily so hopeful about a future for humanity.

Event Horizon, Paul W.S. Anderson, 1997/ *Dark City,* Alex Proyas, 1998

Event Horizon features vampiric entities that are also gateways and whole environments, so that humans who come into their orbit are changed forever. As with Slender Man, once you are "seen" by the vampire there is little chance for escape. *Event Horizon* is set in the not too distant future of 2047 and would seem to be more about humans venturing out into space rather than vampires from another world coming to ours. However, there is a suggestion that the alien entity deliberately orchestrated its encounter with the human astronauts. Furthermore, the film suggests that the ultimate objective of the otherworldly vampires is to land on Earth.

Event Horizon envisages a future on Earth where countries have come together around a shared vision of space travel. By 2040, humans have colonized the Moon and several planets. In an attempt to push further afield, into the outer reaches of the galaxy and beyond, the authorities have built an experimental craft called the *Event Horizon* that is able create its own wormhole and thereby to travel vast distances. The *Event Horizon* thus travels to the edge of the solar system before trying its first test run, but then it vanishes without a trace. The disappearance of the *Event Horizon* is subsequently remembered as the worst disaster in space in human history,

---

82. Curiously, Noland suggests that the Predators themselves are divided between a larger sized caste and a smaller sized one, but this seems a lead-in to further films that never materialized.

where eighteen crew members lost their lives. However, seven years later, the *Event Horizon* mysteriously reappears just beyond Neptune. A rescue ship, the *Lewis and Clarke*, is sent on a secret mission to investigate the vessel. Onboard is the designer of the *Event Horizon*, Dr. William Weir (Sam Neill) who is rather a Renfield-type character insofar as he is more aware of the vampiric presence than he realizes. Indeed, just like Stoker's madman, he becomes increasingly erratic as he closes in on the vampiric entity. On the journey to Neptune, when all the crew are put into stasis, Weir seems to awake to discover that the ship is piloted by his dead wife, who reveals empty eye sockets as she turns to look at him. Screaming, Weir awakens in the real stasis tank just as the ship arrives at its destination. Eyes are thus configured as deceptive receptors that, once in the vampiric world, no longer function as the main receptor of sensory excess.

Once the crew are all awake and gathered together, Weir explains the history and purpose of the *Event Horizon* and its ability to create and travel through black holes. The crew are not happy as they believed they were just going to salvage an ordinary missing spaceship and Lt. Starck (Joely Richardson), gives voice to their incredulity over what Weir has described, "A black hole, the most destructive force in the universe. And you've created one?" (Anderson, 1997). Weir responds with an enthusiastic "Yes," oblivious to the response of his crew. The *Lewis and Clarke* docks with the inert ship, its sensors showing that all environmental systems are offline but unable to confirm if anyone is still alive onboard. Captain Miller (Laurence Fishburne) sends two of the crew, medical officer Peters (Kathleen Quinlan) and Engineer Justin (Jack Noseworthy) to the *Event Horizon* to search for survivors. Once onboard the two go separate ways, with Peters heading to the command deck and Justin to the gravity drive. As Justin arrives at the room with the device that creates the wormhole, a large metal ball surrounded by rotatable metal rings, the room suddenly lights up. Sensing his presence, the ball opens of its own accord, revealing a mirror-like black liquid inside of it. As Justin approaches it, the ball sucks him inside, simultaneously emitting a gravity pulse which damages the *Lewis and Clarke*. Both Justin and Peters are on tethering ropes and they manage to pull the engineer out of the orb, but he is in a catatonic state. Weir denies that the drive could turn on of its own accord, but his denial notwithstanding, the events that follow become increasingly sinister.

Peters catches sight of her son Denny, notwithstanding that he is back on Earth, and his apparition is gravely ill and covered in lesions. Justin suddenly begins to convulse and screams that "the dark is coming" (Anderson: 1997). Weir and Miller investigate the gravity drive, but as Weir crawls into a vent he sees his dead wife again, this time beckoning for him to join her. Meanwhile, fire breaks out in the room containing the metal orb and

Figure 13. Justin (Jack Noseworthy) stands in front of the vampiric gateway to a vampiric world. *Event Horizon*. Directed by Paul W.S. Anderson (Paramount Pictures: 1997).

Miller watches the apparition of a former crewman whom he could not save from burning alive. Thus, the vampire from another world in *Event Horizon* forces its victims to see and experience the most horrific events of their lives, or from the haunted recesses of their imagination, thereby inducing extreme and long-lasting emotional reactions. The crew gathers to discuss these increasingly disturbing events. Starck explains the situation as best s/he can:

> **STARCK:** I think that there's a connection between the readings and the hallucinations the crew have been experiencing like, like they're all part of a defensive reaction, some sort of immune system.... I'm saying that this ship is reacting to us and the reactions are getting stronger. It's as if the ship brought something back with it, a life force of some kind.
> **MILLER:** What are you telling me? That this ship is alive? [Anderson: 1997].

Indeed, the malevolent force proves to be an entire dimension, out of which the gravity drive opens a "living" gateway to a vampiric universe that feeds on emotional excess. The *Event Horizon*'s relationship to this vampiric universe becomes even more pronounced in the film's final sequence. Justin emerges from his catatonic state only to commit suicide because of the psychological trauma triggered by his coma. The crew eventually manage to play the entirety of the damaged final recording of the final moments of the *Event Horizon*'s crew after they activated the gravity drive. The recording reveals the crew in a frenzied excess of violence, mutilation, and pain. Miller orders his crew to evacuate the *Event Horizon* immediately as the repair work on the *Lewis and Clarke* has been completed, but Weir refuses to depart, asserting that he is "already home" (Anderson: 1997).

Peters sees her son onboard the *Event Horizon* and tries to catch up with him, but in so doing falls down a huge shaft. Weir fully embraces the darkness and begins a quest of sensorial overload to feed the vampiric dimension, which begins with him ripping out his own eyes and continues with his destruction of the docking port to the *Lewis and Clarke*, and his murder of a crew member and vivisection of the body, which he displays around the medical bay. Weir prepares to reinitiate the drive and bring the remaining crew into the vampiric dimension when Cooper (Richard T. Jones) smashes the window in the control room so that Weir is sucked out into space. Cooper and Starck set charges to detach the front section of the *Event Horizon* and use it as an escape vessel to return to Earth. However, before Miller can join them, Weir miraculously reappears, having become virtually indestructible due to his newly formed bond with the vampire dimension. The gravity drive engages and begins to pull the craft into the black hole it has created, but Starck and Cooper manage to blast away in time to escape unharmed.

The two survivors put themselves into stasis for the trip back to Earth and seventy-two days later they arrive at their destination. However, not unlike Weir at the beginning of the film, Starck is woken by a nightmare where the first rescuer that enters the craft removes their helmet only for it to be Weir's maniacal face grinning at her. Screaming herself back to reality, she awakes in earnest but is unable to calm down and the actual rescuers call for a sedative for her. However, while they are doing this, the automated hatch closes behind them of its own accord and locks, suggesting that the gateway to the vampiric dimension is not shut but has arrived with Starck and Cooper back to Earth. In this sense, *Event Horizon* becomes a prequel to *Bird Box*, discussed later on in this study, unleashing a vampiric dimension that will suck all the emotional energy from humanity as it turns the Earth into an environment of endless sensorial and emotional excess.[83] If *Event Horizon* suggests the inevitable decline of the human world and its replacement by the world of the alien vampire, the final film in this chapter is a little more hopeful in its conclusions, suggesting that the old world might be gone but the new one is not necessarily a never ending Hell.

Dark City appears to be set on Earth, and in the past, but as the story unfolds these two suppositions are proven false. The urban setting gradually morphs into a dreamlike manifestation of city-life, revealing darker, vampiric forces at play. The mise-en-scene is 1950s American Noir and

---

83. *Event Horizon* obviously shares many features with Clive Barker's *Hellraiser* (1987) though here the gateway to Hell is more for the unwary than a vampiric force wanting to consume the world.

a man, John Murdoch (Rufus Sewell) awakens in a hotel bathtub with no memory of how he arrived in this compromising position. He staggers into the bedroom as the phone rings and a voice warns him to leave immediately as some people, referred to only as the Strangers, are coming for him. While on the phone, Murdoch notices the mutilated body of a dead woman on the floor, but he forces himself to leave just before some mysterious men wearing long dark coats and trilby hats arrive, presumably the aforementioned Strangers. As Murdoch tries to work out the situation, he realizes that he is a suspect in a string of brutal murders, none of which he can remember. He further discovers that the city is in perpetual nighttime and that at the stroke of midnight everyone falls into a deep sleep, all but himself. Indeed, when everyone is asleep, the city changes: buildings transform, streets move, and people change their jobs, their families and their identities upon waking, taking up their new lives in this new city as if they had always been living them. Murdoch gradually realizes that he and the Strangers are the only exceptions to this nightly rearrangement, and furthermore, that they have the power to affect it. The Strangers are not happy about this fact and step up their pursuit of Murdoch, enlisting the help of Inspector Bumstead (William Hurt) of the city police to catch him, believing that he is a serial killer.

Murdoch discovers that he has a wife, Emma (Jennifer Connelly), and that he hails from a place named Shell Beach outside of the city. His quest then turns to escaping an imaginary present (the city) to reclaim a real past (the countryside), eschewing the forms of modern civilization that had attracted the vampires to Earth in the first place. The city is likewise configured as a nexus that consumes memories and overlays them with new pathways, forcing false memories upon its city-dwellers. This corresponds

Figure 14. The Strangers with Mr. Book (Ian Richardson) at their center rearranging the city. *Dark City*. Directed by Alex Proyas (New Line Cinema: 1998).

to Marc Augés' ideas of non-space that describe post-modern spaces such as airports and shopping malls that are architecturally blank, without memory of their own—not full of the usual marks, scuffs, and detritus that signify human habitation and passing—and unable to hold any remembrance of the past (Augé: 2004). The city-dwellers in the non-space that is Dark City similarly are unable to make meaningful memories within the spaces they inhabit, and can only follow the instructions given to them to be able to move through the urban space; i.e., one is told how to use, negotiate and remember a space. Within the context of Dark City the inhabitants of the city are unable to leave it as they are only provided enough memory to negotiate its streets and buildings, not the spaces beyond its boundaries; the city is both source and consumer of the memories of its inhabitants. In this sense the city, and especially the eponymous Dark City, is a vampiric entity, feeding off the memories of those that exist in its space.

Murdoch convinces Inspector Bumstead of the veracity of his story and together they track down Dr. Schreber (Kiefer Sutherland), a human that works for the Strangers but also warned Murdoch of the danger at the beginning of the film. Schreber tells them that the Strangers are in fact a race of alien parasites who act as a collective consciousness—working as a hive mind—who are experimenting with humans in relation to nature versus nurture in order to save their own species. She thereby suggests that the Strangers draw emotional energies from their victims, which dovetails with the city's wider vampiric nature, whereby memories are literally consumed by the ever moving architecture so that with each change in the set-up of the metropolis all residual memory is drained away, making room for new memories that create a constantly renewable energy source for the psychic vampires.

Murdoch, Bumstead, and Schreber pursue their mission to find Shell Beach, as it might offer a way out of the city and the control of the Strangers. However, they discover that it is nothing but a billboard at the edge of the metropolis. Murdoch, in a fit of anger, tries to tear down the poster but pulls away a piece of the wall, revealing a hole into deep space. At this point the Strangers arrive and in the ensuing fight Bumstead falls through the hole and out into the emptiness, showing that the city is nothing but an environment floating in space. The Strangers overpower the remaining humans and take them to their home under the city and force Schreber to inject their collective memory into Murdoch to make him one of them—again reinforcing the notion of memories as a separate entity that can be collected, shared, and/or consumed. However, although Murdoch was formerly an aide of the Strangers, Schreber actually gives him selected memories so that he can control and maximize his powers. Consequently, he breaks free and battles the leader of the Strangers, Mr. Book (Ian Richardson), defeating the alien and taking control of the metropolis. Murdoch's first actions are to bring sunshine back to the city—like many vampires, the Strangers do not like daylight—thereby dispelling the dark from the Dark City and creating a real Shell Beach. He then meets his wife Emma, but she has no memory of him and thus their relationship must begin anew. In the meantime, the Strangers have hidden from the sunlight, preparing to die as they no longer have access to human memories and all new ones are now remaining in the city rather than draining out of it.

This creates a curious ending that forefronts human self-determination but with little indication of how this might play out in practice. The city, while huge, does not constitute a planet and is more like an island floating aimlessly in space. The Strangers were evidently in control of everything from gravity to food and water to supply power, waste services and even cemeteries. Murdoch, who is now a hybrid of sorts—he is described as an "anomaly" in the film, implying that others could be capable of developing and wielding the otherworldly powers of the vampiric parasites—is no less than a god for the Dark City. Thus, the vampire's perpetual present is used to create an unknown human future. The vampires in *Dark City* do not give form to a voracious future that pulls us into its open maw regardless of whether we want it or not, but rather a present that offers change that is just a reconfiguring of the present. There is a sense then, when viewed in relation to *The War of the Worlds*, that the humans (Murdoch) have indeed evolved into the Martians (future humans) but potentially in a way that removes their inherent vampiric nature, enacting something of a decolonization of the future.

Both *Dracula* and *The War of the Worlds* are colonial stories. Each tells of the evils of the colonial imperative with *Dracula* describing reverse colonialism (a reaping what you sow idea) while *War of the Worlds*, though keeping that thought firmly in mind, configures its Martians more as a natural evolution/devolution of colonialism itself; a greed unto exhaustion and dissolution. In Stoker it is the specter of past deeds that will consume the present while for Wells it is the distant future that will suck out its energy. Time plays a pivotal role in the construction of the vampire from another world, often describing anxieties over an unknown future or traumas from the past—this fits in with Wells' own view of two types of people, retrospective or constructive where one continually refers to and is therefore stuck in the past, while the other is constructive and always looking to change things—the monstrosity of the Martians being they continue re-enacting the past while moving into the future (Elder-Aviram: 2021). The next chapter rather sidesteps this, seeing the world of the vampire not as one trying to feed on our own but rather being a mirror to our own vampiric nature.

4

Underworld

This chapter changes focus from the feeding habits of vampires to where they are from. In this instance it is not about a far away world but one that is linked to but separate from our own. More specifically it picks up on the idea of parallel worlds, specifically ones that mirror our own in some way. Thus, the early films in the *Underworld* universe take place in the darkness and shadows of our own world, the sewers, underground tunnels, and hidden communities. The *Underworld* franchise thereby creates a parallel universe which meaningfully intersects with the everyday world on occasion. In this respect, it acts as a carnivalesque excess/jouissance that bursts into reality. This becomes increasingly so in the later installments so that the world of humans actively tries to destroy the supernatural enemy that has suddenly appeared within its midst. Indeed, the worlds created seem to shift and double at will; the world we thought was our own never was, and is itself a parallel plane that, by the later installments, changes from a shadow domain into a dark mirror revealing the vampiric and bestial machinations at the heart of contemporary society. In their role of doppelgängers to contemporary societies many of the worlds discussed here play on ideas of populations divided through historical, racial and ethnic differences as well as economic and sexual exclusion. This is often expressed through ongoing anxieties over technology, which is equally portrayed as the domain of wealth and futurity, but also a means of discrimination and exclusion. The first two films examined in this chapter depict worlds that are removed from our own, though linked to it by their explicit references to distinct historical periods, Victorian England and Weimar Germany respectively.

Perfect Creature, Glenn Standring, 2006/ *The Breed,* Michael Oblowitz, 2001

Standring's *Perfect Creature* is set in an alternate New Zealand in a world that resembles the late–Victorian period with an added flavor of

1940s steampunk. It depicts a society divided between the wealthy and the dispossessed, the latter of whom live in the sprawling slums. According to the backstory of this world, the first vampires were born three hundred years ago in the slums as a side effect of a now banned genetic experiment that created male vampires who were killed at birth. A truce was formed between humans and the vampires who managed to survive, whereby any newborn vampires were taken from their mothers and placed into a religious order called the Brothers whose sole purpose was to serve humanity through spiritual care and scientific research. Humans are accordingly taught in school from an early age that vampires are special and closer to God (more perfect), due to their increased strength, enhanced sight, and resilience to disease. Human loyalists reciprocate by donating their blood to feed the vampires. The vampires in turn give their own blood for special ceremonies that consist of a communion of sorts that involves humans imbibing the vampire blood and thereby triggering hallucinatory visions and out-of-body experiences. As part of the agreement between the humans and the vampires, humans were forbidden from performing any scientific or genetic experiments, making them reliant on the vampires to create vaccines and medicines. Another corollary of this prohibition is that humans are unable to destroy the vampires or gain social independence.

Perfect Creature opens during a long running influenza epidemic that has killed hundreds across the city. The vampires have been unable to develop a successful cure and resentment against them is running high. The tension is ratcheted up by a string of brutal murders of women whose throats have been ripped out. These murders recall the Jack the Ripper murders that took place in the slum areas of Whitechapel, East London in 1888, and which create interesting resonances between our world and the one in which *Perfect Creature* takes place. The narrative makes obvious links between the Ripper case and the one in the slums of the alternate Jamestown; they are shown as being extremely bloody and reveal much violence and brutality in the act, and the killer also purposely leaves evidence to taunt the police. In part, this creates an easy shorthand for the neo-Victorian/steampunk esthetic and associations they are trying to produce in the film, but also suggests a correlation on some level between our world and the vampiric one. In Victorian London the murders took place in some of the most destitute areas of the capital, with the suggestion that the killer came from the wealthy, privileged classes or even might have been part of some secret, religious society (the Freemasons). *Perfect Creature* replicates this with the slums of Jamestown mirroring those of 19th century Whitechapel and further correlates the idea of poverty in our world with being human in the vampiric one. Similarly, the vampires, who are constructed as the religious and administrative authorities in the alternate world, are correlated to the wealthy elites in Victorian London, seeing them as vampiric.

This provides a volatile background to the series of murders. Although the authorities are trying to conceal the murders from the public by cordoning off crime scenes and blaming the deaths on the influenza outbreak, a vampire culprit is suspected—though a fake news story leaked by the authorities is published in newspapers claiming that the killer is a deranged human who thinks he is a Brother. The film reveals that the real killer is the rogue vampire, Edgar (Leo Gregory), who has been sending videos of his crimes to his elder brother, Silus (Dougray Scott) who is prominent in the Brotherhood and is subsequently sent in as an advisor to the police to help solve the crimes. Edgar was once a member of a team of vampires working on a cure for the influenza outbreak and thus his sudden breakdown elicits widespread surprise and is viewed as an expression of the ongoing tensions between vampires and humans. Silus assists in Edgar's capture and subsequently learns that Edgar was part of a secret research team tasked with producing a virus that could be injected into women to force the fetuses to turn into vampires, thereby solving the ongoing problem that no new vampires had been born for seventy years and all were born male. However, Edgar's work did not go to plan and all but one of the women became insane psychopaths. Furthermore, Edgar himself became infected with the virus and subsequently succumbed to madness. On the night of Silus' investiture into the higher realms of the Brotherhood, Edgar escapes, killing the vampires stationed to guard him, and begins to deliberately spread the virus amongst the community of Jamestown.

This is unacceptable to the Brotherhood as it threatens not only their already tenuous relationship to the human community, but also the basis of their power and control within society as a whole. This last is predicated on maintaining strict boundaries, species purity, between the vampires and the humans and the kind of blood pollution/miscegenation that would be caused by Edgar's plan would destroy this balance. Although they quarantine Jamestown to try and contain and kill Edgar before he infects anyone else, he has other plans and has taken control of the local water-plant. There he is planning on contaminating the drinking water supplies with his blood infecting the entire human community. Suitably this is where the final fight between the two brothers occurs, and although Edgar manages to impale Silus on a metal steam pipe, the lead human detective from the original investigation, Lily Squires (Saffron Burrows), is on hand to kill the rogue vampire with another pipe plunged into his head.

During these final scenes Silus has become aware of the location of the final pregnant woman infected by Edger in the original experiments, and unlike the others she did not suffer any mental or physical complications.

Indeed, she's is about to give birth to a baby female vampire. Knowing that this could be the key to altering the power balance between the two communities, Silus tells Squires where the baby is being born and instructs her to take it and keep it safe from the Brotherhood. Silus himself has been excommunicated by the Brotherhood for breaking quarantine and going against their orders to destroy Jamestown and must now permanently hide from them. The film then ends, hinting that miscegenation and hybridity offer both communities a different future, and one that might eventually bring them together, a theme that continues into the next film. *The Breed* depicts an alternate universe which harks back to the 1940s more visibly, with a world that has seemingly also just survived a world war involving a Nazi extermination of the Jewish community.

The Breed creates a world that is neither ours nor sufficiently different from our own to be a world uniquely itself. It thus produces a space that resembles the Count's Castle in Tod Browning's *Dracula*, one that is not completely alien but suggest that the supernatural might intrude at any moment. *The Breed* is set in an unspecified future time that feels distinctly like postwar Europe with noir-esque lighting and 1940s–50s clothing. The community is divided between humans and vampires—the vampire population has come out of hiding to make peace with humanity—though it is an uneasy situation with neither side trusting the other. Vampires are the underdogs of this society, notwithstanding their greater longevity and physical strength, and are forced to live in former Jewish ghettos. They are thus identified with the Jewish community and are similarly shown wearing an identifying symbol stitched onto their clothing, not unlike the Star of David that Jews were forced to wear under Nazi occupation. The male vampires, particularly their leader Cross (Péter Halász), wear long coats and homburg hats. This identification between vampires and Jews is further cemented when the main vampire protagonist, detective Aaron Grey (Adrian Paul) has a flashback to the loss of his wife and child during the war. The correlation between vampirism and Jewishness is not unfamiliar within the vampire genre; indeed it can be traced back as far as the legend of the Wandering Jew at the start of the thirteenth century which became associated with vampires as an undead figure that is cursed to walk the Earth until Christ's second coming (See Davison: 2004, 94–5, and Ní Fhlainn: 2019, 50). Slightly earlier in the twelfth century the blood libels began in England where Jews were wrongly accused of killing and using the blood of Christian children in rituals (see Rose: 2015)—this became a slur against Jewish communities across Europe, and while not linked to vampirism then it has influenced later readings of vampires in European history. In fact, there is no mistaking the reference to it in Stoker's *Dracula* as the Count offers a sack full of babies to his "brides." This was not the only reference to Jewishness in the figure of Count Dracula, the immigrant from the East that no one wanted—at the time of the novel London had become home to many displaced Jews fleeing persecution in Russia and mainland Europe.[84] Many of Dracula's features were based on anti-Semitic stereotypes such as a monobrow and large hooked nose, and his ability to hypnotize his victims copied the gifts of Svengali, a character from George du Maurier's novel *Trilby* (1894) who is often cited as a caricature of a Jew. Not least the vampire is shown to hoard money to serve no other end than to gather dust—Dracula has a room full of gold coins of various currencies. His stereotypically Jewish qualities are still more pronounced in the film *Nosferatu*, where Count Orlok's pointed ears, prominent brow and hooked nose are brought into focus. Furthermore, he is configured as a manifestation of a verminous plague, an accusation often leveled at Jewish communities in Europe. Oblowitz offers a new twist on this identification of Jews and vampires. While the vampires are predominantly shown to be Jewish—some of the main vampire characters in the film, Lucy Westenra in particular, are clearly not Jewish—they are clearly demarcated as unjustly oppressed and vilified and worthy of our sympathy. This is in contrast the human society are aggressive and reactionary with their obvious association with xenophobia and National Socialism, partly through Nazi-style uniforms, increasing our identification with the vampires. As such, this complicates any anti-Semitism that clings to the body of the vampire by revealing the innate racism of the environment around them.

Returning to the film, the mirroring of World War II from our world into this parallel environment makes the real-world conflict the framing reference of the ongoing tension between the humans and the vampires. This tension is typified in a series of mysterious murders of humans by a pale man dressed in black who appears to be invulnerable and possesses superhuman speed and drains his victims of blood. Human detective Steve Grant (Bokeem Woodbine) is put on the case, and is paired with Aaron Grey after the murder of his human partner, in the hope that Grey may give him insight into the vampire community and thereby help him apprehend the killer. As the investigation develops, it becomes clear that the vampire community are at risk, while the humans support a proto-fascist state. This subversion of the conventional power relations between humans and vampires brought home in a scene where Grant and Grey are investigating a lead in the ghetto area and the human detective is taken aback when a young child smiles at him with their fangs suddenly appearing. Grant

---

84. In relation to this Hadas Elbar-Alviram pointed out to me that one of the houses containing Dracula's boxes of soil is located in Chicksand Street in London's East End, the center of the Jewish community in the late 19th century.

immediately realizes they are surrounded by vampires, who actually wish him no harm, but human troops nevertheless round up these vampires and abuse them. In an earlier scene that foreshadows this power abuse, Grant meets Lucy Westenra (Bai Ling)—who is an artist and a vampire and, in many ways, typifies the exoticness of the vampire community with her obvious Chinese heritage, fetishistic fashion choices and pet leopard. While initially repelled and not a little scared of her, Grant eventually becomes romantically involved with her.

As mentioned above, the vampires are generally constructed as symbolically Jewish and the humans as (German/European) fascists, but each group is comprised of many ethnicities and nationalities. Among the vampires, Lucy Westenra is of Chinese descent, Cross and Dr. Orlok (István Gös) are Hungarian, Fusco (William Hootkins) is Italian, and Aaron Grey is English. The humans are equally diverse: Grant is African American and his partner on the police force, Phil (Reed Diamond), was white, while the leader of the human military, Seward, is of Chinese heritage. This mix of backgrounds within each group actually makes ethnicity unimportant as one is defined not by exterior details but by an internal essence. Though, in terms of *The Breed*, ethnicity, as a category of difference, is forced on both the humans and the vampires.

This enforced categorization comes from the leadership above and, and as Grant and Grey discover, beneath the myriad tales of corruption, deceit and betrayal, humans and vampires could coexist if they began to live together rather than in rigidly separate communities, and that this too is imposed from above rather than by their own choice. The leader of the human community, Seward, is so paranoid about the perceived threat of the vampires that he has created a virus that could kill all vampires. Cross has discovered this plan and forces the human scientist who created the virus to reconfigure it in such a way that it could turn all humans into vampires. The film concludes with Grant and Grey defusing the explosive device by drawing on their joint capabilities as human and vampire, having developed a strong bond of friendship and respect. Grant and Lucy's relationship has developed sufficiently for Grant to accept Lucy's invitation to live together in her mansion. He expresses his worry that he will age much faster than her, and that she will still look young while he is an old man—there is no suggestion here that he will be turned into a vampire as in *Twilight* for example. Rather curiously for such a situation, Lucy does not offer easy solutions or platitudes but rather insists that they shall work it out as they go along. This is rather refreshing for a vampire story where the differences between humans and vampires are not resolved, synthesized, or purged but accepted for what that are and negotiated on a day by day basis. This mirror of our world, of its prejudices and horrors, ultimately becomes an example to follow; a doppelgänger that is no longer malevolent but a model to which to aspire.

The Breed is a high point in cinematic human-vampire relations. In the next films under discussion, the use of futuristic alternate worlds often takes center stage to allow the various manifestations of vampiric entities to interact with the human race, even though this vision of tomorrow often looks like the distant past. Thus, *Blood: The Last Vampire* (Nahon: 2009) mixes real world conflict with an alternate world in which victory for one side spells the annihilation of the other, even if the humans are wholly unaware of the battle.

Blood: The Last Vampire, Chris Nahon, 2009/ *Priest*, Scott Stewart, 2011

Blood: The Last Vampire is a live action version of an earlier anime film of the same name by Hiroyuki Kitakubo (2000). Targeted at a wider international audience, the live action film unnecessarily complicates the plot of the anime, but it thereby offers the possibility of a mutual respect growing between humans and a certain kind of vampire. The story in both films is set in real-world Japan that is negotiating a changing relationship with America after World War II, but in an alternate reality where demons (vampires) actually exist. While the two films differ in their categorization of the "vampires"—the original anime defines them more definitively as vampires whereas the live action movie shifts toward blood-drinking demons—both agree that the main protagonist, Saya, is a vampire hunter. The indeterminate nature of who or what the vampire is in the films is understandable as Japan did not have such creatures as they are known in the West until the Americans arrived in the early 20th century (see Melton: 2011, 389, and Hudson: 2017, 470) with the first vampire novel, *The Death's Head Stranger* by Seishi Yokomizo, appearing in 1939 (Kotani: 1997, 189), and the first vampire film, *Vampire Moth* by Nobuo Nakagawa, in 1956.[85] Japanese mythology and folklore has many hungry ghosts (gaki), corpse-eaters (jikininki), and blood (life)-drinking demons (jubboko) but nothing that specifically correlates to the western popular tradition of romantic, fanged bloodsuckers. China, which has heavily influenced Japan on occasion, has

---

85. It should be noted that *Vampire Moth* did not feature a real vampire but rather a masked thief, not unlike the French film *Les vampires* (Feuillade: 1915) that was about a gang of crooks. However, Nakagawa's 1959 film *Vampire Woman* has much more of a supernatural flavoring to it. Of interest in relation to *Blood* is that, as Susan Napier observes, vampires in Japanese literature and film, at least up until the mid to late 19th century, have been predominantly female (1998, 106).

hopping green vampires which, golem-like, can be animated by placing a specific text on their foreheads, or removing it. Consequently, the film itself is predicated on the idea of colonialism where Japanese "vampires" (blood sucking demons) are trying to kill American vampire killers—the demons can assume human form but look not unlike plump, winged raptors. The anime makes this idea even more explicit where the Japanese vampiric shapeshifters, which are huge, batlike creatures, are called Chiropterrans—coming from chiroptera, the name for the mammalian order of bats.

Saya herself looks like a young girl though it is suggested she is much, much older; in the anime she is called an "original" and in the live-action she is the daughter of the original demon, Origen (Koyuki). The live-action film shows Saya (Ji-Hyun Jun) in the employ of The Council, a high-powered secret order, that is tasked with destroying all the blood-drinking demons. While they are supposed to be a global organization, Nahon's film explicitly connects them to the United States—all their operatives other than Saya are American and they pretend to be the CIA throughout, and do seem to have powerful connections in Washington, D.C. As such, they strongly appear to represent America and western culture trying to dispel Japanese culture and identity as symbolized by the demons. The film opens in 1970—the anime was set 4 years earlier—with the United States using Japan as a base for their ongoing operations in Vietnam. This also marked a time of change in the relationship between the USA and Japan with the latter becoming increasingly independent. Saya is sent into a military school to track down some demons and to lure out their creator, Origen. In the anime Saya kills the Chiropterrans that have infiltrated the school and moves on, leaving the institution's nurse as the only witness to the events. The live-action version complicates this by having

Figure 15. Japanese vampires. *Blood: The Last Vampire*. Directed by Chris Nahon (Asmik Ace Entertainment: 2009).

Saya save Alice McKee (Allison Miller), who is the daughter of an army general, after she witnesses the vampire hunter killing two demons in the guise of fellow students. This is further complicated not only by the arrival of Origen and a dramatic increase in the number of demons in the vicinity, but also a coup of sorts within the ranks of The Council where the second in command to Saya's handler decides to take matters into his own hands and kill all those who are complicating their current mission; this includes both Saya and Alice.

In the anime Saya remains true to herself—an isolated, hybrid anomaly in a world to which she does not belong, engineered by personal history to destroy her own past and hence facilitate the forces of American colonialism. In the live-action film, the relationship between Saya and Alice is supposed to heal the antagonism between America and Japan, mooting the possibility of reconciliation and mutual respect (see Gelder: 2012, 97). Yet in this parallel world the American contingent appears to have very little to justify its usefulness and indeed is lost in the world of demons and nightmares that are largely beyond its comprehension. In many ways this is not surprising as the narrative increasingly becomes not just about Japan's past consuming the present but actually entering the dream world of Saya herself. As the film gradually reveals, Saya is approximately 400 years old and the daughter of a great warrior/vampire hunter. It would also seem that her mother is none other than Origen herself meaning that she is half human and half demon—or potentially not human at all. Furthermore, Saya requires human blood to survive, which is kept in bottles in her refrigerator so one assumes it has been sourced from a blood bank rather than slain victims, and her own blood is poisonous to the demons. Her samurai heritage is depicted through many flashbacks where she is raised and mentored by her father's trusted friend Kato (Yaduaki Kurata)—her father was killed by Origen. These flashbacks show her growing realization of the dangerous nature of her demon self, particularly in her dream of drinking the blood of her best friend only to awake and find him dead next to her with his throat ripped out. This provides the catalyst for Saya's self-hatred, her vampire hunting symbolically enabling the destruction of the demon inside herself but also of her past. The past that she symbolically destroys is also the national history of Japan that has made her into the hybrid monster that she has become. Her all-consuming quest to kill Origen—literally her point of origin—is one to free herself from her past and to prove that she is human rather than a demon. However, the film's conclusion is open-ended, leaving many of these issues unresolved.

The film establishes that the procedure for unmasking a demon involves looking into their eyes to expose the lack of a soul. Saya initially sees little difference between the demons and herself, but toward the end of the film, Alice looks into her eyes and confirms her humanity. The film tries to make this a pivotal moment, yet it is quickly diffused in the battle between mother and daughter when Origen says to Saya, "You think the more demons you kill the more human you become, don't you? How naïve" (Nahon: 2009). Saya appears weakened by this comment and Origen is on the point of victory until Alice, who has been forgotten for most of the preceding fight, suddenly appears behind the demon and seriously wounds her. Saya, sword in hand now, stands above her prone and bleeding mother but not before Origen tells her that if she kills her, she will become her. Saya of course kills her, literally slaying her demons, but also symbolically destroying the world where such entities exist. By killing her mother, Saya symbolically destroys Japan's history and cultural heritage, and thus the parallel world collapses and becomes one with the real world, where the war in Vietnam is happening and tales of demons and blood-suckers are no more than myths. The film thus ends with Alice telling her story to the authorities. Asked where this "Saya" is, Alice stops talking and her gaze turns toward the camera, but drifts off slightly with a curious mix of knowledge and madness flickering across her face. Alice thus signals her knowledge of Saya's whereabouts and her unwillingness to divulge it. Yet, her ambiguous expression suggests that Alice might be harboring a darker secret.

Alice is established as a rebellious teenager who loves her father but does not respect what he stands for as part of the American armed forces currently invading Vietnam. Thus, one may argue that Alice has knowingly released a demon into the world who is set upon reintroducing the old ways to the new world, not least with a view to liberating Japan from colonial forces. Thus, the closing shot of the film depicts Saya working in a rice field, a traditional occupation in a traditional setting, marking a return to a Japan of the past where the world was full of demons and Japan took pride in its myths. Consequently, while Alice respects Saya, she realizes that vampires and humans can never exist in the same world and she decides that the real-world colonial American version is not one she wants to be part of. Something of this occurs in *Priest*, which pictures a similar antipathy between vampires and humans with the former being indigenous and the latter colonialists, though here the narrative is far more metaphorical and takes place on an entirely different world.

Priest (Stewart: 2011) is set on what appears to be an alternate Earth that is inhabited by humans and vampires. The film itself borrows much from the earlier Western, *The Searchers* (Ford: 1956), which shows a Civil War veteran rescuing his niece from the Comanches. Indeed, the mise-en-scene of *Priest* is very in keeping with that, showing "reservations," farmsteads in the wilderness, and even towns in which buildings are connected by a network of railways lines and steam trains. All of this recalls American frontier towns of the 19th century, even though Priest himself is shown riding on an amazingly fast and futuristic motorcycle of some kind. The treatment of the vampires then becomes analogous to the conditions forced upon the Native American communities by the ever-increasing expansion of the settlers.

The film suggests that the humans and vampires have always been at war, at least until the undated point that the humans retreated from the plains into large fortified cities. Here, humanity turned to the Church, a homogenous organization, that produced the Priests, extraordinarily gifted men and woman who were made into vampire hunters. The Priests were so successful that the vampires were forced back onto large reservations—the use of the word in the film is purposeful and highlights the subtext of the narrative, that of the colonization of Native American land[86]; the correlation is not without its complications, not least in monsterizing these that have been colonized, although it does highlight the kinds of propaganda used in such ventures[87]—where they are not allowed to breed or regroup. The vampires themselves are human-sized feral creatures that live in huge communal hives and act like bees or termites with a Queen ruling over the rest who are drones. This situation has remained in place for a number of years with the "hives" located in the radiation-saturated and largely barren wastelands of the planet while the humans, ruled over by the Church, are grouped together in mega cities joined by a network of railway lines—the Church here is something of an overdetermined version of the Catholic Church. Indeed, the peace seems so complete that the Priests are seen as surplus to requirements and many of their number are being integrated back into society. That is until a small search party, Priest (Paul Bettany), Priestess (Maggie Q), and Black Hat (Karl Urban), go to the Sola Mira Hive to check on some unusual activity. Once there they discover something is not quite right and suddenly realize they have walked into a trap. Priest and Priestess escape but Black Hat is captured and assumed to have been killed by the vampires.

Priest returns to Cathedral City, the headquarters of the Church, to warn them that the vampires are beginning an uprising, but he is not believed. While in the city Priest learns that his niece Lucy (Lily Collins) has been taken by the vampires[88]—Priest is in fact her father but because his order are not supposed to have children she is being raised

---

86. See Dalton: 2011, and Bacon: 2020.
87. In terms of *The War of the Worlds* this would see the Martians representing humanity as monstrous savages that need to be controlled or exterminated.
88. There is a possible connection to Lucy Westenra from *Dracula* here that would see Priest and his helpers as the vampire slayers though no other character names from Stoker's novel are used in the film.

by Priest's brother Owen (Stephen Moyer). Priest immediately goes to his brother's farmstead in the wasteland to glean more information from Owen, and proceeds to the nearest reservation to search for Lucy. In the reservation, he finds the guards dead, with only human familiars guarding the hive—familiars are humans that have been infected by the vampires and have become more feral in appearance and behavior and guard the hive while the vampires sleep during the day—and learns that Lucy has been taken to the Sola Mira Hive. Priestess joins him and together, along with Lucy's suitor, Hicks (Cam Gigandet), they go to the Hive to find it abandoned, discovering that the vampires are headed toward the town of Jericho.

There is a strong sense in the film that as the vampires make their way to Jericho, and then on to Cathedral City, they are reclaiming land that has been taken from them, and that their monstrosity is the manifestation of the violence and greed of humanity itself. This equally applies to the level of violence inflicted on humans by the vampires, part of which is seen in the familiars mentioned above, which exemplify the well-known vampiric trope of miscegenation to warn of the dangers of being in the proximity of those seen as socially abject. This is further complicated by the reappearance of Blackhat, who was not killed but infected by the blood of the Queen herself. Unlike the other familiars seen in this alternate world, who are hairless, pale and have pointed ears—very much in the Orlok tradition—Blackhat looks just as he did in life except with the addition of fangs and gold-colored eyes. He is also extremely strong, agile, and gifted with a malevolent intelligence. While there is much of the "white savior" in Blackhat's construction—only a white man is capable of saving the "savages" that are the vampires—he also represents the perfect synthesis between human and vampire with the "best" characteristics of both. But his hybridity does not bring the two species together but is geared toward resolving the conflict in favor of those more closely connected to the planet.

This too correlates the vampires to Native Americans where both are seen as indigenous; a community that has evolved in close relation to the environment seeing its ongoing existence as vital to the wellbeing of the planetary ecosystem.[89] Much of this is shown, not just in the vampires' dependence on hives that are inextricably part of the landscape but in humanity's distancing themselves from all that is natural; walling themselves up in mega cities; a dependence on technology and traveling across the surface of the planet in trains that protect them from interacting with the outside world. By using train carriages to deliver a deadly cargo of

---

89. In terms of *The War of the Worlds* this would equate to the special, evolutionary bond that the inhabitants of the Earth have with their home world and which ensures their primacy over outside invaders such as the Martians.

vampires into Cathedral City, Blackhat not only associates himself with the vampires but more closely with the planet, framing his actions as an attempt to restore balance by, if not destroying humanity, certainly returning it to a dependency on the environment. Interestingly the wastelands to which the vampires are banished and where Owen and other pioneers are setting up farmsteads are said to be recovering from high doses of radiation, suggesting that this came about due to the earlier conflict between the two species and more specifically because of humanity.

As the film reaches its denouement Blackhat and the vampires are approaching Cathedral City on the speeding train. Priest, with the help of his friends, manages to stop the train with a large number of explosives strapped to a motorcycle. Yet, although they find Blackhat's distinctive black cowboy hat, his body is nowhere to be found. Although the world of humans thinks it can rest easily again through acts of violence that caused the problem in the first place, Priest knows the solution is more elusive. And as the film ends he goes to the Monsignor (Christopher Plummer) in Cathedral City and throws the head of a vampire at his feet exclaiming, not unlike the look given by Alice at the end of *Blood: The Last Vampire*, that "the war has just begun" (Stewart: 2011).

The next two films also feature an Earth far removed from our own, so much so that it resembles an alien planet. On this Earth, humanity has migrated to the city for protection, not from vampires but from contagion initiated by the humans themselves. This Earth thus forms an allegory of urbanization, albeit one where cities are a concentration of humanity, whereas in our world the city is an insatiable all-consuming creature (vampire) that spreads ever wider across the surrounding environment. These films depict a humanity so far removed from its natural environment that it has become an increasingly engineered, non-natural creation very much in the way that H.G. Wells envisioned future-humanity as Martian vampires that cannot safely exist outside their metallic exoskeletons. In this world of sparse population, all aspects of life from architecture to fashion are sophisticated and technologically advanced, underscoring humanity's distance from the natural world.

Ultraviolet, Kurt Wimmer, 2006/ *Aeon Flux*, Karyn Kusama, 2005

Ultraviolet shows humanity completely removed from the natural world, in an environment so manufactured that even the diseases are synthetic. One of these, the hemoglophagic virus, originally created to produce stronger and more agile troops, has escaped from a laboratory, infecting the population. Once they contract the virus, the victims grow fangs and become preternaturally strong and endowed with regenerative powers. But their lifespan is also reduced to twelve years from the moment of infection. The infected are known as "Hemophages" (vampires) due to these symptoms and are spurned by the rest of society. Their situation worsens when Vice Cardinal Ferdinand Daxus (Nick Chinlund), who is the leader of both the church and the government, determines to exterminate all hemophages and so the infected unite to form an underground resistance movement. The uniting of Church and state here resembles that seen in *Priest*. The main protagonist, Violet (Milla Jovovich), was pregnant when she became infected so was taken in by the authorities to be studied but managed to escape and join the Hemophage Underground. It is in this role, just before her twelve years are over, that Violet infiltrates the Archministry and manages to steal a case supposedly containing the ultimate weapon against the hemophages which will wipe them all out.

Violet's entry into the secure government facility manifests a transformative vampirism that is grounded in the mutability of Violet herself both in terms of her internal mutation and external transformations. Part of the essence of Bram Stoker's Count Dracula was his ability to change, appearing in the novel as a bat, a wolf, elemental mist, and even changing his human appearance—he was old and hirsute in Transylvania but young and virile in London. This "more than human" or super-human aspect of the vampire has been used by theorists Gilles Deleuze and Felix Guattari (1987) and Donna Haraway (1991) to describe not just human becomings in terms of individual subjectivity but also cyborgian hybridity—becoming here denoting a trajectory, or movement, away from normative binaries and subjectivities (Deleuze and Guattari: 2004, 105), and cyborg a transgressive interconnectedness beyond containment (Thweatt-Bates: 2012, 90–1): both of these states work from societally accepted ideas of what is normal, usual, and even universal and are largely configured around dominant white, patriarchal, heteronormative, anthropocentric ideology so that paths or trajectories of deviance from that can be described as "becoming." Vampiric bodies thus exceed the limits of the merely human through biological becoming—drugs, transplants, and body modification—or through technological implants, namely mechanical, electronic, nanotech "hardware." The performative nature of the vampire plays an additional role in this model, through the characteristics, choreography, and the ways in which the vampire engages with and affects the environment around it.

Violet embodies many of these aspects. When she arrives at the facility she is dressed as a motorcycle courier who has arrived to collect and deliver the package containing the secret weapon. She successfully passes through extensive security checks, including strip searches, that confirm her DNA and identity, and she is able to change the design and color of her clothes and her hair color once they are returned to her, and she can produce weapons seemingly out of thin air. These weapons and augmentations are not just an extension of her physical self but inherently part of who she is—she literally becomes "Violet" because of these deviations from normality. In fact, it is her ability to constantly transform—a trajectory of becomings—in relation to the complete inability of change in the armored, male guards that try to stop her that further categorizes her as vampiric. Indeed, her very presence charges the space that she inhabits with a dangerous transgressiveness, not unlike that experienced in the vicinity of Count Dracula and his castle. As such, these transformational characteristics, along with her internal biological evolution, see Violet as performatively a vampire, even though we never see her drink blood.

The future world of Violet recalls its counterpart in *The Breed*, with the divisions between humans and vampires, the secret plot to exterminate one of the species, and the exotic, performative nature of the vampires—it is not surprising that the only other character who seems able to transform as much as Violet, Vice Cardinal Ferdinand Daxus, turns out to be a Hemophage as well.

Violet disobeys her instructions and opens the stolen case, discovering

Figure 16. Violet (Milla Jovovich) becoming vampire in the face of the anonymous guards of normativity. *Ultraviolet*. Directed by Kurt Wimmer (Sony Pictures Entertainment: 2006).

a young boy inside it named Six (Cameron Bright), as he is the sixth of eight clones developed by Daxus. Violet escapes with the boy and brings him to a scientist friend who discovers Six is not dangerous to vampires but actually only to humans. Her friend also discovers the boy has a tracking device implanted in him and consequently forces her to leave. It is not long before Violet and Six are tracked down and she is killed in the ensuing fight. However, due to her regenerative powers, and with the help of her friend, she comes back to life, literally becoming undead.[90] Once awake, Violet realizes that Six might still be alive—she assumed he would be killed upon being captured—even though Daxus has him back at the Archministry. Violet, now returned to her vampiric self, breaks into the government building just in time to stop Six from being dissected—the boy, who was originally thought to carry an antigen that would kill hemophages, is actually cloned from Daxus himself and so was actually a weapon to turn all humans into vampires to ensure his own superiority in the world order. However, Six is designed to live for only 6 hours and so Daxus needs to take samples to recreate his weapon. Violet defeats all the soldiers guarding the facility culminating with a final battle with Daxus, though not before she discovers that he too is a hemophage, and it is through the biological enhancements due to the disease that he has ensured his rise to power. Daxus loses the battle and Six is saved. It is discovered that the tears that Violet shed over him earlier passed on her disease to him which has nullified the effects of the antigen in his body so that he will now life a normal life span—effectively becoming a vampire has made him human again. As such Six will become a source for finding the antidote for the virus, though not quickly enough for Violet as bringing her back from the dead has not affected the fact that she is due to die extremely soon.

The film ends with Violet on the edge of death, and Six ensuring the survival of both the vampires and the humans. Curiously, though, this can equally be seen to be purging the planet of vampires, even if it is achieved by turning them all into humans—this is rather reminiscent of *The Omega Man* (Sagal: 1971) where all the vampires, even the African American ones, are white, destroying ideas of difference as everyone is the same. Indeed, this shows a contrast in the handling of difference in *Ultraviolet* and *The Breed*. The latter allows for difference and there is no "cure" because none is needed; both species can learn to get along with each other. In contrast, arguably *Ultraviolet* sees the sharing of the Earth as impossible as only humans will be left alive. This is confirmed by the cure offered by Six as it is not just a way of extending the limited lifespan of the vampires but of returning them to ordinary humanity; there is no "becoming" in this

90. Interestingly in the animated series that came out of the film Violet dies at the end of every episode only to be brought back to life for the next installment.

scenario for it does not embody change, only eternal stasis. Much of this framework is seen in *Aeon Flux* (Kusama: 2005) and particularly in the performative nature of the vampire body.

Aeon Flux is also predicated on a plague devastating humanity, but this one does not turn them into vampires but simply kills them. Ninety-nine percent of the Earth's population is killed before a cure is found and by this time the remaining survivors have retreated into one city named Bregna. As with *Priest*, the city is walled in as protection from the contagion, but it also effectively incarcerates the people inside. The movie opens four hundred and four years after the plague, with the city in a state of unease as people mysteriously disappear and many of the inhabitants suffer from nightmares. The opening sequences of the film resonate with the vampire genre, with imagery of a closed eye in closeup and a fly landing near it and walking toward the lashes, which quickly open and trap the insect. The eye, out of context of a face, is a Venus flytrap, a vampire plant that features in F.W. Murnau's *Nosferatu* that is shown as synonymous with the vampiric state. The fingers that suddenly appear and grip the fly, but do not kill it, belong to Aeon Flux (Charlize Theron). The speed of her movements and strength in her eyelashes intimate her more- or other-than-human, vampire-like character. The society plagued with nightmares and vanishing citizens likewise resonates with vampire tropes.

This vampiric undercurrent reinforces the vampiric becomings that Aeon manifests throughout the film, including extreme speed and powerful body strength, as well as the aforementioned entrapping eyelashes. Aeon is part of a resistance group called the Monicans who are trying to break the stranglehold that the scientific elite have held over society since the original outbreak—not unlike that seen in *Perfect Creature*. All the members of

Figure 17. Handler (Francis McDormand) communicates to Aeon via telepathy and telekinesis. *Aeon Flux*. Directed by Karyn Kusama (Paramount Pictures: 2005).

the group keep in touch through telepathy and via the guidance of Handler (Francis McDormand), a mysterious figure who seems to guide all the movements of the resistance (see image above) as well as supply them with high-tech devices—these are either elaborately transferred between group members, as seen in a kiss between Aeon and a stranger she meets in the street who thereby passes a device from his mouth to hers while avoiding the ubiquitous surveillance cameras, or via telepathic dreams—these often involve a dream version (avatar) of Aeon standing in front of Handler while information is passed between the two. Aeon's first mission is to destroy a surveillance center, which she performs off-handedly by using her inherent gymnastic skills to overcome armed guards and infiltrate and exit the facility unnoticed—like many vampires, she is a creature of stealth, silence and darkness. However, upon returning home, she discovers that her sister, Una (Amelia Warner), is missing, and she concludes that Una has been taken by the authorities as a suspected Monican. Her next mission is to kill the leader of the government, Trevor Goodchild (Marton Csokas)—the descendant of the original scientist that found a cure for the plague.

This mission explicitly showcases Aeon's vampiric nature, and indeed, the vampirism of the parallel world of the film. As Aeon arrives at the perimeter of the government facility, she is joined by her colleague in the resistance, Sithandra (Sophie Okonedo), who is equally more-than-human and has had her feet replaced with hands allowing for increased acrobatic ability. As the pair somersault and dive across the grounds leading to the main building, the fruit in the nearby trees fires poisoned metal shards at them. Aeon crawls at speed on just her fingertips and toes—oddly similar to the sight of Count Dracula crawling down the side of his castle. As they approach the building, the landscape becomes increasingly transformative and dangerous, and even the grass becomes weaponized as it mutates into literal blades. Leaving Sithandra outside, Aeon enters the building and a map of the facility emerges from her raised skin tissue after she taps the inside of her forearm. Aeon successfully makes her way to a theater auditorium where Trevor is practicing a speech. She easily sneaks up on him with a gun, but just as she is about to shoot him, he looks at her and vivid memories flood her mind, leaving her paralyzed and unable to resist arrest. She subsequently escapes her prison cell with the aid of intelligent, explosive metal balls. As she leaves the building, she encounters one of the members of the central committee and forces them to reveal what is actually going on. She learns that the original cure created by Goodchild also makes everyone sterile and thus cloning has become the only viable way to maintain the population, but in the fullness of time this process has inflicted increasingly worse nightmares on the new clones in the form of the memories of their earlier lives. Trevor has been conducting experiments to try and solve this problem and apparently Aeon's sister Una was the first success in producing a natural birth rather than a manufactured one. This was the cause of Una's death, as Trevor's brother Oren (Johnny Lee Miller) is attempting to destroy all the naturally born citizens in order for the Goodchild family to maintain their control over the city. In this respect, the entire society could be construed as immortal or undead, given that their DNA and memories are resurrected time and again. Aeon likewise discovers that she is cloned from the DNA of the original Trevor Goodchild's wife Katherine. She is the first clone produced from Katherine's DNA since the original Katherine died.

Fortunately for Aeon and Trevor, the film does not conclude like most vampire narratives featuring eternal love, that is in the death (sometimes redemptive) of the vampire, but with the collapse of the oppressive society. Aeon realizes that Handler was in fact an agent of Oren and that her acts of resistance were meant to reinforce the corrupt society she was trying to bring down. Consequently, she unites with Trevor to try and eliminate Oren and his agents. To this aim, Aeon speaks to The Keeper (Pete Postlethwaite), who guides a huge dirigible above the city that watches everyone as well as storing all the memories they have ever had—in a sense he is the true King Vampire overlooking the resurrections of the undead citizens below and it was his doing that Katherine was reborn in Aeon. She sets an explosive device on the dirigible and escapes, with The Keeper's blessing, resulting in the craft's explosion as it collides into the wall of the city and opens a large breach in it. The citizens are amazed as they were always told that the vistas beyond the wall are dangerous wasteland when in fact, they form a lush green landscape ready to be reinhabited. Thus, synthesis between the normal and the deviant remains unachieved because the film ends on the suggestion that given the choice, the resurrected undead would happily become human again.

The next two films feature parallel worlds that are connected to the real world in some way suggesting that they are not only parallel to, or mirror, our world but are joined with our world in ways where one can affect the other.

John Carter, Andrew Stanton, 2012/ *The Matrix,* The Wachowskis, 1999

John Carter opens in 1868 where a Union colonel arrests John Carter (Taylor Kitsch) in the hope of using his military background in the current conflict against the Apache. Carter is disinclined to help and escapes. Pursued by the U.S. Cavalry and, not long after, the Apache as well, he seeks refuge in a cave on sacred ground. He is surprised by the sudden appearance of an alien, that we later discover is a Thern, who is equally startled and attacks Carter with a knife. Carter manages to kill the alien but activates a medallion it was carrying which transports him to Barsoom (Mars). Carter's life changes drastically on Mars, notwithstanding that the alien planet corresponds remarkably to the American Western landscape back on Earth with its associated colonial intent over the Native Americans.

Carter soon discovers that Barsoom is divided into two species, the Green and the Red Martians. The Green Martians, the Tharks, are shown as animalistic in the vein of the vampires in *Priest*, albeit less feral. They are quickly correlated with Native Americans, exiled to a reservation far from any of the areas populated by the Red Martians—as with *Priest* above there are many complications in such like-for-like conflations of otherness and more so as Carter only seems to use his growing knowledge of the Tharks to his own advantage.[91] The Red Martians are human in appearance and divided into two warring factions, those centered in the city of Helium and those in the city of Zodanga. This division allegorizes the armies of the North and the South in the American Civil War with the Native Americans caught in between—the American Civil War ended scarcely three years prior to opening of the story. The conflict between these two factions seems to have been ongoing since the founding of the cities but appears to have entered into a new and deadly phase due to the intervention of the Therns. In the original novel(s), the Therns are more akin to a religious order, but in the film they are constructed as an alien race (alien to Mars) that travel the Galaxy, causing strife between the inhabitants and then "feeding" off the resultant energies produced—they are never shown to eat but seem able to control and transform energy. They are curiously similar in appearance to the Strangers (vampires) in *Dark City* (see above), in that they are hairless and extremely pale.

The Therns exhibit more vampiric traits than the Strangers, as they are able to transform their appearance, very like Count Dracula in Stoker's novel, with the additional advantage that they are able to shapeshift into a likeness of anyone—we see their leader Matai Shang (Mark Strong) transform from a maid, to a guard, back to himself, then another guard in the blink of an eye.

The Therns' need for conflict is quickly established in the film by way of a powerful weapon that Matai Shang gives the Zodangan leader, Sab Than (Dominic West), in order to prolong his conflict with the forces of Helium. The weapon is powered by the mysterious "ninth ray" which seems to be akin to another wavelength in light or a hidden energy inherent in the

91. This correlation to Native Americans is taken from Burroughs' original novel as noted by Stecopoulos: 1997, 179, and DeGraw: 2007.

Figure 18. Matai Shang (Mark Strong, left) leader of the Therns, with Prince Sab Than of Zodanga (Dominic West). *John Carter*. Directed by Andrew Stanton (Walt Disney Pictures: 2012).

universe itself. Its almost spiritual nature is shown as the film progresses and Carter travels to an ancient religious site on Mars which acts as something of a focus for the energy—the novel suggests it was a world-making factory that produced the living environment on Mars but had now fallen into disrepair[92]—and although dormant when Carter arrives, it sparks into life as he touches a particular spot on its surface. The Therns soon arrive and attack the trespasser. While the religious site suggests strong links to Mars, it is also clear that the medallions the Therns used to travel to Earth also hold the coordinates to other worlds, and the fact that they are thinking of moving to Earth next as Mars is dying intimates this could just be another stage on an ongoing interplanetary odyssey where they vampirize an ever growing number of worlds.

Matai Shang then instructs Than on what to do to take control of Mars, forcing the conflict to a point where Helium has no option but to offer him the hand of their leader's daughter, Dejah Thoris (Lynn Collins), in marriage. Matai Shang has no intention of allowing peace to return to Mars and rob him of his source of nourishment, but his plans are derailed by Carter, who during the course of the story has fallen in love with Dejah, and who leads the forces of the Tharks against Zodanga and the Therns. Once victory for the forces of peace is achieved, Carter himself marries Dejah, but not long after this Matai Shang sends him back to Earth. The film concludes

---

92. This resonates with a similar idea in *Total Recall* (Vorhoeven: 1990)—taken from the short story "We Can Remember It for You 'Wholesale'" (1966) by Philip K. Dick—where a planetary power plant on Mars, constructed by the original inhabitants, is purposely kept dormant so a corporation from Earth can control all the settlers.

with Carter luring Matai Shang down to earth, where he manages to kill the Thern and return to Mars to reunite with Dejah.

The Therns follow in the footsteps of Wells' Martians insofar as their "greedy eyes" are leading them from planet to planet, though as mentioned above it is not explicit that Mars is their actual home world. Indeed, their ongoing journey suggests more the aliens in *Independence Day* that are seen as intergalactic scavengers/parasites that leave a trail of destruction behind them before moving on to "younger more virile" lands. That said, the Therns are unusually insidious in their machinations—they do not directly intervene in life or death battles but are rather the instigators of conflict. The construction of the Therns as a third force, an outside influence, suggests that they may bear some relation to the contemporaneous real-world events on Earth. As mentioned before, Carter was a Civil War veteran who fought on the side of the Confederates. However, he has become disillusioned about such conflicts. The correspondence in the film between the two factions of Red Martians and the Union and the Confederacy suggests that the American Civil War was likewise fueled by outside forces who seek to prolong the conflict for personal gain. These forces are curiously impersonal—while Mark Strong as Matai Shang is very distinctive as an actor, the rest of the Therns are largely interchangeable in their identical grey robes, deathly pale skin and bald heads—they are literally the faceless grey men. This impersonality is further reinforced by their ability to shapeshift at will, as though they have no "true" shape, only the one they most regularly choose because of their surroundings. As such, they more clearly embody an energy that creates physical and emotional extremes for its own sustenance. Carter thus seeks to spare the Earth from the self-destruction that took hold of Mars—though the World War I and World War II, amongst others, are evidence enough that he failed in this endeavor. Consequently, even though Carter might have saved Mars from the Therns, it is highly unlikely that they are rendered useless or ineffectual and will have just moved their base of operations elsewhere. Like many of the texts to follow, and an inherent part of the vampire genre, the resolution at the end of the narrative promises naught but temporary peace. More so, the vampire is configured as the embodiment of a certain ideology or way of life, which is brought to the fore again in the next film, *The Matrix*.

As mentioned earlier, both *The Matrix* and *The Terminator* series of films are predicated on a similar idea of machines/computers becoming sentient and exploiting, subjugating humans. Indeed the treatment of robots and/or AIs (artificial intelligences) by humans as seen in films like *A.I. Artificial Intelligence* (Spielberg: 2001), *I, Robot* (Proyas: 2004), *Automata* (Ibáñez: 2014), and *Ex Machina* (Garland: 2014), to name but a few, reveals why the antagonism toward humanity is completely justified—while all the films listed culminate in very different AI-human relationships, they all feature scenes of abuse and denigration of robots. However, while the machines in *The Terminator* are determined to totally destroy all humans, *The Matrix* has a slightly different tack where humanity becomes a resource to be exploited, not just disposed of. The reason for this is partly seen in the framing of the technological entities within the film. The Terminator is centered largely on the physicality of machines. In contrast *The Matrix*, while showing robot-like elements throughout the narrative, is more focused on the idea of intelligence itself, and particularly the idea of artificial intelligence in terms of computers, information, and networks. In this sense the war between humans and machines is not a physical one, as in *The Terminator*, but rather a mental one so that it becomes more about control rather than destruction. This also begins to describe the vampiric nature of the man/computer relationship as human intelligence is at first copied, exceeded, and eventually consumed by the machine.

Although *The Matrix* describes the early stages of the conflict as physical, with humans exploding nuclear weapons to cause dust clouds to deprive machines access to solar power, the battlefield quickly shifted to energy transferences. The machines capture the humans and use them as batteries, but rather than just drain them of life, they exploit humanity's mental and emotional states as enduring power sources.

Consequently, human subjects are plugged into life support and energy transference connectors as well as neurological links that hook them up to a kind of computer mainframe. Here, the various human consciousnesses are

Figure 19. Human batteries. *The Matrix*. Directed by The Wachowskis (Warner Bros.: 1999).

linked into something akin to a MMORPG (Massive Multiplayer Online Role Playing Game) where the players do not realize that they are in fact in a simulation/game—which would be the ultimate conclusion of *Stay Alive* mentioned earlier. This allows the matrix to vampirically draw energy from those engaged in this ongoing, never-ending dream state. Curiously, this dream-state is not a vision of a perfect world, but of the humdrum, pointless existence that people had before the machine wars began.[93] Of particular interest here is Neo (Keanu Reeves), who also becomes the "white savior" of the film who works at a huge software company, but is also a computer hacker, and simultaneously circumvents, exploits, yet also supports the system that keeps everyone locked in their own little office cubicles—Neo stays locked in his own apartment and never lets anyone in.[94] Nearly all the people who feature in the early stages of the film in the dream world are engaged with computers in some way, from Neo to the people who come to his door asking him to do "jobs" for them to the staff in his workplace. The authorities, led by Agent Smith (Hugo Weaving), appear, transform, and disappear in consummate vampiric fashion, functioning as part of the system that ensures its smooth operations. They accordingly terminate any source of interruption to the flow of energy from the humans. Thus, not unlike the Therns, the Agents represent the real-world capitalist system itself, facilitating the ongoing vampirism of the population. The power of the Agents and their connection to the system is most clearly shown in one scene where they are questioning Neo. As punishment for his refusal to provide them with desired information, they alter the matrix to seal over his mouth, literally silencing him for his refusal to speak.

As with *John Carter*, there is a glitch in the vampire's plan, namely the humans who have not been assimilated into the system. The vast majority of humanity is hooked up to the vampiric machines, but a small group of resistance fighters inhabit the underground caverns below the surface of the Earth—the nuclear explosions that blackened the sky also decimated the planet's surface and therefore the machines and the free humans alike live underground. The free humans have found a way to "dial" in and out of the dream world, but if they are killed by Agents while in the matrix, they also die in the real world. The human resistance and the Agents are thus configured, respectively, as viruses and computer programs, a reading that is continually reinforced by the appearance of characters such as

93. Apparently, the machines trialed the system in a perfect world and the humans quickly got bored and could not cope with it.
94. Arguably Neo is of the same category of people that created computer intelligence in the first place and so are in some way implicated in the rise of the machines, and the downfall of humanity, very much in the same way that the Francis Lawrence's *I Am Legend* (2006) sees Robert Neville (Will Smith) as a doctor, in the same category as those that created the vampire plague, creating a cure for it.

Oracle (Gloria Foster), who seem to be on neither side but are an inherent part of the system—this becomes more and more convoluted as the franchise unfolds with an increasing number of unaffiliated characters and an internal power struggle to control the system itself.[95] This rather blurs the boundaries between competing groups within the world, which also spills over into the real world—though the franchise blurs this by having entities that can only exist in the virtual world which is effectively the "real" world to them. This makes the real world seem even more imaginary and Gothic than the virtual one, since many of the characters are doubled between the worlds, and given the surreal nature of the tentacled hunter machines that seem to move in the air as though floating on water. Consequently, as the films unfold, the barriers between the worlds within the film grow increasingly permeable until they seem to disintegrate altogether. *The Matrix* thus undermines its own explicit theme, namely the struggle of humanity to disengage itself from the computer/dream-world. As with Neville in *The Omega Man*, Neo is blessed with a special power that runs in his blood, his essence, that marks him out as different and somehow able to save humanity from the dreamworld (nightmare) of the vampires. Yet even this seems to be subject to the same kinds of permeability that plagued the dreamworld itself.

Neo appears to be "the chosen one." From outside the dream world he is spotted by Morpheus (Laurence Fishburne), the leader of one group of the human resistance, and offered the chance to remain in the dream world, or to be awoken to reality: Neo chooses the latter. Although Morpheus and the rest of his group understand the dreamworld is not real, they are nevertheless susceptible to death within it. Neo, however, is fully able—at least by the end of the first installment—to link the two separate worlds, with his real body manifesting the marks of violence from within the world, but also able to control the dream world itself and "kill" the Agents—erase programs from the system. As such, there is a sense in which Neo is more vampiric than the system, or rather is of the same order as the machines that are coded as vampires—we see the "agents" in the virtual world able to inhabit and vampirize other entities (human constructs), not unlike that seen in *Get Out* or *The Host* earlier, but Neo can resist and control that, and even vampirize the agents themselves. Both worlds are thus a single universe of vampires with no sustainable barrier between the woken and dream worlds. This is reinforced by the vampiric

---

95. As mentioned to me by Andrew M. Boylan, in the later film *Matrix Reloaded* (The Wachowski Brothers: 2003) it is suggested that the Moravingian, his wife, and their guards are vampires. This is explicitly shown in the game *Enter the Matrix* (Shiny Entertainment: 2003), which is part of the franchise. The guards in there can only be killed after being staked and this is underscored by the fact that there is a Hammer vampire film on in the mansion).

nature of the humans and the machines in the real world. Part of the process of preserving the humans in their regenerative cells is feeding them a high protein liquid diet, and in a world which has been burned black, the only possible food source is humanity itself, as explained by Morpheus, in a lengthy but informative monolog:

> We don't know who struck first, us or them. But we do know it was us that scorched the sky. At the time, they were dependent on solar power. It was believed they would be unable to survive without an energy source as abundant as the sun. … The human body generates more bio-electricity than a 120-volt battery and over 25,000 BTU's of body heat. Combined with a form of fusion, the machines had found all the energy they would ever need. There are fields … where human beings are no longer born, we are grown … [where they] liquefy the dead so they could be fed intravenously to the living [Wachowskis: 1999].

The human resistance are nowhere near as well fed, but seem to find some kind of basic foodstuffs from somewhere, though they are so bad that one of their number, Cypher (Joe Pantoliano), permanently reenters the dream world just to experience eating "proper food" again. Even as Neo rises victorious at the end of the first film, and the humans win the battle for their survival at the end of the trilogy, there is the sense that no matter the outcome of the war, the world has become irreparably vampiric. This idea of planets or even universes becoming inherently vampiric is explored in the last two films in this chapter.

Interstellar, Christopher Nolan, 2014/ *The Cloverfield Paradox,* Julius Onah, 2018

Interstellar and *The Cloverfield Paradox* both take place in the future and on a version of the Earth that is on the verge of death. The Earth's decline is largely attributed to the vampiric habits of humanity: in *Interstellar*, the world's crops are decimated by blight and drought, presumably caused by climate change, and in *The Cloverfield Paradox*, planetary war is imminent due to energy shortages. Each film locates the solution to Earth's problems in outer space, driving humanity into the clutches of a vampiric entity.

Interstellar suggests that the world is drying out through cataclysmic changes in the weather, not unlike those seen in Richard Matheson's *I Am Legend*, where storms blow dust and pestilence across the continents. *Interstellar* suggests that the world is running out of energy: energy for crops to grow, to fight off infection, and even humanity itself has ceased its progress with all technological innovation at a standstill and the surviving population reassigned to work toward saving life on Earth—energy here is configured as a kind of biological life force that motivates everything from plant to human thought. Consequently, the production of motor vehicles, televisions, and all non-vital equipment is suspended, leaving people to make do and repair anything ready to hand. One such handyman is Joe Cooper (Matthew McConaughey) who was once a test pilot, but now runs a farm while looking after his son and daughter. It is 2060 and the United States is now completely agrarian. Yet Cooper's farm features no livestock and its crops are dying. His son is marked out to be a farmer once he graduates and comes of age but his daughter, Murph (Mackenzie Foy, until age 10, and as an adult Jessica Chastain), desires a different life, while complaining of ghosts shifting objects in her room. After a rare family outing the Coopers return to find the dust in Murph's bedroom formed in perfect lines on the floor. Cooper suspects that the lines might be coded coordinates and tests this hypothesis by driving to the destination that they indicate, as Murph hides in the back of the vehicle. Cooper and Murph arrive at a secret facility searching for hospitable planets out in deep space, which they are hoping to reach via a wormhole near Saturn. The facility has sent twelve spacecraft through this hole, but received only three messages in return, signaling potentially habitable worlds. The planets all orbit a massive black hole that they have nicknamed Gargantua, which is the size of the Earth's sun but of a mass fifty million times greater. The facility conveniently lacks a pilot to send on the mission to discover which of the three worlds is habitable, while also gathering information from the black hole that will provide a solution to the formulae that will allow the facility, which is actually a centrifugal space-station, to defy gravity and save the last survivors of Earth. Thus, they ask Cooper to lead the mission. Murph is unhappy about her father's mission, but Cooper insists on accepting it, notwithstanding that her "ghost" lets it be known that he should stay home. He leads a four-person crew that departs Earth and arrives at Saturn two years later. Locating the wormhole, they travel to an area of space ten billion light years from Earth. They lose one crew member and much time on the first planet, and another crew member and the landing craft on the second planet. After a prolonged struggle with the astronaut from the original mission, Mann (Matt Damon), Cooper manages to get onboard what is left of his ship and join the remaining crew member, Brand (Anne Hathaway), but with no possibility of returning to Earth. Cooper devises a plan to use the ship's two landing crafts to give it enough propulsion to reach the last remaining, potentially habitable planet. However, for the weight ratios to work he must blast off on one of the landing crafts, propelling the main ship toward the planet and leaving Brand to survive alone.

Once free of the spaceship, the landing craft is pulled into the super massive black hole. It is at this point that the vampire of the film reveals itself and shows that it has actually been present for most of the film.

As the craft is dragged faster and faster toward the black hole, it begins to break up and Cooper ejects himself, but rather than being torn apart by the huge gravitational forces he seems to travel faster and faster until he finds himself inside something akin to a huge venting system, but which also seems not unlike the wooden lath used to support plaster in walls. He realizes that these slats afford a view on his daughter's room, back into the past when she was a young girl. Cooper has thus been saved by a version of humanity from the far distant future that is no longer constrained to four-dimensional space. This version of future humanity thereby provides Cooper with the means of saving the human race of his present day. Cooper discovers how to send Murph messages via dust patterns in her room—he is the ghost she experienced when young—and manages to manipulate a watch that she received from him as a gift to send her the quantum information she needs to make the centrifugal space station work, via Morse code. Having passed on the information that will save humanity, the future humans return Cooper to the orbit near the wormhole around Saturn, where he is picked up by space rangers moments before his oxygen is due to run out. It is now sixty years in the future and humanity now lives in space on a variety of huge space stations with regular patrols around the galaxy. Cooper, who has been unconscious all this time, awakens in a hospital bed to discover that Murph is now ninety years old and on the verge of death. He goes to see her, but she tells him no parent should see their child die and sends him away. Realizing he has no place in this world of the future, he decides to depart through the wormhole and find Brand.

While there do not appear to be many vampires involved here, the fantastical, dream-like qualities of the film's ending resonate very strongly with other space films that do. In this respect *Solaris* (Tarkovsky: 1972/ Soderbergh: 2002) is of particular interest where astronauts on a space station orbiting the planet Solaris experience dream-like hallucinations linked directly to their emotional states, especially toward those they have loved deeply but feel they let down in some way—very much like Cooper's relationship with Murph. In fact, as the two films proceed it becomes clear that the planet does not just react to the emotional states of the humans but somehow feeds off them, often sustaining them in an endless dreamlike state so that it can feed off their emotional states—not unlike *The Matrix*. This is explicitly seen in Tarkovsky's version where the main protagonist cuts from the spacecraft crashing into the surface of Solaris to his father's cottage in the woods where he is watching the weed in the water in a nearby stream; in actuality we see him on a small island on the liquid surface of the planet. The idea of vampiric entities in space creating emotionally charged dream states in their victims is also seen in *2001: A Space Odyssey* (Kubrick: 1968)—a black hole—*Gravity* (Cuarón: 2013)—the Earth itself—*Event Horizon* (Anderson: 1997)—a wormhole as discussed earlier. Black holes, being energy vampires in real life, fit this bill very well, and Gargantua as a vampiric entity provides a far more reasonable solution to the end of the film than the actually illogical nature of the narrative itself. As such, Cooper, once in the grip of Gargantua, is held in an unconscious stasis and all the events that happen afterwards are just a dream, and one that is guided by the two most emotional events that occur in the film, his abandonment of Murph and then Brand. His dream specifically centers on these two events, allowing the black hole to feed off the emotional energy created by both—interestingly the robot that has, supposedly, followed Cooper into Gargantua notes the importance of emotional attachment, and Cooper himself realizes they—his higher beings are in fact Gargantua—are using the strength of his love (emotional energy) for Murph to guide his mission (dream). As with the humans in *The Matrix*, and *Solaris*, this is a dream from which Copper will never wake, and in fact, he would not want to. The last film in this chapter takes the idea of the vampire from another world to its most extreme form, not just a planet or a black hole but the size of an entire universe.

The Cloverfield Paradox is the third film in the *Cloverfield* series which features a series of mysterious incursions of alien creatures into the Earth's environment. In the first two films they appear to be from outer space, but the third installment suggests that they might be due to something more catastrophic. The film begins in an unlikely version of the not-so-distant future of 2028 where oil and fossil fuels have been exhausted and all the available alternatives are inadequate. There appears to be only one way to avert warfare and the eventual desiccation of the world, and that is the Shepard Particle Accelerator on the *Cloverfield* space station orbiting the Earth. The Accelerator is designed to extensively amplify a small amount of energy, though with unknown side effects—in a curious way it's not unlike *Event Horizon* where a mysterious device is designed to open up a wormhole onboard a ship but unleashes deadly vampiric forces into the universe. The catastrophic potential of the accelerator is summed up briefly during a television report where the interviewed expert replies to a question regarding why he fears the test:

> Because that accelerator is a thousand times more powerful than any ever built. Every time they test it, they risk opening the membrane of space-time, smashing together multiple dimensions, shattering reality. And not just on that station, everywhere. This experiment could unleash chaos, the like of which we

have never seen. Monsters, demons, beasts from the sea.... And not just here and now. In the past, in the future, in other dimensions [Onah: 2018].

This mirrors a similar response to human tampering with unknown forces in *Event Horizon* where one character angrily shouts at the creator of the wormhole making device, "When you break all the laws of physics, do you seriously think there won't be a price?" (Anderson: 1998). This sets up the events that unfold after the accelerator becomes operational. The crew soon realize that they are no longer orbiting the Earth, but they cannot discover their position as the ship's gyro (compass) has vanished. They hear screaming from a lower deck and discover a woman behind a wall panel fused into the cabling, and are further perplexed when, after extensive medical intervention, she appears to be acquainted with a member of their crew.

One of the crew members, a Russian named Volkow (Aksel Hennie), begins acting strangely and his right eye suddenly turns 180 degrees of its own volition. Panicking, Volkow scratches at his face but eventually the eye returns to its original position, but as though it is staring at the person whose face it has found itself in. Volkow then reacts as though he hears someone speaking, who may be the owner of the eye, and agrees with them; his standing in front of the mirror makes this appear as if there are two people, each containing a part of the other. Where the other Volkow, or whoever it is, might have come from is not clear but it soon becomes apparent that the Accelerator has wrought serious damage. Volkow then attacks the crew member in charge of the Accelerator, Schmidt (Daniel Brühl), accusing him of sabotage, but then collapses and dies. Another crew member, Mundy (Chris O'Dowd), loses his arm as it is bitten off by a wall panel, but once he pulls himself free, the stump is perfectly healed as though he had sustained the loss long ago. The arm itself becomes a separate entity, not unlike Volkow's eye. Indeed, the arm writes the crew a message, telling them that the missing gyro is in Volkow's body. Once they reinstall the gyro, they discover that the Earth has not vanished but is on the other side of the sun. They then reestablish contact with the planet and realize that they are in a different version of the universe, and that the Accelerator has shifted them into another dimension where the *Cloverfield* exploded and war is ravaging the Earth. Thus, the woman they found onboard, Mina Jensen (Elizabeth Debicki), is from this dimension and is acquainted with the mirror world crew of the *Cloverfield* that exploded.

The vampiric nature of the other dimension becomes increasingly apparent. It seeks to kill and/or consume those that have come from the other world. Indeed, it seems to act as a malevolent entity in its own right, causing irreparable harm to Volkow and Mundy and also killing Tam (Ziyi Zhang), Schmidt's assistant who was replaced by Jensen in the other dimension. Finally, it causes the ship to consume Mundy later in the film. In an odd way, the other dimension acts as a kind of King vampire, controlling the environment to attack the unwary—in this sense the *Cloverfield* bears much resemblance to the *Demeter* in *Dracula*, whose crew are killed one by one with the ship tossed and turned by the influence of the vampire. Indeed, this connection to Dracula permeates the film: the clashing together of worlds with one intent on consuming the other, creatures of the night (to be discussed later), and the changing and mind-control over the main characters. In this sense Volkow is a Renfield character, drawn between his own world and the commanding call of his new master. More interesting still is the figure of Mina Jensen, not least as the central female character in Dracula is called Mina. Mina Jensen is a character that has already been infected by the vampire. When we see her in the medlab she is deathly pale with blonde hair drawn back and wearing a hospital gown that looks to all intents and purposes like a shroud—in a vampire film she would be a bride of Dracula.

She is ingratiating, duplicitous, menacing and preys on the most vulnerable woman onboard, Hamilton (Gugu Mbatha-Raw), who lost her child in her own world but not the version of Earth in this dimension. Mina encourages Hamilton to stay in the vampire dimension, while maintaining that she does not want to leave either. The rest of the crew are keen to leave and after Tam is trapped by the ship in a condensation chamber, drowned, frozen and shot out into space, Kiel (David Oyelowo) declares "We can't stay here. This dimension is eating us alive" (Onah: 2018). The remaining crew decide they must return to their own dimension at any cost. Mina seems spurred on by their

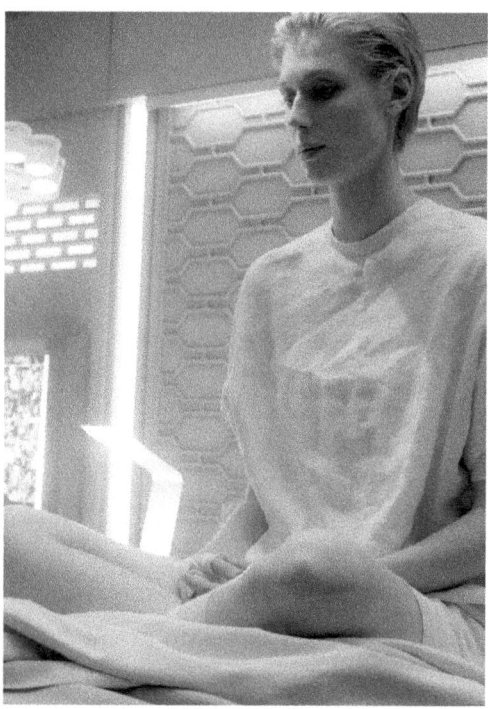

Figure 20. Mina (Elizabeth Debicki) returning from the dead as the vampire's bride. *The Cloverfield Paradox*. Directed by Julius Onah (Netflix: 2018).

newfound determination and tries to kill the remaining crew in an attempt to keep the Accelerator in her dimension.

The crew then try to reenact the experiment that brought them to the alternate dimension in the first place, but Mina foils their plans, subduing Hamilton, killing another crewman, and wounding Schmidt. However, Hamilton revives, and struggles with Mina, causing a bullet to crack an observation window in the craft. The hole produced is at the exact height of Mina's heart—a virtual stake—and the vacuum of space pulls her into the hole, cracking the glass further and shooting her out into space. Hamilton manages to revive Schmidt, and with the new data provided by Tam before she was killed, successfully start the Accelerator and return to their own dimension, hoping to save their own Earth. However, while only the *Cloverfield* has crossed over to the other dimension, very different kinds of entities had made the reciprocal journey from the vampiric universe; behomothic creatures of the night that are consuming the Earth.

The parallel dimension in *The Cloverfield Paradox* exemplifies that once the gateways to vampiric worlds/dimensions have been opened, they can very rarely be fully closed. This film does not even leave us with a sense of unease at its closing but shows us that the monsters have been unleashed in our world; insatiable creatures that will never rest as they have no way to return home; they will only die when the world can no longer support them.

In many ways *The Cloverfield Paradox* would seem to signal a return to the idea of the inherent malevolence of space toward humanity, but there is much to suggest it is equally environmental; it is the alien environment that is existentially antagonistic to our own and more specifically life on Earth. The *Cloverfield* begins attacking its own human crew from our world; the alternative Mina tries to kill the human crew from our world; the monsters from the alien dimension are intent on killing humanity on our Earth—this is more clearly seen in the earlier installments of the franchise. These environmental factors return to the fore in the final chapter, sometimes in relation to alien entities that come to our world from outer space, but also in terms of those arising from "alien" environments from our own; however, nearly all of them envision a time when our only value to the planet is as a foodstuff.

5

The Thing from Another World

This chapter focuses on non-human life forms, often from other worlds, that depend on humankind for sustenance. Many of these are plant-based organisms that seem to have developed a penchant for human blood or life force, a craving that sometimes expands to wider ecologies or environments. An early version of this trope can be found in the "red weed" that arrives from Mars with the aliens in *War of the Worlds*. The weed does not explicitly feed on blood, but it thrives as the blood-sucking Martians thrive. Conversely, as the invaders die the red weed expires as well, reinforcing the suggestion that they are physically connected and that the blood that invigorates one species from Mars also provides energy to the other. Steven Spielberg's 2005 adaptation of the novel is one of the few that makes this connection explicit, when the main character Ray Ferrier (Tom Cruise) happens upon a farm that the aliens have used as a base for siphoning blood from their victims. The ground is soaked in blood and the red weed is growing virulently over the entire area, visually a vegetative extension of the pools of red fluid. Wells suggests that the weed is "slain" by the same "putrefactive and disease bacteria" (Wells: 2018, 106) that kills the Martians, further intimating the similarity between the two alien species and the idea that Mars itself—as an environment and/or ecosystem—would also consume humanity given the chance. In contrast to Stoker's novel, published the same year as the serialized version of *War of the Worlds*, makes no real reference to vegetation in that way, though one of its first adaptations (unofficial) into film, *Nosferatu* (Murnau: 1922) cites a direct correlation between the natural environment and the vampire. The film directly links the undead to vampire plants, such as the Venus flytrap, or vampiric microbes like polyps that ensnare and absorb their prey, suggesting that vampires are part of the natural world and a wider planetary, even galactic, ecosystem. An intelligent form of flora is thus central to this chapter, as an expression of a non-anthropocentric vision of evolution and one that is often specifically anti-human. Ecological readings of such vampiric entities are irresistible in a time of impending climate catastrophe and many of the films under discussion invite such readings. While such ideas often include much of the same theoretical framing as colonialism, most of the examples below also speak of a certain kind of decolonization where humanity is firmly removed from the spotlight of planetary and environmental development and only remains of importance as either a link in the food chain or a chemistry set for experiments in biological hybridity.

The Thing from Another World, Christian Nyby, 1951/*Queen of Blood*, Curtis Harrington, 1966

The Thing from Another World invites readings from a 21st century perspective, not just because of John Carpenter's seminal 1982 adaptation, but because of its setting in the North Pole. In an age of oncoming environmental disaster, the melting ice caps have become symbolic of the dramatic effects of human on the planet. Granted, *The Thing from Another World* was released in 1951, before the environmental consequences of human actions came to the forefront of public discourse, but just on the cusp of such public awareness. With the end of World War II and the detonation of atomic bombs, the cataclysmic effects of human activity came into sharp focus, not least in the fields of culture and the arts that speculated on the possible effects of radiation and "science"—a term that became synonymous with mankind's uncontrolled penetration into the natural world and its inevitable creation of monsters. While *The Thing* would appear to be more about the alien invasion associated with Cold War anxieties, the extraterrestrial body in *The Thing from Another World* invites other readings of a more ecological nature.

While the characters in *The Thing from Another World* perceive the entity that they discover under the ice as an alien, a vampire from another world that seems to subsist on human blood, the film suggests that it may hail from closer to home. The film opens on an inhospitable North Pole, a space that is extremely unwelcoming to humans.[96] We next see an officers' bar in Anchorage where news reporter Ned "Scotty" Scot (Douglas Spencer) is looking for something to report on. He joins a group of men to see if there's anything newsworthy going on at the moment and one of the men mentions a lot of scientists seem to have arrived at the North Pole recently. Later that night another of the group at the bar, Captain Patrick Hendry (Kenneth Tobey): is told he is to be in charge of a recovery mission

---

96. Interestingly there no inference at the start of *The Thing from Another World* that creatures from outer space have been visiting or crashing on the Earth—Carpenter's remake of the film makes this explicit as does *AVP* (Anderson: 2004), mentioned earlier and which shares many plot similarities.

regarding a strange aircraft found at the North Pole. Hendry invites Scotty to join his team and they fly to the outpost nearest the site of the possible crash where they meet a team of scientists gathered there. When the members of Polar Expedition Six leave their remote outpost to investigate reports of an unusual aircraft crashing in the area, nothing untoward is expected. Interestingly when they arrive at the site there are no signs of a crash of any sort, just a frozen landscape covered in snow. Even when they discover an object under the ice it really does not appear to have just crash landed but rather to have been buried under the surface for many, many years. As such, it is more like digging back to the past rather than discovering something from the future. This impression continues as the crew set thermite charges around the circular perimeter of the object to melt the ice, only for the detonation to destroy the craft completely. All that is left is the craft's occupant, almost as if the vehicle were a gateway delivering the vampire from the past into the world of the present. The creature from the world of the past, of a time when mankind was nowhere near the top of the food chain and was part of a far more symbiotic relationship with the environment, is not immediately released into the present but is contained within a block of ice that is taken back to the scientific outpost to be studied further.

Once unearthed, it is not futuristic science that facilitates the vampire's movement from one world to another, but something more mundane and oddly symbolic of humanity's effects on the planet, namely an electric blanket. Man-made heat literally releases the monster/vampire from the melting ice—this ties into recent anxieties around contagion,[97] more clearly seen in Carpenter's film, but also more recent concerns over global pandemics being set free/revived due to melting ice caps as seen in *Blood Glacier* [Blutgletscher] (Kren: 2013)—where once free the contagion from the past begins a reign of terror in the confined spaces of the facility. *The Thing from Another World* constructs the creature as a sophisticated alien life form that has conquered space travel, but it is nevertheless disoriented and violent upon awaking. Indeed, its actions seem much more in line with a creature abruptly launched from the past into the present rather than an alien race that one assumes is familiar with the sensations that accompany the encounters with new species on new planets. The entity manages to free itself from the confines of the base only to be attacked by sled dogs, to which it loses an arm. The humans find the arm and deliver it to the team of scientists on the base led by Dr. Carrington (Robert Cornthwaite) who discover that it is plant-based in composition. Furthermore, the arm is alive in its own right and separate from the body from which it detached

---

97. See Goudarzi: 2016, Fox-Skelly: 2017, and McCall: 2020.

and appears capable of producing "seeds" to reproduce itself. The appearance of the "Thing" is obviously inspired by James Whales' 1932 monster in *Frankenstein*, featuring a large, powerful body and head with a pronounced brow. But while Frankenstein's creature was composed of dead parts that were given life, the alien in *The Thing from Another World* is made of parts that are independently alive.

Given that one of the killed sled dogs was drained of blood, the scientists conjecture that the creature requires blood to survive. Their supposition proves correct when Carrington learns that "baby" aliens feed on blood. The scientists decide that the creature must be an advanced species of plant that is vastly superior to humanity, not least in that it has traveled to the earth across space, and that it should be studied further, but the rest of the members of the outpost think it needs to be killed as soon as possible.

This vision of an advanced species dependent on (human) blood is of course reminiscent of Wells' *The War of the Worlds* and even his earlier scientific romance, *The Time Machine*, where vampiric creatures embody visions of a future past. In *The War of the Worlds*, the Martians are a (colonialized) vision of humanity's future where we have evolved to a point where we are only able to nourish ourselves by directly ingesting liquid proteins (blood). *The Time Machine* takes a different tack, as humanity divided into two evolutionary branches, with those that support and create a livable Earth (the Morlocks) residing underground while the rest live a life of leisure on the surface (the Eloi). However, the price for this class division is that the Morlocks are literally farming the Eloi for food. There is a sense then that the alien from the ice, in Nyby's film, is from a future vision of the Earth, or a return to its distant past, where plants are/were the dominant species that "farm(ed)" animals and/or humanoids for sustenance.

Figure 21. The Thing (James Arness) as monstrous ecological revenge. *The Thing from Another World*. Directed by Christian Nyby (RKO Radio Pictures: 1951).

It can be argued then

that the craft under the ice is a time-capsule left in waiting, ready for a time when human technological development would change the Earth's environment sufficiently to uncover it—hence the lack of evidence of a crash around the area that the craft carrying the Thing was found. It thus functions as a kind of ecological regulator. Once the occupant of the capsule is released, it would be charged with stalling mankind's advancement and the consequent demise of the planet's ecosystem, a mission that proves ultimately unsuccessful in the film. At the movie's denouement, the Thing, unlike Frankenstein's creation, is not enlivened by electricity but reduced to a pile of ash—earlier attempts with fire proving useless. Though it is possible to conjecture that the monster may yet return, in the vein of the Gothic genre. Carpenter's adaptation ends on an ambiguous note, with two human survivors who may or may not be an alien replica/clone. But in Nyby's version of the story, the Thing does not replicate via copying or cloning its victims but rather via spores or seeding itself. In this sense it becomes a forerunner to *The Girl with All the Gifts* (McCarthy: 2016), discussed later on in this chapter, where the monster plant's reduction to ash actually catalyzes its reproduction, allowing it to spread far and wide. *The Thing from Another Planet* never makes such a suggestion explicitly, but the reporter Scotty opens his broadcast at the end of the film with the warning "Tell the world. Tell this to everybody, wherever they are. Watch the skies everywhere. Keep looking. Keep watching the skies" (Nyby: 1951). On the surface, his words refer to invaders coming from the heavens—or Soviet spies entering American society—but they can equally be taken to refer to spores/seeds falling from the sky. The next film takes this advice to heart, but not as a warning so much as a chance to make contact with new species. *Queen of Blood* (1966), directed by Chris Harrington, features vampires from another world not already on the Earth, but on a far distant planet, who cross paths with humans who are as developed and evolved as the aliens.

Queen of Blood is set in the far distant, space-traveling literate future of 1990. The film opens with the following exposition:

> The year 1990, the problem of traveling to the Moon has been solved for many years. Space stations have been built there and authorized personnel come and go as they wish, but the Moon is a dead world. And the great question about space still remains, does life exist on another planet? To seek an answer to this question, the major powers of the world have been actively preparing at the International Institute of Space Technology to explore the planets Venus and Mars [Harrington: 1966].

The Institute of Space Technology has been receiving signals from a distant planet whose inhabitants are keen to meet and discuss future relations, and it is excited by the opportunities afforded by this prospect. The

5. The Thing from Another World 153

representatives of this planet agree to send an ambassador to Earth but their craft crashes on its journey and thus a rescue ship, the *Oceano*, is sent to the location of its last contact in the vicinity of Mars. They discover the wreckage of the alien ship on Mars but only one dead crew member and therefore speculate that a rescue ship must have already been sent for the survivors. Two of the human crew are sent to try and locate the alien rescue ship and they find it on one of Mars' moons, Phobos. This ship apparently crashed as well and the scouting ship from the *Oceano* discovers only an unconscious female alien left alive in it. They bring her back to the main ship to run a medical examination on her and ensure she is not hurt, but she does not speak nor eat and she refuses to allow them to examine her. The medical officer Anders Brockman (Robert Boon) observes:

> This is more than some childish fear of the needle. Perhaps she has an extremely low pain threshold. Perhaps…. But we mustn't do anything that may affect her health adversely. She is probably the most valuable specimen for scientific research in the history of our planet. To get her back to Earth safely has to be our first consideration [Harrington: 1966].

The only female member of the crew of the *Oceano*, Laura James (Judi Meredith), notices that the alien only smiles at the men on the ship, who in return quickly develop a fascination with her. That night Paul (Dennis Hopper) watches over her and quickly falls under her spell. He is quite literally glamored by the luminous glow from her eyes. Caught in a kind of intense, incapacitating sexual attraction, Paul is unable to resist her advances as she bites his neck and drains his body of blood.

Not unlike the scientists in *The Thing from Another Planet*, the surviving crew of the spaceship try to learn more about the alien species and deduce from her green skin color that she is a plant-based life-form that requires blood to survive. The question of why the aliens from another world would evolve to survive on blood is never addressed, but this trope can be traced back to *The War of the Worlds*. The vampire Queen's behavior resembles that of predatory plants on Earth such as the Venus flytrap or the Sundew plant that display features that

Figure 22. The Queen of Blood (Florence Marly) glamoring her victims. *The Queen of Blood*. Directed by Curtis Harrington (American International Pictures: 1966).

draw their prey to them, namely distinctive coloring and glistening drops of a sugary substance. H.G. Wells penned a short-story on a similar theme, "The Flowering of the Strange Orchid" (1894), where a vampiric plant uses the beauty of its flowers to lure unsuspecting humans (colonials) into its vicinity where it sedates them and feeds upon them. Predatory plants of this kind evolve to draw a specific kind of prey into their deadly embrace which does call into question just why the Queen of Blood would develop these specific talents if humans or humanoid species were not present on her home world.

The hypnotic influence of the alien appears to be heterosexually based as it only works on members of the opposite sex. One of the (male) scientists postulates that this heterosexuality derives from the fact that the alien species is organized in a social structure of hive-mentality, from which the Queen has escaped to further the existence of her species.[98] This configures the alien species as insectile, not unlike the aliens in *Starship Troopers* and *Priest*, but also oddly elevates the male scientists as it is only them that the Queen is interested in. This goes in the face of what is seen in the movie where it is just Laura, the only female crew member, who resists the influence of the alien and recommends they get rid of the unwelcome visitor. The men, both on Earth and onboard the ship, insist that they must study this unknown species further.

The male scientists decide to bring the vampire Queen back to Earth and sustain her by feeding her the ship's supplies of plasma from the medical bay. But the Queen glamors the captain of the *Oceano*, Allen Brenner (John Saxon). Just as she is on the verge of claiming her next victim, Laura intervenes, struggling with the alien and pushing her away. The Queen escapes as Laura turns to help Allen. Once Allen has returned to his senses, he begins to search for the alien together with Laura. They find her dead, stretched out on her bed with a large pool of green fluid on the floor. They realize that she must have been scratched in the fight with Laura and bled to death, her chlorophyll laden blood unable to clot. They are surprised to discover a tray of red, pulsating eggs in a thick green gel that could compensate for the knowledge they had lost with the Queen's death. Allen urges the destruction of the eggs after his experience of losing control at the hands of the alien, but Laura points out that it is for the authorities back on Earth to decide the fate of the eggs. Yet, Laura happens upon another tray of the eggs onboard, suggesting that not all the eggs have been found and that perhaps the humans have invited in more aliens than they intended— much here resonates with *The Thing from Another World* and alien "seeds"

98. The director of *Queen of Blood*, Curtis Harrington, has suggested that this aspect was used by Ridley Scott in his seminal alien/vampire film *Alien* (1979) see Harrington: 2005.

and *Alien*, where the xenomorphs seem to magically appear from nowhere no matter how thoroughly the crew ensures they are all dead. The next two films take up this theme of uninvited vampiric entities from other worlds making their way to Earth with catastrophic consequences for those who encounter them.

The Relic, Peter Hyams, 1997/*The Day of the Triffids*, Steve Sekely, 1963, & *The Day of the Triffids*, Nick Copus, 2009

The Relic correlates with the tale of Count Dracula and it resonates with themes of a vampire from another world. The entity in question, though not an alien from outer space, is an alien from another world, not just beyond modern civilization but beyond the realm of reason and normalcy. The story opens with a colonial expedition into the unknown led by a white, American man, a trope not uncommon within vampire tales. The film is set in the South American rainforests, configuring them as a space of otherness, an otherworldly place of savagery, superstition and danger, at least for those who hail from the soft, degenerate West. This dichotomy of a dangerous, enticing East, and a safe but decadent West can be found in vampire stories from the 19th century onwards, where novelists, inspired by the evolutionary theories of Charles Darwin, sought natural explanations for supernatural phenomena—something of the difference between science-fiction and fantasy is an emphasis on the former or the latter. Thus, for example, Phil Robinson's *The Last of the Vampires* (1893) follows the exploits of an anthropologist from a German university who travels to South America in search of a mysterious winged creature that local legend described as a vampire, which he finds and endeavors to bring back to Europe. *The Relic* opens with a similar premise, as an anthropologist, Dr. John Whitney (Lewis Van Bergen) from the colonial center of the modern world, America—more specifically the Natural History Museum of Chicago—travels to the alien world of the primitive past of the Brazilian rainforest. He thus enacts the kind of reverse colonialism (vampirism) seen in *Dracula* where the expected processes of the colonial endeavor, i.e., the vampirism of other less advanced nations, is turned around and the colonial "home" nation is attacked, or vampirized, by the victim of its actions. Thus, it is the plundering of other, less "developed" nations and cultures enacted by the Museum and other cultural institutions that results in the "infection" of the home nation.

In the rainforest, Dr. Whitney takes part in a tribal ritual of summoning an ancient god called Kathoga, during which he drinks a potion concocted from a red fungus that grows on a particular kind of leaf—one does think of Wells' Martian red weed. Later on in the film, Dr. Whitney finds himself on a cargo ship arguing with its captain, whom he tries to convince to offload the crates marked for the Museum before setting sail. The captain refuses and consequently Whitney stows away onboard as the ship leaves for the United States. Six months later the ship docks in Chicago. There is no sign of Whitney, but all the crew are dead, their heads severed from their bodies. The crates, however, are untouched and are taken to the Natural History Museum, very much resonating with Count Dracula's journey on the *Demeter*.

This early part of the story oddly bears much resemblance to the earlier parts of *Dracula*, and more so the Tod Browning version from 1931. Browning's *Dracula* saw a young professional travel to the land beyond the trees, from the modern world of reason to the past of superstition. Once there he goes mad and travels back to his homeland with a deadly cargo that leaves the crew of the ship carrying him, the *Vesta*, dead—in Browning's film the name of the Demeter is change to the *Vesta*. Only the cargo is untouched and that is safely delivered to its final destination, Whitby.[99] In *The Relic*, the deadly cargo is as vampiric as Stoker's Count, and its intentions are equally malevolent. The ship, the *Santos Morales*, thus acts as a conduit between worlds, bringing the monsters (vampires) from the past to feed on the energy of the present. However, just as the *Demeter* in *Dracula* was not the only conduit of the past, but also the naive young professional, so too in *The Relic*, it is the young travelled academic, the Renfield/Whitney, that becomes the focus of porosity between the present and the past.

Meanwhile the crates have arrived at the Museum in time for a new major exhibit on superstition—this also echoes the idea of superstition/urban legend mentioned in Chapter 3 with the Kothoga as a legendary creature from the environment it comes from. Many of the staff are wondering why Whitney has not returned with his crates while Dr. Margo Green (Penelope Ann Miller) looks in on the team responsible for organizing the items that have arrived from Brazil. One of the artifacts is a mysterious stone carving, which another member of the team, Dr. Frock (James Whitmore), explains is in fact a carving of Kothoga, who is particular to one tribe in Brazil, "[the] South American tribe, the Zenzera, long thought to be extinct—They made a deal with Satan to vanquish their enemies. So Kothoga was born—Son of Satan." This description recalls the name

---

99. As noted by Hadas Elber-Aviram there is something of a resonance between the names the point of Dracula's arrival in England, Whitby, and the anthropologist whose office is the point of arrival in Chicago, Dr. Whitney.

"Dracula" that is roughly translated from Romanian into English as "Son of the Dragon or Son of the Devil" (Grumeza: 2010, 1).[100] Frock further elaborates that Kothoga was a chimera, a hybrid creature made up of many different animals. Dr. Green notices that the statuette is wrapped in green leaves covered in red fungus, the same kind we saw earlier used in the potion that Whitney consumed. Intrigued by the red egg-like growths, Dr. Green sends some of them away to be tested, while the rest are incinerated just in case the fungus is dangerous.

Shortly afterwards, deaths begin to occur at the museum with the victims' heads removed and part of their brains missing, much like the crew of the *Santos Morales*. The postmortem examination discovers that the portion missing from the victims' brain is the hypothalamus, which influences human emotions, especially interpersonal bonds. Dr. Green begins to examine the leaves and the red fungus back in the laboratory, upon which she discovers that red fungus is made of the same hormones excreted by the human hypothalamus and its consumption can additionally trigger mutations. A beetle makes its way into one of the boxes of leaves and escapes her notice, and when she returns to the lab the following morning, the insect has grown to the size of a rat. Only just managing to catch it and examine it, she shows her findings to Dr. Frock who tells her of the "Calysto Effect"[101] which is a sudden evolutionary jump creating an aberrant (new) species. Interestingly what *The Relic* suggests is that once that happens it ignites a chain event of mutation and monstrosity, capturing the kinds of colonial anxiety that hangs around miscegenation and hybridity. This is seen explicitly in the beetles that have suddenly embarked on this trajectory of speeded up evolution and hybridity. Fueled by the fungus, they have become monsters of excess, vampiric entities that must consume more and more of the hormone provided by the fungus, no matter where it comes from.

The creature loose in the Museum, Kothoga, is a Calysto hybrid that depends on the hormone for its survival—hence the leaves in the boxes to sustain it—and thus when the leaves are destroyed the only source left for the hormone is the human hypothalamus itself. Thus, in their own world the Kothogas can exist solely on leaves, but in our world, they become vampires. Furthermore, given the hypothalamus's effects on the human body, the Kothogas appear to feed on human affection, or love. Kothoga is thus a love vampire. Kothoga requires substantial "love" to survive and must therefore kill and draw out the "love" out of a large number of humans. Indeed, the Zenzera apparently only use the fungus to summon Kothoga

---

100. Bram Stoker also believed Dracula to mean "son of the devil," from his notes, and also gave the count the pseudonym Count De'Ville, see Eighteen-Bisang and Miller: 2008.
101. Spelling according to IMDb.

when outsiders invade their world, allowing the creature to kill all those who are unaware of the danger it poses and therefore mark themselves as outsiders to their society. This hypothesis is substantiated by the results of tests run on a sample from the creature, which reveal that it contains Dr. Whitney's DNA, establishing that the anthropologist himself had undergone the Calysto effect after drinking the potion given to him at the start of the film. The creature goes on a killing spree in the museum, in the course of which it expresses a predilection for Dr. Green. At one point Kothoga slowly licks her face in a purposely gratuitous scene that is often repeated in horror films featuring violence toward women. Dr. Green quite literally fights fire with fire, finally igniting an explosion that consumes the vampire in flame.

Day of the Triffids is both similar to and different from *The Relic*. Like *The Relic*, *The Day of the Triffids* follows a trajectory of reverse colonialism, at least in the later adaptation of it by Copus (2009), but unlike *The Relic* the vampire plants require blood, the more traditional vampire fare, as their sustenance. The original novel *Day of the Triffids*, written by John Wyndham in 1951, contained something of the gist of Richard Matheson's *I Am Legend* from four years previously, attributing the impending apocalypse to the hubris of science.[102] Matheson saw the mysterious effects of radiation as the likely culprit while Wyndham sees secret government testing in the USSR as the initial cause. The titular triffids are unusually large mobile carnivorous plants that produce a highly desirable fuel for which they are farmed across the globe. The triffids become a threat after a meteor shower—though Wyndham speculates this could be weaponry on orbiting satellites—sparks the possible end of humanity. The first film adaptation by Steve Sekely changes this premise, reconfiguring the triffids' origins into vampiric plants from another world which are intent on human destruction—not unlike Wells' Martians.

In Sekely's film the plants originally arrived on Earth via a meteor shower that dropped spores into the atmosphere. The meteor shower produces a searing bright light that permanently blinds a vast proportion of the Earth's population, creating perfect conditions for the attack of the vampiric vegetation from another world. The film centers on Bill Masen (Howard Keel), who is a merchant sailor—in the book he was a biologist who worked with triffids—who has been in hospital with injured eyes and so had bandages over them during the meteor shower. Left to his own devices—all the hospital staff have been affected by the meteor shower—he removes the bandages to discover that everyone around him

---

102. Wyndham himself cited Wells' *The War of the Worlds* as an influence (Morris: 2003).

is blind. As he leaves the hospital, he witnesses groups of people stumbling around, with many squabbling over supplies. The film thus posits that within the space of a few hours, blindness has triggered the collapse of civilization. Sight is thus configured as both humanity's greatest strength and its greatest weakness, thereby revealing the supremacy of the visual within contemporary society as well as its inherently fractured nature. Triffids are not affected as they have no eyes, but they are able to sense the humans, while a similarly eyeless condition leaves humanity helpless. One assumes that the triffids are capable of sensing radiation from the humans such as heat/infrared, much as flowers are capable of tracking light. In some of the adaptations, the triffids make clacking noises, which might also intimate some form of radar/sonic distancing within their organic makeup.

The triffids are larger than a human, with a single flower on a long stem which functions both as its "head," a delivery system for the venom it is able to whip at its victims and blind them, and a feeding mechanism. An extensive and muscular root system spreads from its base. The triffids might not be physically intimidating, but it is their otherworldliness that works in their favor. The triffids make nonsense of conceptual categorizations that assume humans to be the apex predator, and they reveal that even the most ridiculous of monsters, under the right conditions, can become an existential threat. The esthetic of the film creates a vision of an Earth that has been overtaken by an alien dimension where the humans are incapable of comprehending or coming to grips with the situation. In contrast, the triffids adapt swiftly and efficiently go about their business of blinding and consuming humans—just as mankind harvested these plants as a unique and invaluable source of energy (at least in Wyndham's book and Copus' mini-series), so the triffids now return the favor. Indeed, the plants echo Count Orlok in *Nosferatu* as he left his world and entered the new one of commercial Germany. Orlok spreads disease and chaos with ease, because the "civilized" world knows nothing about him or his weaknesses. Indeed, Orlok anticipates the triffids insofar as he is visually correlated with predatory plants. Similarly, in the 2009 film adaptation *The Day of the Triffids*, the newcomer "Triffidus Celestus, brought to Earth on the meteorite" is also paralleled with the Venus Flytrap, which is also cited by Professor Bulwar (John Gottowt) in *Nosferatu*: "In nature's scheme of things, there are certain plants which are carnivorous, or eating plants. The Venus Fly Trap is one of the best known. … Just how these plants digest their pray has yet to be explained. There is much still to learn about these fascinating eating plants" (Murnau: 1922).

In fact, it is partially science's inability to fully understand these non-human life forms that gives the clue as to why the collapse of civilization in *Day of the Triffids* is so fast and complete; it is not just contemporary society's dependence upon the visual, but its inability to comprehend how dangerous the world had suddenly become—much of this is repeated in *Bird Box* discussed later. Masen thus becomes a witness to chaos and soon learns that the surviving humans are as dangerous as the triffids, none more so than the sighted. Thus, after Masen and his companion escape London and sail across the Channel to France, they find a school for the blind that is well adjusted to the new situation because they had far longer to develop their other senses. But a gang of sighted men appear in short order and behave abusively and violently toward the pupils. In something of an anticlimax, and one not unlike the ending of *War of the Worlds*, saltwater proves highly corrosive to the plants and they can be easily defeated by covering them with it, restoring order between the worlds. A later version by Nick Copus is less easily resolved and is worth examining briefly for its framing of reverse colonialism.

Copus' miniseries (two episodes) looks back more to Wyndham's book than Sekely's film and sees Masen as a biologist working with triffids. The triffids in this adaptation have no connections to the extraterrestrial or Cold War scientific experiments gone awry but are naturally occurring plants from Africa. This part of the narrative re-enacts the framing of *The Relic*, and it adds a more detailed backstory to Masen, positing that his parents were biologists and triffid specialists working with the plants in Zaire. But their work goes awry and his mother is killed by one of the plants, though a native mask—which is a recurring part of the trauma of that moment which Masen constantly relives—seems to hold the key to handling the triffids safely. As he matures into an adult, Masen becomes a lead scientist on a triffid farm just outside London, as the oil produced by the plants has now replaced all fossil fuels in a bid to prevent global warming. This narrative complicates the notion of straightforward solutions to ecological problems, calling attention to the fact that these solutions often involve blatant exploitation of other countries, or another nation's ecosystem—the scenes in Zaire are supposedly from the late 1970s but their construction and feel invite comparisons with *The Relic* and its criticism of white civilization in worlds that they seek to exploit for financial gain, which they do not understand and to which they do not belong. Plant liberation activists break into the triffids farm on which Masen works and attempt to free the triffids. During the break-in, Masen's eyes are contaminated with triffid poison and he is taken to a hospital. A huge solar flare blinds 95 percent of the world's population while Masen is recuperating in the hospital. Masen awakes up to chaos and, slowly removing his bandages, he realizes that his sight has remained intact, but the hospital is in turmoil with everyone stumbling around and screaming for help. The situation is still more dire outside of the hospital, as planes crash into the iconic skyscrapers of the City of London just outside the hospital.[103] The world is thus transformed, to a greater degree than in Sekely's film, becoming a post-apocalyptic Hell on Earth.

The blind are correspondingly more zombie-like, shambling through the streets in hordes and mobbing the sighted. The triffids are released into this maelstrom, as one of the protesters who broke into Masen's farm awakes in his cell to realize he alone is still in possession of his sight, easily evading guards to open the gates to all the compounds holding the plants. The triffids in this adaptation are far more dangerous, moving faster on long ,whip-like and extremely agile root systems that likewise easily ensnare their prey. As in the earlier adaptation and the original book, the groups of human survivors are often as deadly as the plants, but the film's denouement attempts to bridge the gap between worlds to provide a solution to the vampire plants from another world. Masen ends up at his father's house, where the mask from his dream hangs from the wall. The triffids attack the house and Masen and his companion discover that the mask was created by the village elders back in Zaire as a means of protection from the triffids. Wearing the mask during the triffids' venom attack makes the wearer invisible to the triffids. Thus, in this contemporary adaptation, the Earth provides no easy solutions such as corrosive sea water. Masen and other survivors have travelled to the Isle of Wight off the south coast of Britain where there were no triffid farms, and they plan to retake the mainland at some point in the future. But for now, the vampires from another world are in control. The triffids offer no possibility of hybridity or symbiosis with the human community, a characteristic that features in the next pairing of films, though *Venom* does suggest that certain scenarios might offer a middle ground.

Splinter, Toby Wilkins, 2008/ *Venom*, Ruben Fleischer, 2018

Toby Wilkins's *Splinter* and Ruben Fleischer's *Venom* reconfigure the specifically plant-based vampire into a non-specific organism with floral qualities, producing a biological jouissance, an excess of life that consumes living matter. Both films feature otherworldly entities who are intent on conquering the Earth. The life-form at the center of *Splinter* hails from an environment so alien that it leaves no doubt of its otherworldliness. The film opens with a gas station on the edge of a large area of woodland. The attendant is sitting in a chair by a patch of fairly short grass near the gas

---

103. The hospital would be approximately where the Barbican Centre is in London, and the exterior street scenes were filmed in or near that location.

station when he hears a strange noise and some rustling behind him. He goes to investigate and something unseen attacks him. The scene cuts to a couple driving through the woodlands, Polly (Jill Wagner) and Seth (Paulo Constanzo), who stop to pick up a female hitchhiker whose boyfriend suddenly appears brandishing a gun. The two strangers, Lacey (Rachel Kerbs) and Dennis (Shea Whigham), get in the car with the couple but as they all drive away something causes a front tire to burst, forcing them to pull over. They assume that they have hit an animal so while two of them change the punctured tire the others go to investigate the dead creature. However, upon approaching they see that the creature appears to be a slowly reanimating pile of flesh. They quickly drive off, but upon realizing that their fuel has almost run out, they pull into the nearest garage. No attendant mans the station and thus they help themselves to fuel and snacks from the shop. Lacey then decides to go to the bathroom that is outside at the back of the gas-station. As she pushes her way into the cubicle she is attacked by the attendant, who acts and looks like a broken doll covered in long spines that lunges toward its prey, knocking Lacey to the floor as she tries to make it back to the safety of the shop. The others have now locked themselves inside the shop, but Dennis leaves the safety of the locked shop in an attempted rescue. Lacey has already transformed into a monster, however, and he barely escapes, crushing her hand in the shop door as he slams it shut. However, the severed hand reanimates and scuttles after the survivors inside the shop—this scene instantly links back to *The Thing from Another World*, and its remake by John Carpenter, where each part of the creature is able to exist autonomously from the rest.

Of particular interest here is the way it is uncontrollably drawn to animals and more particularly humans. At the start of the film we assume the creature in the grass that assimilated/infected the attendant was originally a smallish animal, and the creature knocked down by the car was formerly a deer, but these are posited as more the means to an end which is assimilating humanity. Once humans have come into the vicinity of the parasite, they become its total focus, as seen in the unfolding drama at the gas station. The three surviving humans are now trapped in the shop with the hand that tries to "bite" them—make them part of itself—until they trap it in a cool cabinet where the cold seems to make it inactive—again not unlike the creature in *The Thing from Another World*. The "bite" indeed increases the entity's vampire credentials as the titular "splinters" that stick out of the infected limbs and body masses recall fangs that penetrate the skin to infect the blood of its victim.

The main body then tries to find a way into the shop, and decides to climb onto the roof to try and find an entrance there. At this point a police woman arrives to investigate, only to be killed and attached to the corpus of the creature as it drags itself onto the roof of the gas station, tearing the body of the officer in half as it does so—curiously the part that falls off remains uninfected. This drive to assimilate reflects Franco Moretti's aforementioned reading of Dracula as the perfect consumer who is driven to forever accumulate. The parasite in *Splinter* likewise fits this description, intent on accumulating ever greater layers of human flesh so that it turns all living matter into part of itself. The survivors inside the shop come up with a plan to escape as they realize that the creature is drawn by body heat and if one of them, Seth, can make himself sufficiently cold, he will become invisible and so could escape the shop and get in and start the police car. Seth could then drive up to the shop door for the rest to get in and escape before the vampiric creature can react. Unsurprisingly, the plan begins to unravel, but Polly and Seth eventually manage to escape, immolating the vampire in a pillar of flame as the gas station explodes.

The entity here then has many traits that link it to other examples in the vampire genre in general and more particularly with films discussed here. As mentioned, there are several points of resonance with *The Thing from Another World*, not least the in the ability of separate parts of the vampiric creature to survive independently. It equally seems able to communicate and/or join back to the main body, suggesting a hive-mentality, as with *Queen of Blood*, and *Priest*. Such an idea is seen in Count Dracula himself, who infects others to become part of his growing vampiric body (Mina becomes increasingly joined to him the closer she gets to being a vampire), and more recently *The Strain* (del Toro and Hogan: 2014–17) also explicitly shows this with the Master vampire controlling the minds of all those he makes/infects, assimilating them into himself. In this sense the parasitic creature does not so much feed off its victims as it infects them with a kind of organic, biological energy. It is no simple contagion.

Thus, *Splinter* can be read as a sustained meditation on the potential of organic life, and a narrative more akin to *Annihilation* where the alien is an aspect of life itself, an unstoppable biological jouissance that melds, transforms, and hybridizes all life forms together: animal, human, vegetation, flora and fauna into a single affirmation of existence. It thereby sets itself in opposition to the forms of individuality, identity and hierarchy that are the foundation of the human world, and particularly twenty first century America where it is set.

As the film ends only the original couple survive, a symbol of the continuing propagation of humanity—itself an all-consuming biological/ideological force—yet as their car drives away through the rows of trees the camera rises to an aerial view of the surrounding woodlands. The tree is still there and as we watch a rabbit hops near its base as a protuberance darts out and infects it; it is only a matter of time before the vampires from another world invade again as the forces of life are unstoppable. The next film follows in this vein, but the vampires are far more focused in their uses of organic jouissance.

Venom (2018) by Ruben Fleischer is part of the recent spate of superhero films, not least in making it explicit from the start that the vampiric parasite here is from space. As with *Event Horizon* mentioned earlier, the vampiric parasite in *Venom* intentionally lands on Earth, as the parasites themselves confirm. The story opens with the return to Earth of a space shuttle owned by the Life Foundation. Though its mission has been successful, its return is less so and it crashes into the jungle in Malaysia. Four alien creatures called symbiotes have been onboard from the surface of an asteroid, where thousands more are to be found. The entities are kept in special containment pods as they are unable to survive in the oxygen-heavy atmosphere of Earth. But one of these pods has broken in the crash, allowing one of the symbiotes to bond to the single surviving astronaut, who subsequently escapes from the site before Life Foundation security personnel arrive. The other containers are returned to the headquarters of the Life Foundation in San Francisco where the scientist Carlton Drake (Riz Ahmed) is explaining his vision of the future of humanity—this part of the story is very like *Dracula* where the alien from another world is invited in to the heart of civilization, and in both cases the invitation was engineered by the vampire from the outset. Drake is a visionary who feels the Earth will only be capable of sustaining mankind for another generation at most and sees the only way forward as hybridity between humanity and an alien species, which would increase humanity's chances of survival on Earth as well as in other planetary ecosystems. His program of space exploration has been specifically geared toward this aim, and while our solar system has proved uninhabitable, the passing asteroid has been a godsend to him.

In the high-security section of Drake's facility the symbiotes are kept in their containment tubes inside transparent walled-in quarantine rooms. The staff in the facility are experimenting on human subjects, kidnapping "volunteers" from the homeless and poor communities around the city in the knowledge that they will not be missed. The symbiote is released from its container during the experiment, from which it emerges in the form of a viscous black fluid in zero gravity as it engulfs its victim. Unlike the vampiric parasite in *Splinter* or *Slither*, this entity does not violently penetrate the test subject nor flow in through an orifice but rather absorbs through the skin, bonding with the organs beneath. However, the symbiote tends to satiate its hunger by consuming the victim's internal organs, and thus only a select few human beings survive the process. The symbiote must consume its food while the food is still living, thereby feeding its organic jouissance and fueling its ability to transform, mutate and regenerate at impossibly fast rates. Drake's experiments are not going as well as he expected due to the voracious nature of the symbiotes, which causes irreparable damage to the human subject's lungs, liver and other organs even in cases where the symbiosis was initially successful. The protagonist, reporter Eddie Brock (Tom Hardy), becomes the first successful human host, after he infiltrates the facility with the help of a disillusioned doctor in Drake's employ. Eddie spots a homeless woman he had befriended and breaks into the containment room in which she is held, only for the symbiote within her to leap from her body and into his.

The symbiote engages in performative vampirism, doubling as cyborgian appendage and species hybridity that makes the combined body of host and parasite more than human; a becoming that is almost supernatural in its actualization. The symbiote calls itself Venom, and it exists within/with Eddie as a separate entity, while having access to his thoughts and memories but not sharing its own. Venom needs "meat" to sustain itself and although it tries a variety of foodstuffs, including rotten meat, it soon realizes that only live food will work for it and subsequently it eats live lobsters in a restaurant and bites the heads off armed personnel from Life Corporation who are trying to kill it and its human host.

Venom exhibits many vampiric qualities, from its fanged mouth to the mutability of its body from a miasmic mist to a mercurial liquid to a huge multi-limbed monster. Venom thereby mirrors Dracula's ability to pass through locked doors, become a huge wolf, and even affect the weather. The symbiotes plan to send up further shuttles to bring over the rest of the alien colony and consume all the live food on the Earth before moving on. Not unlike Jonathan Harker or Mina, Eddie has been chosen due

Figure 23. The performative vampirism of Venom and Eddie Brock (Tom Hardy). *Venom.* Directed by Ruben Fleischer (Columbia Pictures: 2018).

to his "soft" nature and "hysterical" disposition—interestingly both Eddie and Mina share secretarial skills which facilitates the vampires' dissemination through the world—which also points toward the shared femininity of their respective bodies as ones that are open to being controlled and manipulated by a vampiric presence.

Where the creature veers away from Stoker's vampire is that it is already one of many, and it does not replicate itself; if its host dies then so too does the alien. However, the union seems to work so well between Venom and Eddie—we are never told exactly why this is so other than Venom seems to like Eddie—that the alien decides to prevent the rest of the symbiotes from landing on Earth. The symbiote that escaped the shuttle crash site, Riot, then makes an appearance in San Francisco and enters the body of Drake. There is another Life Corporation shuttle due to be launched and Riot/Drake wants to use it to bring more symbiotes to Earth. Venom/Eddie attempt to thwart their plans in a protracted final battle, and they manage to send the recently launched spacecraft off course, causing it to crash into Riot and Drake—the symbiotes seem largely indestructible except that they are vulnerable to fire and have an extreme reaction to high frequency sounds which cause them to detach from their hosts. Venom was also apparently killed, but he is now so bonded to Eddie (and in the hope of sequels) that he survives, offering a rare case in this chapter of a successful integration of a vampire from another world into our own. It certainly does not describe a future of hybridity and human evolution, but at least it describes a future where humanity might still be alive. The next pairing also shows vampires that have come to Earth from space but, as with earlier examples, they have no intention of bonding with humanity.

A Quiet Place, John Krasinski, 2018/ *Bird Box*, Susanne Bier, 2018

In both *A Quiet Place* and *Bird Box*, aliens seem to appear from almost nowhere. Their vampires are most definitely not from Earth but they seem to have been spun from the essence of contemporary life, as if the psychic excesses of the early 21st century were given physical embodiment. These vampires are almost entirely focused on humanity, suggesting that they are manifested from within us or our lifestyles. The films accordingly trace a purposeful turn away from contemporary civilization and its associated technology that is presented as the only means of survival.

In *A Quiet Place*, the vampires from another world consume all living flesh, but they soon narrow their preferences to the human variety—presumably, the larger mammals and birds were dispatched quite quickly, given the insatiability of the creatures' appetite. The creatures bear some similarity to the xenomorphs from *Alien* in that they are nominally quadrupedal, they lack eyes and would be unable to make their own way to Earth unaided,[104] but possess acutely sensitive hearing, with their heads designed as a floral-shaped sound receiver with teeth.

This hypersensitivity to sound is accompanied by great speed and agility, meaning they can cover large distances quickly and thus their victims often seem to vanish in a blur of movement. Their predatory style is not unlike that of the vampires in *30 Days of Night* (Slade: 2007) that literally "vanish" their prey. As with the xenomorphs, it is hard to imagine a home world where they would evolve naturally without consuming its resources in a short space of time.[105]

The film rather neatly sidesteps these questions by focusing on the Earth in the aftermath of the apocalypse—the earliest scene is eighty-nine days after the initial invasion, at a point at which human civilization is already decimated.[106] The Abbott family, upon whom the film is focused, are shown walking barefoot through a town which is deserted. Flyers for "Missing Persons" hang on the wall of the shop as they search for medications for their eldest son Marcus (Noah Jupe). These flyers suggest that the catastrophe was not cataclysmic but gradual, prompting people at its early stages to believe that their loved ones might have lost their way rather than died in their confrontations with this all-consuming alien vampire. However, as the film opens, nearly three months into the vampire occupation, even the birds have gone quiet. The Abbotts walk silently and carefully through an abandoned and derelict town that was once a center of commotion and noise. Indeed, even in the town's current state, it is still deemed uninhabitable by the Abbotts. The abandoned town thus reinforces the impression that the sheer volume of noise and chaos in 21st-century life attracted the aliens in the first place and that they consequently remain near modern hubs of life as if they contain some residual energy. Indeed, the Abbotts seem to have survived the onslaught thanks to the remoteness of their home—they live on a family farmstead a long way from the town and even further from a major city.

104. In the Alien Versus Predator crossover universe it is suggested that the xenomorphs are brought to Earth at some point in ancient history—during the period of the Aztec civilization—and put in a kind of "game reserve" deep under the surface of Antarctica, but manage to escape their imprisonment at the start of the 21st century.
105. It is never explicitly shown that the creatures eat humans, or consume anything for that matter, though their imperative to kill larger animals suggests they get sustenance from them in some form.
106. It should be noted that a sequel/prequel, *A Quiet Place Part II* (Krasinski) is set for release shortly after this book goes to press and may provide answers to some of these questions or even change details established in the first film.

A Quiet Place further suggests that the Abbotts' continued survival can be partly attributed to the fact that they have a daughter who is deaf and have consequently all learned sign language. Thus, deafness and/or sensorial non-normativity becomes an evolutionary advantage in this new, post-apocalyptic world, a proposition that *A Quiet Place* shares with *The Silence* (Deafness) and *Bird Box* (Blindness) that also use conditions often described as disabilities as positive traits—*The Day of the Triffids* also intimated that the congenitally blind coped better with the new world order. However, *A Quiet Place* purposely complicates this suggestion with the death of the youngest son, Beau (Cade Woodward), as it is partially caused by his sister Regan's (Millicent Simmonds) inability to hear. Yet by the end of the film, *A Quiet Place* has firmly championed the value of human frailty and individual persistence.

A Quiet Place centers largely on the struggles of daily existence in a world where making any noise is potentially deadly, a problem exacerbated when Evelyn Abbott (Emily Blunt) is pregnant and near her due date. Her husband, Lee Abbott (John Krasinski), has set up surveillance cameras all around the property and a silent alarm system that flashes red lights when set off to alert the family of intruders. The Abbotts appear to have developed a workable survival strategy until Lee and Marcus come across a man in the woods. The man is standing by the body of his dead wife and breaks into a wail, thereby effectively committing suicide by monster. The creatures arrive swiftly and kill him, consequently becoming aware of the possibility of other prey in the area. As Lee and Marcus rush back to the house, a chain of events quickly unfolds, leaving Lee dead, and Evelyn, her new baby, Marcus and Regan trapped in the cellar while an alien searches for them on the premises. Regan takes stock of her surroundings and notices among various hearing aids, mechanical parts and speakers in her father's workshop, some scribbled notes written by her father, one reading "what is their weakness?" She then recalls two scenes earlier on in the film when feedback from her hearing aid had caused extreme distress to an alien in her vicinity. She quickly switches on an implant processor on the counter, which immediately begins emitting a high-pitched squealing that causes the creature in the basement considerable discomfort. She then places the processor by a microphone and turns on some speakers. The burst of sound incapacitates the alien, allowing Evelyn to grab a shotgun and kill it. The mother and daughter look at the surveillance monitors and see many creatures making their way toward the house, but now they feel ready to face them.

The use of the hearing aid as a weapon harks back to *The War of the Worlds*. In Wells' story the common cold saves mankind from the alien invaders. Rather than a symbol of human frailty, humanity's susceptibility to the common cold is revealed to have built-up an immunity that enables its survival. A similar revelation occurs at the end of *A Quiet Place*, where a hearing aid, a symbol of human frailty (deafness) becomes a weapon against the vampires from another world. Indeed, the aural feedback from it, which is an annoyance to human beings, proves deadly to the aliens. Furthermore, the key role of the hearing aid complicates the film's initial antipathy toward technology. Indeed, technology proves vital to the Abbotts' survival in more ways than one—Lee deploys surveillance equipment, he has accumulated radios to try and contact other survivors, and he works with technology to try and fix Regan's cochlear implant. *A Quiet Place* is thus not altogether Luddite, but rather warns of a danger inherent within certain types or uses of technology, i.e., technology without a utilitarian purpose. This warning finds its clearest expression in the death of Beau. While the Abbotts search for medications for Marcus at the opening of the film, Beau finds a toy rocket. His parents quickly divest him of the toy, knowing he could use it to make noise and thus attract the aliens. But as they leave the pharmacy, Regan grabs the toy and gives it to Beau without her parents' knowledge. Yet her little brother, who unbeknownst to her has also taken the batteries for the toy, soon places them in the rocket and causes it to blast into life, summoning the creatures who pounce on him and kill him. Thus, technology for toys, games and/or the leisure industry is framed negatively as a waste of energy for nonessential purposes—an aural and sensorial excess—that brought the alien vampires to Earth in the first place. *Bird Box* picks up on this theme.

As in *A Quiet Place*, *Bird Box* opens on a post-apocalyptic world, five years after the catastrophe, but unlike *A Quiet Place*, *Bird Box* provides more detailed descriptions of the apocalypse in flashbacks. The story centers around a pregnant artist named Malorie Hayes (Sandra Bullock), who lives in an unnamed town in California. She is visited by her sister Jess (Sarah Paulson) who describes Malorie as "detached" based on her paintings—emotional detachment becomes important as the story unfolds. Malorie watches the news on television with her sister, which relates a story about a sudden surge in mass suicide in Romania. A similar surge occurs in Siberia and spreads eastward across Europe. Malorie, accompanied by her sister, goes to visit her obstetrician at the hospital, but as they depart, a woman begins banging her head against the wall. Outside of the building they emerge into chaos, screaming, shouting and cars crashing and they realize the "violence" from Europe has arrived in the United States. As they drive home through the carnage, Jess' eyes turn a peculiar color and she appears to be hallucinating as the car crashes and flips over. They both survive but as they attempt to escape Jess purposely walks in front of a moving truck. Malorie escapes on foot and as she nears her house her landlord, Douglas (John Malkovich), warns her away, even as his wife warmly invites her in just as her eyes glaze over and she proceeds to enter a car on fire. Another survivor, Tom (Trevante Rhodes), ushers Malorie into a house sheltering survivors, where they are soon joined by Douglas. The survivors begin to recount their recent experiences and collectively realize that the catastrophe is caused by an invisible force that compels those who "see" it to commit suicide. A member of the group named Charlie (Lil Rel Howery) suggests that the menace is made up of demons who have arrived on Earth and inflict upon their victims a vision of their greatest sadness or worst fear, thereby driving them to suicide. The vampiric alien invasion thus provokes deep and excessive emotional responses in all who "see" it, making the victims the perfect food source for energy vampires. This impression is reinforced by the chaotic scenes in the city that amplify and exaggerate everyday scenes in a metropolis where people, cars and trucks rush in all directions and cacophony attends them. The excess provoked by the vampires is thus merely an extreme form of everyday excess.

The survivors board up the windows in the house and cover the gaps with cardboard and paper, blocking the outside view and thus the visions conjured up by the creatures. But a member of the group, Greg (BD Wong), offers to use the installed surveillance equipment to check if the entity approaches the house, and consequently he "sees" the entities on screen and is thus driven mad. As the film unfolds, they welcome a newcomer into the house named Gary (Tom Hollander), who claims to have fled from inmates who have escaped the insane asylum and are now forcing people to look at the entities. Although he seems unaffected, it is not long before he reveals himself to be one of the insane, while Malorie and another woman go into labor. Gary begins to remove hand-drawn illustrations of the "beautiful" entities out of his bag and even these approximate likenesses propel him to a state of excitation.

He consequently goes on a murder spree and tries to force the survivors to look out the windows, from which he has now torn down the coverings. The majority of the survivors are killed, including the other woman who went into labor, but Tom manages to overpower Gary and kill him.

Gary's illustrations of the entity tellingly resemble Count Dracula in his misty form. The entity exists as a cloud of energy that only takes form in the eye/mind of the beholder. The entity carries Lovecraftian undertones as it exceeds human comprehension. It constitutes a hyper-object whose scale not so much opens a doorway into another world or state of being as makes it impossible to carry on living in our own. The state of emotional excess that it conjures does not last long, allowing Malorie and some other survivors to withstand it due to their natural emotional detachment. While this quality was initially posited as a negative attribute detrimental to the protagonist's ability to raise children, it enables Malorie's survival and thus places her in

5. The Thing from Another World   171

Figure 24. The many forms of the energy vampire. *Bird Box.* Directed by Susanne Bier (Netflix: 2018).

charge of two children, her own and the child of the woman killed by Gary. Indeed, her detachment comes to the fore when she names the two children "Girl" and "Boy." This detachment allows her to focus on the task at hand without getting caught up in the emotional turmoil unfolding around her and thus, where all others in the house have died, she has survived.

The survival of Malorie and the children in her care is further contingent on her decision to leave the city and lead them deeper into the wilds beyond it. Malorie leads the two children, now aged about five years old, on a symbolic journey downriver from the dangers of 21st-century civilization to sanctuary in the past. Indeed, the journey downriver is equated with the journey of life, shot through with flashbacks to the house that emphasize what she is leaving behind as they are carried along by the current. Malorie and the children thus symbolically travel along the mythical Styx, but rather than passing from life to death, they pass from death to life: away from the cities, the places of death, to the countryside which symbolizes life, and away from the toxic present to the pristine past. The mystical element of this journey comes to the fore in the blindfolds that Malorie and the children wear for the duration of their forty-two-hour journey. The boat eventually capsizes but they all make it safely to the shore where the entities tempt the three to remove their blindfolds as they approach their final sanctuary. This temptation further invites a reading of the entities as demons of some kind trying to tempt the faithful to a world of sensorial excess and away from the true path of abstinence.

The escape from the vampires from another world is thus predicated not just on emotional detachment but on visual abstinence as well. Indeed, the theme of blindness runs through the film, just as deafness did in *A*

Quiet Place. In *Bird Box*, blindness is almost penitential in nature, associated with blocking out the sights of the city while they are in the house, and wearing blindfolds once outside and on the river to limit sensorial overload at all points of the journey—in the book *Bird Box* (2014) by Josh Malerman, from which the film was adapted, the children are shown to have heightened senses of hearing, touch, etc., due to their effective blindness from birth. Once at the Sanctuary, they are immediately out of danger, notwithstanding that the entities await just outside, and are thus able to remove their blindfolds. The Sanctuary is a school for the blind, though not everyone there is unsighted, and it is represented as a veritable Garden of Eden with unmistakable religious undertones. The Sanctuary is thus configured as an alternative space in a culture that is visually focused/dependent, making it literally invisible to the entities. Sanctuary is thus a return to an idealized past before such sensorial overload attracted the vampires from another world to the Earth, when there was no television nor internet and where the protagonists can make a fresh start, rather like Noah on the arc. This new start is symbolically signaled by Malorie's bestowal of new names to the two children in her care. Of course, the entities have not left the world, they are only unable to enter the compound, so while the ending offers a sense of hope it is difficult to see just how it will play out when the two worlds of alien vampire present and the human past are irreconcilable. Consequently, *A Quiet Place* and *Bird Box* envisage the modern world as monstrous, a space from which humanity has become so detached that the only method of survival is to retreat to the past. The final two examples discussed in this volume return to the idea of alternative, plant-like forms of intelligent life that offer different interpretations of the past and the possible futures that might replace them.

Stranger Things, The Duffer Brothers, 2016–present/*The Girl with All the Gifts,* Colm McCarthy, 2016

Stranger Things is a television series set in the 1980s, specifically catering to the nostalgia felt by people of a certain age in the late 2010s. Indeed, it capitalizes on nostalgia so overtly that one could argue that it vampirizes the past. Yet notwithstanding its heavy-handed nostalgia, *Stranger Things* also configures the past as an undead monster, unable to change and held permanently in a form and meaning that the present fixes upon it. The series thus complicates its use of nostalgia, utilizing some of it to highlight the effects it has on our vision of the past and also the kinds of future it might bring forth. *Stranger Things* thus builds a narrative that focuses on the Cold War tensions between the United States and the Soviet Union to construct a mirror world of demons and monsters intent on destroying the rose-tinted view of the American past. The world is aptly named the Upside Down and seems as antithetical to humans as the world that the bodachs in *Odd Thomas* came from.

Stranger Things centers on a group of children in a small American town named Hawkins. Through these children and their trials and tribulations, it explores the cultural anxiety that encompasses a lingering distrust of 1960s hippy culture, mind-altering drugs, little green men and secret government experiments that feed into the perceived menace of Communism and paranoia regarding its destruction of the United States and the American way of life. This exploration configures change as the greatest bogeyman in a world that is retrospectively labeled as idyllic, thereby redoubling the lens of nostalgia. *Stranger Things* thus creates a world that is simultaneously framed as "perfect," as seen through the eyes of a group of twelve-year-old friends, and as fleeting, given that the protagonists are on the verge of adolescence and eventually adulthood. The protagonists thus act as a synecdoche of the wider society and culture that likewise cannot remain fixed in time. Yet the experiences of the adults in the series are tainted by broken and/or abusive relationships that reveal their ostensibly perfect world as a beguiling illusion. Consequently, the invasion of this world by another is not only inevitable but actively sought, not as a manifestation of a cultural death-drive but as a means of revealing the inherent nature of America to itself. Inevitably then it is the children who create, discover, fight, and solve (if only temporarily) the existential crisis of the vampires from another world that threatens to destroy their America—America being synonymous with the (known) world within the narrative.

Stranger Things is set in Hawkins, Indiana, in the early 1980s. Not unlike Stull in *Nothing Left to Fear* and Sunnydale in *Buffy the Vampire Slayer* (Whedon: 1997–2003), Hawkins is a natural gateway to another world. A government research facility runs clandestine experiments near Hawkins and is the cause for the events that follow. Its experiments are conducted on subjects endowed with "gifts" such as telekinesis and telepathy. One subject, Terry Ives (Aimee Mullins), gives birth while in the facility, notwithstanding that the father of her baby remains unknown and implies a supernatural cause to her pregnancy. Her baby is taken by the lead scientist, Dr. Brenner (Matthew Modine), and raised under laboratory conditions to develop her skills, initially in order to eavesdrop on a Russian spy by traveling to another dimension. This dimension is not uninhabited as first assumed and the girl, Eleven (Millie Bobby Brown), awakens creatures from this other world and inadvertently allows them to enter our own. Her entrance into the other dimension creates a gateway from it into our world, which becomes the center of the experimentation taking place at the site. This premise configures nostalgia as a process that creates an alternative dimension in order to "eavesdrop" on and reinterpret the past, which awakens vampires and monsters intent on consuming the present. The alien world has been slowly making inroads into Hawkins, and when Eleven escapes the government facility, it becomes apparent that the other dimension is approaching our world and on the verge of consuming the town.

There seems to be only a thin layer separating the two domains with our world existing on one side of a continuous skin with the Upside Down on the other. The Upside Down is a mirror image of our own world, as demonstrated in its flashes of dark copies of scenes from Hawkins covered in fungal vegetation. In the first season particularly, much of the growth seems focused on the Byers house just out of town. The youngest boy in the family, Will (Noah Schnapp), becomes a focus for the Upside Down and is infected by it, thereby fulfilling a Mina Harker role in the narrative. He is subsequently able to see into the Upside Down version of Hawkins and to envisage the consequences should the vampiric world below break into our own. The vegetative growth from the Upside Down appears in the Byers house and spreading out like veins or root systems. It thereby serves as a forerunner of and accompaniment to the alien invasion, while also marking the spots where the alien invasion has occurred, not unlike the red weed in *The War of the Worlds*. As the story of the first season reaches its climax, the alien world has spread a root-like system under the entire town and is on the verge of consuming the population. Will's visions of the town do not just involve the decayed and rotten looking plant-life but are increasingly apocalyptic, overseen by a huge spider-like figure towering over it called a Mind Flayer—while the Mind Flayer is first seen in season 2 it was its influence that caused the events in season 1. The Mind Flayer, it later transpires, is connected to all the life in the Upside Down and seems to be able to control it and those that have been infected by it, seeing it act as something of the King Vampire of the realm. However, not all the growth in the Upside Down is purely plant-like in nature and one of the more dangerous entities are the Demogorgons who are more the real vampires from another world in the story.[107] The Demogorgons are mainly humanoid and can move on either two or four limbs, yet they are plantlike in their construction as their

---

107. In many respects it is not unlike the vampire in the eco-system on Pandora as seen in *Avatar* (Cameron: 2009). This is an interesting correspondence as the environment on Pandora rises up to defend itself from human invasion, and curiously suggests that such might be the case for the Upside Down and that the incursion into it by Eleven, with its associated attempts at exploitation by the government scientists, has initiated a form of reverse colonialism. In fact, this is a theme that runs through all three seasons so far, where both the Americans and Russians (Soviets) attempt to use the Upside Down as a resource for their own ends.

heads, while at first appearance smooth, open up like large flowers with each "petal" covered in teeth on their inside edges—not dissimilar to the creatures in *A Quiet Place*.

The Demogorgon exhibits many vampiric qualities. It is exceedingly strong, impervious to bullets, possesses telekinetic abilities, heals swiftly, and is highly sensitive and attracted to human blood. The Demogorgon is focused on killing humans when in our world, and more specifically tracking down Eleven—in many ways Eleven is something of their Van Helsing and is the only person that can resist the Demogorgons and kill them. Indeed, at the end of season 2 it is Eleven that is able to defeat the Demogorgons and seal the gateway at the government facility. However, although the Upside Down is apparently contained, it is still connected to Will, its living gateway to this world. By season 3 the metaphorical Soviet menace is made real, and Communist spies have taken control of the experimental facility in Hawkins and reopened the gateway to the Upside Down—there is much correlation between the Soviet Union and the Upside Down and it is not surprising that at the end of season 3, Demogorgons have been taken into captivity in Siberia. Not unlike the alien world, the Soviets too have spread their tentacles far and wide under Hawkins and beyond, with a base in the town's shopping mall—the heart of the town in season 3 and indeed symbolic of wider America—and agents who seem able to attack and kidnap people at will across America. Once again Eleven and her group of friends manage to close the gate, but this time as the series ends the vampires from

Figure 25. The Demogorgon, vampiric hybrid of fauna and flora. *Stranger Things*. Created by The Duffer Brothers (Netflix: 2016–).

another world, the Demogorgons, are left on our side of the gateway. The Demogorgons are so alien to Earth that hybridity or coexistence with humanity is inconceivable. However, this is not the case in the final film discussed in this monograph, *The Girl with All the Gifts*.

The Girl with All the Gifts is set in an apocalyptic future where the world is under attack by a mysterious fungus that bonds with its human host to turn them into mindless, violent, flesh-eating monsters called "hungries." The fungus is supposedly a mutation of Ophiocordyceps unilateralis, which is found in the rainforests of South America and in its original form attacks ants, causing them to lose control of their actions and subsequently climb to a high point in the undergrowth so that fungal spores can be released from their heads. The real fungus protects itself and the community of ants it "feeds" on, creating a rather vampiric symbiotic relationship with them. Similar to the real fungus, the fictional fungus in *The Girl with All the Gifts* attaches itself to its host's central nervous system, taking over the host's body and its functions and movement. This process seems to energize the host's muscles and imbues it with the desire to eat human flesh, which in turn passes on the fungal infection. Yet the process is different when the fungus attaches itself to children, more specifically children yet unborn at the time of their mother's infection. The fungus seems to fuse more smoothly with these children and is less parasitic in nature and more of an evolved hybrid. Thus, while the children occasionally lose control of their bodies, they also have long periods of lucidity and autonomy. The UK government has thus set up a facility under the auspices of Dr. Caroline Caldwell (Glenn Close) to study the symbiosis between the fungus and these children, in the hope that this research could lead to a cure.

The facility is for all intents and purposes a high security prison where the inmates/children are kept in individual cells, but it is also a school where they have classes all day. Although the classes seem to be largely a pretense that provides a gloss to the study of these children, at least one student, Mel (Sennia Nanua), seems to respond positively to the classes and particularly to the idea of stories and fairytales taught by Helen Justineau (Gemma Arterton). Dr. Caldwell has been choosing students meanwhile in order to examine the fungus's bond with their spinal cord and whether there is a possibility of creating an antidote. However, she must dissect their bodies to this end, and remove their brains and spinal columns. Mel soon comes to Dr. Caldwell's attention, not just because she is extremely intelligent, but because unlike the other children she seems able to master her violent impulses. Much to Justineau's distress, Dr. Caldwell decides to vivisect Mel, but the facility is overrun by hungries before she can carry out her plan. The human world is

5. The Thing from Another World   177

apparently losing the fight against the fungus, and Dr. Caldwell, Justineau, Mel and some military personnel are forced to flee the facility. They decide to head to Beacon across London. This is a journey not without its risks as the hungries tend to migrate to areas of (former) high population.

London has transformed into a post-apocalyptic city, where groups of motionless hungries have "shut down" due to the lack of food, reactivating as a response to noise. Weeds and plants have grown in paths and roads that have long since been abandoned by people, and they grow all the more virulently as the group approaches central London. The environs of the BT Tower proliferate with weeds that are complemented by piles of decomposing hungries out of which further vegetation is emerging. The vegetation that emerges from the corpses winds its way up the Post Office Tower, producing pods which contain fungal spores that will become airborne upon release and spell the end of humanity. The fungus thus reproduces its own natural habitat—the jungle is claiming the modern, technological metropolitan space of London. Indeed, like the real fungus, this fictional counterpart turns its victims (ants/humans) into a vehicle for spreading its spores. The film suggests that a central intelligence might be driving the spread and ongoing mutation of the fungus, not unlike the Upside Down. Thus, the hungries are merely the first stage that prepare this new world for a new age. They will be followed by a secondary infection, once the fungus has become more enmeshed and integrated with human DNA, creating a hybrid that can maintain and defend the fungus' environment. Mel cannot be the only successful second-stage hybrid for this to work, and indeed, she finds a pack of feral children in London that are likewise bonded with the fungus and yet in possession of their higher faculties. She quickly establishes herself as their leader, and while Dr. Caldwell and the surviving group believe she is protecting them, she is in fact establishing a bridgehead for the next stage of the fungus' evolution.

The team discover an abandoned solar-powered mobile laboratory by the BT Tower, which they take charge of as a basecamp. Mel, Helen, and Sgt. Parks (Paddy Considine) are eventually knocked out by Dr. Caldwell, who drags Mel into the mobile laboratory. She plans to use Mel's brainstem to create an antidote and thereby save humanity before the release of the spores on the BT Tower. Mel wonders if Caldwell believes that she is no longer acting like a human. Dr. Caldwell grants that Mel is alive, to which Mel responds, "Then why should it be us who die for you?" Mel threatens to bite Dr. Caldwell and manages to escape the laboratory. Dr. Caldwell attempts to follow her but is attacked by the feral children and killed. Mel goes to the base of the fungal tower and sets light to it, thereby opening the pods and filling the air with a thick cloud of spores. Returning to the lab, Mel hopes to find Sgt. Parks and Helen safely locked in the hermetically sealed vehicle but discovers the soldier slumped to the ground, overcome by the fungal infection. Knowing his time is up, in a despairing voice he says to Mel "It's over. It's all over." Mel looks back at him and calmly replies "It's not over. It's just not yours anymore" (McCarthy: 2016). As the dust finally settles, Helen awakens in the laboratory. The first sight that greets her is the group of feral children sitting on the ground, kept in check by Mel. She asks Helen to tell them a story, just as she did to the children back at the facility. Helen declines, but as Mel points out, they now have plenty of time for her to tell one.

The ending has much of *I Am Legend* to it where unbeknownst to Neville there is however another species that has survived the plague, a vampire-human hybrid that is the future of life on Earth. In *The Girl with all the Gifts* the hungries are the zombie/vampires, and Helen becomes the last human, the legend, just like Neville. *The Girl with All the Gifts* purposely reverses the tropes from *I Am Legend*; the last human is a woman not a man, and she is not violent like Neville and so is able to survive. The children are then the hybrids, the third option that can survive and provide a future for life on Earth. Keeping Helen alive is then an interesting choice, and one which creates a specifically non-masculine ending when read beside *I Am Legend*. Neville's actions in the dying world are continuously selfish, penetrative, and violent. The new species has no option but to kill him as he has killed so many of their own. Helen provides a specifically feminine riposte to this, being the one who provides Mel with a motherly figure and does all she can to protect her. And, unlike Neville, who uses his knowledge to destroy the vampires and try and save humanity at their expense, Helen is a nurturing educator. In this way her legend is in not being the end of the story of humanity but the beginning of a new species learning to write its own stories for an unknown future.

In *The Girl with All the Gifts*, humanity, in its present state, is doomed to die out. The hybridity and rebirth heralded at the end of the film use human life force as a fuel to propel it into a new, often hybrid world, rather than just a self-sustaining meal as so often seen in the examples discussed in this book. As such, it is worth a quick comparison with the two focal texts used throughout the volume and picking out important exceptions to the general rule encountered so far of "consume and move on." *War of the Worlds* offers no room for hybridity. Such an idea is unacceptable to both the Martians and the humans; the only future is if one kills the other or if humanity evolves into the future that the hungry eyed aliens foretell. *Dracula* is more open to the idea. While the colonial vampire hunters are against the idea, the vampire is more generous with its affections and while hybridity on the scale of *The Girl with All the Gifts* might not be its preferred route of moving into the future, transgression of norms and the pleasures of miscegenation are absolutely acceptable. Identity politics for the vampire from another world are far less demarcated and fractured than in ours. Texts that speak of species in terms of commonalities rather than differences—*Ultraviolet, Aeon Flux, The Girl with All the Gifts*, and even *Splinter*—see a future that is free from its past and in many ways open to develop in new and unthought of directions. Humanity as we know it is not sacred and unchangeable in these instances, but like the past is a palimpsest that can be overwritten.

This would seem to go against the solution found in *The Breed*, one of the few films looked at here where the vampires and the humans find a way to coexist. In one sense it shows an uneasy future where two different societies try to learn to coexist. However, the romance between Grant and Lucy suggests a greater merger. It is never explored in the film whether humans and vampires can create hybrid offspring, but the fact that the two are also African American and Chinese implies that White, Western normativity is already a defunct category and that new trajectories and becomings are there to be discovered. Arguably then, vampires from another world are there to serve two functions. The first and most obvious, as seen in *War of the Worlds*, is to act as a mirror: to show the unacceptable behavior of our own world, largely focused on exploitation of others and insatiable consumerism, and with this an unwillingness to change or accept difference. The other is to show that change is inevitable and present ways in which we might prepare for it. Deleuze and Guattari's term "trajectories" is particularly useful here as it opens up the idea of individuality and uniqueness but seeing all those embarked upon one moving forward. In part this describes *The Breed*. All the characters are putting the past behind them and moving into the future. Exactly what that might mean for them they do not know, but they are embarking on the trajectory anyway. *The Girl with All the Gifts* would seem slightly different, until one looks at it a little more closely. The fungus that is melding to the children's spinal cord would seem to bring out their similarities rather than differences, the driving impulse to eat flesh overriding anything else. However, Mel shows there is more to it than that; she can understand the commonalities she has with the others but also knows who she is, a girl that loves stories. And while she loves fairytales from the past she is also engaged in writing the story of the future. Which is possibly the most important aspect of vampires from another world in taking us to a future that we do not know. *War of the Worlds* actually foretold our future, effectively creating a loop of consumerism that was impossible to leave. *Dracula*, however, offers something slightly different. At story's end, the vampire appears to be dead, yet still an air of unease hangs over the present where the future might change in ways we cannot predict; our world, no matter how much we think we "own" it, is beyond our control. Our future, like that of Grant, Lucy, and Mel, is to embrace the trajectory of the vampire and become whatever future awaits us.

Filmography

Abraham Lincoln: Vampire Hunter, dir. Timur Bekmambetov (20th Century-Fox: 2012)
Aeon Flux, dir. Karyn Kusama (Paramount Pictures: 2005)
A.I. Artificial Intelligence, dir. Steven Spielberg (Warner Brothers: 2001)
Alien, dir. Ridley Scott (20th Century-Fox, 1979)
Alien Resurrection, dir. Jean-Pierre Jeunet (20th Century-Fox, 1997)
Alien³, dir. David Fincher (20th Century-Fox, 1992)
Alien vs. Predator [AVP], dir. Paul W.S. Anderson (20th Century-Fox, 2004)
Alien vs. Predator: Requiem [AVPR], dir. The Brothers Strause (20th Century-Fox, 2007)
Aliens, dir. James Cameron (20th Century-Fox, 1986)
The Andromeda Strain, dir. Robert Wise (Universal Pictures: 1971)
Annihilation, dir. Alex Garland (Paramount Pictures, 2018)
Armageddon, dir. Michael Bay (Buena Vista Pictures: 1998)
The Astronaut's Wife, dir. Rand Ravich (New Line Cinema, 1999)
Autómata, dir. Gabe Ibáñez (Contracorrientes Films: 2013)
Avatar, dir. James Cameron (20th Century-Fox, 2009)
Beast from Haunted Cave, dir. Monte Hellman (Allied Artists Pictures: 1959)
Beyond Skyline, dir. Liam O'Donnell (Vertical Entertainment: 2017)
Bird Box, dir. Suzanne Bier (Netflix, 2018)
Blade, dir. Stephen Norrington (New Line Cinema, 1998)
Blade: Trinity, dir. David S. Goyer (New Line Cinema, 2004)
Blade II, dir. Guillermo del Toro (New Line Cinema, 2002)
Blood Glacier, dir. Marvin Kren (Allegro Film: 2013)
Blood: The Last Vampire, dir. Hiroyuki Kitakubu (Production I. G.: 2000)
Blood: The Last Vampire, dir. Chris Nahon (Pathé: 2009)
Bloody Mary, dir. Richard Valentine (Echo Bridge Home Entertainment: 2006)
Boogeyman, dir. Stephen Kay (Sony Pictures: 2005)
Boogeyman 2, dir. Jeff Betancourt (Sony Pictures Home Entertainment: 2007)
Boogeyman 3, dir. Gary Jones (Stage 6 Films: 2008)
The Breed, dir. Michael Oblowitz (Columbia TriStar: 2001)
Buffy the Vampire Slayer, created by Joss Whedon (20th Television: 1997–2003)
The Bye Bye Man, dir. Stacy Title (STX Entertainment: 2017)
Candyman, dir. Bernard Rose (TriStar: 1992)
Carmilla, dir. Gabrielle Beaumont (Warner Brothers: 1989)
Christine, dir. John Carpenter (Columbia Pictures, 1983)
Citadel, dir. Ciaran Foy (Citadel Films: 2012)
The Cloverfield Paradox, dir. Julius Onah (Netflix: 2018)
Contact, dir. Robert Zemeckis (Warner Brothers: 1997)
Cronos, dir. Guillermo del Toro (October Films: 1993)
Dark City, dir. Alex Proyas (New Line Cinema, 1998)
Daughters of Darkness, dir. Harry Kümel (Showking Films, 1971)
The Day of the Triffids, dir. Steve Sekely (Allied Artists, 1963)
The Day of the Triffids, dir. Nick Copus (BBC, 2009)

182 Filmography

The Day the Earth Stood Still, [a.k.a. Farewell to the Master, and Journey to the World], dir. Robert Wise (20th Century–Fox, 1951)
The Day the Earth Stood Still, dir. Scott Derrickson (20th Century–Fox, 2008)
Daybreakers, dir. the Spierig brothers (Lionsgate, 2009)
The Devil's Plaything, [Der Fluch der schwarzen Schwestern], dir. Joseph W. Sarno (Retro Seduction Cinema, 1973)
Doctor Sleep, dir. Mike Flanagan (Warner Brothers: 2019)
Dracula, dir. Tod Browning (Universal Pictures, 1931)
Dracula, dir. John Badham (Universal Pictures: 1979)
Edge of Tomorrow, dir. Doug Liman (Warner Bros. Pictures: 2014)
Enter the Matrix, dir. The Wachowskis (Shiny Entertainment: 2003)
Eve of Destruction, dir. Duncan Gibbons (Orion Pictures, 1991)
Event Horizon, dir. Paul Anderson (Paramount Pictures, 1997)
Ex Machina, dir. Alex Garland (Universal Pictures, 2014)
The Fearless Vampire Killers, or Pardon Me, Your Teeth Are in My Neck, dir. Roman Polanski (Metro-Goldwyn-Mayer, 1967)
Female Vampire, dir. Jess Franco (Bruce International Pictures: 1975)
First Man into Space, dir. Robert Day (Metro-Goldwyn-Meyer: 1959)
Fright Night, dir. Tom Holland (Columbia Pictures:5)
Get Out, dir. Jordan Peele (Universal Pictures: 2017)
Ghosts of Mars, dir. John Carpenter (Screen Gems: 2001)
The Girl with All the Gifts, dir. Colm McCarthy (Warner Bros. Pictures, 2016)
Gravity, dir. Alfonso Cuarón (Warner Brothers Pictures: 2013)
Groundhog Day, dir. Harold Ramis (Columbia Pictures: 1993)
Halloween, dir. John Carpenter (Compass International Pictures: 1978)
Heartless, dir. Philip Ridley (Lionsgate: 2009)
Hellraiser, dir. Clive Barker (Entertainment Film Distributors:7)
H.G. Wells' War of the Worlds, dir. David Michael Latt (The Asylum: 2005)
The Host, dir. Andrew Niccol (Open Road Films, 2013)
I Am Legend, dir. Francis Lawrence (Warner Bros. Entertainment, 2007)
I, Robot, dir. Alex Proyas (20th Century–Fox: 2004)
Independence Day, dir. Roland Emmerich (20th Century–Fox, 1996)
Independence Day: Resurgence, dir. Roland Emmerich (20th Century–Fox, 2016)
Interstellar, dir. Christopher Nolan (Warner Brothers, 2014)
Invasion of the Body Snatchers, dir. Don Siegel (Allied Artists Pictures: 1956)
Invasion of the Body Snatchers, dir. Philip Kaufman (United Artists: 1978)
Island of the Burning Damned [Night of the Big Heat], dir. Terence Fisher (Planet Film Productions, 1967)
Island of the Doomed [La isla de la muerte], dir. Ernst von Theumer (Orbita Films, 1967)
It: The Terror from Beyond Space, dir. Edward L. Cahn (United Artists, 1958)
John Carter, dir. Andrew Stanton (Walt Disney Studios Motion Pictures, 2012)
Jupiter Ascending, dir. the Wachowskis (Warner Bros. Pictures, 2015)
The Last Man on Earth, dir. Sidney Salkow and Ubaldo B. Ragona (American International Pictures, 1964)
The Last Sect, dir. Jonathan Dueck (Peace Arch Entertainment Group: 2006)
Let Me In, dir. Matt Reeves (Hammer Films, 2010)
Let the Right One In, dir. Tomas Alfredson (Sandrew Metronome, 2008)
Life, dir. Daniel Espinosa (Sony Pictures: 2007)
Lifeforce, dir. Tobe Hooper (TriStar Films, 1985)
The Lost Boys, dir. Joel Schumacher (Warner Brothers, 1987)
Marble Hornets, created by Joseph DeLage and Troy Wagner (YouTube: 2009–14)
The Matrix, dir. The Wachowskis (Warner Brothers, 1999)
The Matrix Reloaded, dir. The Wachowskis (Warner Bros. Pictures: 2003)
Metropolis, dir. Fritz Lang (Parufamet, 1927)
Monster from Green Hell, dir. Kenneth G. Crane (DCA, 1958)
The Mummy, dir. Alex Kurtzman (Universal Picture, 2017)
Nadja, dir. Michael Almereyder (October Films, 1994)

Filmography   183

Night of the Living Dead, dir. George A. Romero (Continental Distributing, 1968)
Nosferatu, dir. F.W. Murnau (Fine Arts Guild, 1922)
Nosferatu the Vampyre, dir. Werner Herzog (20th Century-Fox, 1979)
NOS4A2, created by Jami O'Brien (AMC: 2019–present)
Not of This Earth, dir. Roger Corman (Allied Artists, 1957)
Not of This Earth, dir. Jim Wynorski (Concord Pictures, 1988)
Not of This Earth, dir. Terence H. Winkless (Concord Pictures, 1995)
Nothing Left to Fear, dir. Anthony Leonardi III (Anchor Bay Films: 2013)
Odd Thomas, dir. Stephen Sommers (Future Films: 2013)
The Omega Man, dir. Boris Sagal (Warner Bros. Pictures, 1971)
The Omen, dir. Richard Donner (20th Century-Fox: 1976)
The Originals, created by Julie Plec (Warner Bros. Television, 2013–18)
Perfect Creature, dir. Glenn Standring (Magna Pacific, 2006)
Planet of the Vampires, dir. Mario Bava (American International Pictures, 1965)
Predator, dir. John McTiernon (20th Century-Fox, 1987)
The Predator, dir. Shane Black (20th Century-Fox, 2018)
Predator 2, dir. Stephen Hopkins (20th Century-Fox, 1990)
Predators, dir. Nimród Antal (20th Century-Fox, 2010)
Priest, dir. Scott Stewart (Screen Gems: 2011)
Prometheus, dir. Ridley Scott (20th Century-Fox: 2012)
The Quatermass Experiment, dir. Rudolph Cartier (BBC: 1953)
Queen of Blood, dir. Curtis Harrington (American International Films, 1966)
A Quiet Place, dir. John Krasinski (Paramount Pictures, 2018)
A Quiet Place II, dir. John Krasinski (Paramount Pictures, 2021)
The Recall, dir. Mauro Borelli (Minds Eye Entertainment: 2017)
The Relic, dir. Peter Hyams (Paramount Pictures: 1997)
Rise: Blood Hunter, dir. Sebastian Gutierrez (Samuel Goldwyn Meyer: 2007)
Rosemary's Baby, dir. Roman Polanski (Paramount Pictures, 1968)

The Satanic Rites of Dracula, dir. Alan Gibson (Hammer Film Productions, 1973)
The Silence, dir. John R. Leonetti (Netflix: 2019)
Siren X, dir. Hideo Jôjô (Shintoho Company: 2008)
Skyline, dir. The Brothers Strause (Universal Pictures: 2010)
Slender Man, dir. Sylvain White (Sony Pictures Releasing)
Snowpiercer, dir. Bong Joon Ho (The Weinstein Company, 2013)
Solar Crisis, dir. Alan Smithee (Trimark Pictures: 1990)
Solaris, dir. Andrey Tarkowsky (Mosfilm, 1971)
Solaris, dir. Steven Soderbergh (20th Century-Fox, 2002)
Son of Dracula, dir. Robert Siodmak (Universal Pictures, 1943)
Species, dir. Roger Donaldson (Metro-Goldwyn-Mayer, 1995)
Species II, dir. Peter Medak (Metro-Goldwyn-Mayer, 1998)
Species III, dir. Brad Turner (Metro-Goldwyn-Mayer Home Entertainment, 2004)
Species: The Awakening, dir. Nick Lyon (Metro-Goldwyn-Mayer Home Entertainment, 2007)
Splinter, dir. Toby Wilkins (Magnolia Pictures, 2008)
Stake Land, dir. Jim Mickle (Dark Sky Films, 2010)
Starship Troopers, dir. Paul Verhoeven (Sony Pictures: 1997)
Stay Alive, dir. William Brent Bell (Universal Pictures: 2006)
The Strain, created by Guillermo del Toro and Chuck Hogan (20th Television, 2014–17)
Stranger Things, created by the Duffer brothers (Netflix, 2016–present)
10 Cloverfield Lane, dir. Dan Trachtenberg (Paramount Pictures: 2016)
The Terminator, dir. James Cameron (Orion Pictures, 1984)
Terminator 2: Judgment Day, dir. James Cameron (TriStar Pictures, 1991)
Terminator 3: Rise of the Machines, dir. Jonathan Mostow (Warner Bros. Pictures, 2003)
The Thing, dir. John Carpenter (Universal Pictures, 1982)
The Thing, dir. Matthijs van Heijningen, Jr. (Universal Pictures, 2011)

184 Filmography

The Thing from Another World, dir. Christian Nyby (RKO Radio Pictures, 1951)
30 Days of Night, dir. David Slade (Sony Pictures, 2007)
30 Days of Night: Blood Trails (seven-part miniseries), dir. Victor Garcia (FEARnet, 2007)
30 Days of Night: Dark Days, dir. Ben Ketai (Sony Pictures Home Entertainment, 2010)
The Tomorrow People, created by Roger Price (ITV: 1973–9)
Total Recall, dir. Paul Verhoeven (TriStar Pictures: 1990)
Transformers: Revenge of the Fallen, dir. Michael Bay (Paramount Pictures: 2009)
Twilight, dir. Catherine Hardwicke (Summit Entertainment, 2008)
2001: A Space Odyssey, dir. Stanley Kubrick (Metro-Goldwyn-Mayer: 1968)
Ultraviolet, dir. Kurt Wimmer (Screen Gems, 2006)
Ultraviolet: Code 044, dir. Osamu Dezaki (Animax: 2008)
Underworld, dir. Len Wiseman (Screen Gens, 2003)
Us, dir. Jordan Peele (Universal Pictures: 2019)
Vampire Moth, dir. Nobuo Nakagawa (Toho: 1956)
Vampire Wars: Battle for the Universe, dir. Matthew Hastings (Nu Image Films: 2005)
Les vampires, dir. Louis Feuillade (Gaumont: 1915–16)
Vamps, dir. Amy Heckerling (Anchor Bay Films: 2012)
Venom, dir. Ruben Fleischer (Sony Pictures: 2018)
Virus, dir. John Bruno (Universal Pictures: 1999)
The War of the Worlds, dir. Byron Haskin (Paramount Pictures: 1953)
The War of the Worlds, dir. Steven Spielberg (Paramount Pictures, 2005)
The War of the Worlds, created by Craig Viveiros (BBC: 2019)
War of the Worlds, created by Greg Strangis (Paramount Domestic: 8–90)
War of the Worlds, created by Howard Overman (Fox: 2019)
War of the Worlds II: The Next Wave, dir. C. Thomas Howell (The Asylum: 2008)
What We Do in the Shadows, dir. Jemaine Clement and Taika Waititi (Paramount Pictures: 2014)
What We Do in the Shadows, created by Jemaine Clement (20th Television: 2019–present)
World War Z, dir. Marc Forster (Paramount Pictures, 2013)

Bibliography

Arata, Stephen. 1996. *Fictions of Loss in the Victorian Fin de Siècle*. Cambridge: Cambridge University Press.

Auge, Marc. 2004. *Non-Places: An Introduction to Supermodernity*, trans. John Howe. London: Verso.

Bacon, Simon. 2019. *Dracula as Absolute Other: The Troubling and Distracting Specter of Stoker's Vampire on Screen*. Jefferson: McFarland.

Baring-Gould, Sabine. 1892. *Margery of Quether*. London: Heinemann and Balestier.

Baudrillard, Jean. 1994. *Simulacra and Simulation* [1981], trans. Sheila Faria Glazer. Ann Arbor: The University of Michigan Press.

_____. 1995. *The Gulf War Did Not Take Place* [1991], trans. Paul Pattern. Bloomington: Indiana University Press.

Benjamin, Walter. 2019. *Illuminations: Essays and Reflections*, trans Harry Zohn. Boston: Mariner Books.

Bernstein, Albert J. 2012. *Emotional Vampires: Dealing with People Who Drain You Dry*. New York: McGraw-Hill.

Blackwood, Algernon. 27 February 2011. "The Transfer" [1911], Algernonblackwood.org. http://algernonblackwood.org/Z-files/Transfer.pdf. Accessed 21 August 2019.

Boylan, Andrew M. 2012. *The Media Vampire*. Morrisville: Lulu.com.

Burdett, Carolyn. "Darwin and the Theory of Evolution," *Discovering Literature: Romantics and Victorians*. 15 May 2014. https://www.bl.uk/romantics-and-victorians/articles/darwin-and-the-theory-of-evolution. Accessed 19 May 2020.

Burroughs, Edgar Rice. 2012. *Mars Trilogy: A Princess of Mars* [1912]; *The Gods of Mars* [1913]; *The Warlord of Mars* [1914]. New York: Saga Press.

Cohen, Jeffrey Jerome. 1996. *Monster Theory: Reading Culture*. Minneapolis: University of Minnesota.

Craft, Christopher. 1994. *Another Kind of Love: Male Homosexual Desire in English Discourse 1850–1920*. Berkeley: University of California.

Dalton, Stephen. "Priest," The National. 12 May 2011. https://www.thenational.ae/arts-culture/priest-1.479495. Accessed 20 May 2020.B

Daniel, Carolyn. 2006. *Voracious Children: Who Eats Whom in Children's Literature*. Abingdon: Routledge.

D'Arcy, Uriah Derick. 1819. *The Black Vampyre: A Legend of St. Domingo*. Available at: http://jto.common-place.org/just-teach-one-homepage/the-black-vampyre/. Accessed 20 May 2020.

Darwin, Charles. 1964. *On the Origin of Species: A Facsimile of the First Edition* [1859]. Cambridge: Harvard University Press.

Davison, Carol Margaret. 2004. *Anti-Semitism and British Gothic Literature*. Basingstoke: Palgrave Macmillan.

DeGraw, Sharon. 2017. *The Subject of Race in American Science Fiction* [2007]. Abingdon: Routledge.

Deleuze, Gilles, and Felix Guattari. 1987. *A Thousand Plateaus: Capitalism and Schizophrenia*. Minneapolis: University of Minnesota Press.

_____. 2004. *A Thousand Plateaus: Capitalism and Schizophrenia*, trans. Brian Massumi. London: Continuum.

del Toro, Guillermo, and Chuck Hogan. 2009. *The Strain*. London: Harper.

186 Bibliography

_____. 2010. *The Fall*. London: Harper.
_____. 2011. *The Night Eternal*. London: Harper
Dickens, Charles. 2012. *A Christmas Carol* [1843]. Mineola: Dover Publications.
Dijkstra, Bram. 1988. *Idols of Perversity: Fantasies of Feminine Evil in Fin-de-Siècle Culture*. Oxford: Oxford University Press.
Dodd, Kevin. 2019. "'Blood Suckers Most Cruel': The Vampire and the Bat in and Before Dracula," *Athens Journal of Humanities & Arts*, Volume 6, Issue 2. 107–132.
Donald, Ralph. "America's 'Great Satan' Then and Now." *American Studies Today Online*. 20 February 2014. http://www.americansc.org.uk/Online/Great_Satan.htm. Accessed 11 July 2017.
du Maurier, George. 1894. *Trilby*. New York. Harper.
Eighteen-Bisang, Robert, and Elizabeth Miller. 2008. *Bram Stoker's Notes for Dracula*. Jefferson: McFarland.
Elber-Aviram, Hadas. 2021. *Fairy Tales of London: British Urban Fantasy, 1840 to the Present*. London: Bloomsbury.
Fox-Skelly, Jasmin. 2017. "There Are Diseases Hidden in Ice, and They Are Waking Up." *BBC*. 4 May. http://www.bbc.com/earth/story/20170504-there-are-diseases-hidden-in-ice-and-they-are-waking-up. Accessed 20 May 2020.
Gelder, Ken. 2012. *New Vampire Cinema*. London: Palgrave Macmillan.
Gibson, Matthew. 2006. *Dracula and the Eastern Question: British and French Vampire Narratives of the Nineteenth Century Near East*. London: Palgrave Macmillan.
Goudarzi, Sara. 2016. "As Earth Warms, the Diseases That May Lie Within Permafrost Become a Bigger Worry." *Scientific American*. 1 November. https://www.scientificamerican.com/article/as-earth-warms-the-diseases-that-may-lie-within-permafrost-become-a-bigger-worry/. Accessed 20 May 2020.
Grumeza, Ion. 2010. *The Roots of Balkanization: Eastern Europe C.E. 500–1500*. Lanham: University Press of America.
Haraway, Donna. 1991. *Simians, Cyborgs, and Women: The Reinvention of Nature*. London: Free Association Books.
Harrington, Curtis. 2005. "Retrospective in Terror: An Interview with Director Curtis Harrington." *The Terror Trap*. April. http://www.terrortrap.com/interviews/curtisharrington/. Accessed 20 May 2020.
Heinlein, Robert A. 2010. *Starship Troopers* [1959]. New York: Ace Books.
Heller-Nicolas, Alexandra. 2018. "Joseph DeLage and Troy Wagner's Marble Hornets (2009–2014)—New Media Horror." In Simon Bacon, ed., *Horror: A Companion*. Oxford: Peter Lang.
Hill, Joe. 2013. *NOS4A2*. New York: William Morrow and Company.
Hilton, J.L. 2014. "'Odd Thomas' Is 'Ghost Whisperer' for Men?" *Contact Infinite Futures*. 15 July. https://contactinfinitefutures.wordpress.com/2014/07/15/odd-thomas/. Accessed 20 May 2020.
Hudson, Dale. 2017. "Vampires and Transnational Horror." In Harry M. Benshoff, ed., *A Companion to the Horror Film*. Chichester: Wiley Blackwell, 463–82.
Hurley, Kelly. 1996. *The Gothic Body: Sexuality, Materialism, and Degeneration at the Fin De Siècle*. Cambridge: Cambridge University Press.
Lauro, Sarah Juliet. 2018. "Ron Honthaner's The House on Skull Mountain (1974)—Zombie Gothic." In Simon Bacon, ed., *The Gothic: A Reader*. Oxford: Peter Lang.
Lee, Tanith. 1980. *Sabella, or, The Bloodstone*. New York: DAW.
Le Fanu, Sheridan. *Carmilla* [1872]. Maryland: Wildside Press, 2005.
Le Rouge, Gustave. 2015. *Prisoner of the Vampires of Mars* [1908]. Lincoln: University of Nebraska Press.
Lindqvist, John Ajvide. 2008. *Let the Right One In* (Låt Den Rätte Komma In) [2005], trans. Ebba Segerberg. New York: St. Martins Giffen.
Malchow, Harold L. 1996. *Gothic Images of Race in Nineteenth-Century Britain*. Stanford: Stanford University Press.
Malerman, Josh. 2015. *Bird Box: A Novel*. New York: Ecco.
Marryat, Florence. 2010. *Blood of the Vampire* [1897]. Brighton: Victorian Secrets.
Marx, Carl. 2007. *Capital: A Critique of Political Economy: The Process of Capitalist Production—Part 1* [1867]. New York: Cosimo Classics.
Matheson, Richard. 2007. *I Am Legend* [1954]. London: Gollanz.

Mavis, Sophia. 2017, "How Dating Changed in 1970." *Medium*. 30 September. https://medium.com/@fundatejar/how-dating-changed-in-1970-268ca9c75fae. Accessed 20 May 2020.

McConnell, Frank. 1981. *The Science Fiction of H.G. Wells*. Oxford: Oxford University Press.

Melton, J. Gordon. 2011. *The Vampire Book: The Encyclopedia of the Undead*. Detroit: Visibke Ink Press.

Meyer, Stephenie. 2005. *Twilight*. London: Atom Books, 2005.

———. 2006. *New Moon*. London: Atom Books.

———. 2007. *Eclipse*. London: Atom.

———. 2008. *Breaking Dawn*. London: Atom Books.

Moretti, Franco. 1988. *Signs Taken for Wonders: Essays in the Sociology of Literary Forms*, trans. by Susan Fiscer, David Forgacs and David Miller. London: Verso.

Morris, Edmund. 2003. "Introduction." In John Wyndham, *The Day of the Triffids* [1951]. New York: Modern Library, xi–xv.

Napier, Susan J. 1998. "Vampires, Psychic Girls, Flying Women and Sailor Scouts: Four Faces of the Young Female in Japanese Popular Culture." In D.P. Martinez, ed., *The Worlds of Japanese Popular Culture: Gender, Shifting Boundaries and Global Cultures*. Cambridge: Cambridge University Press, 91–109.

Ní Fhlainn, Sorcha. 2019. *Postmodern Vampires: Film, Fiction, and Popular Culture*. London: Palgrave Macmillan.

Pappas, Stephanie. 2012. "5 Mars Myths and Misconceptions." *Live Science*. 3 August. https://www.livescience.com/22102-5-mars-myths-and-misconceptions.html. Accessed 20 May 2020.

Pullman, Philip. 1995. *Northern Lights*. New York: Scholastic Point.

———. 1997. *The Subtle Knife*. New York: Scholastic Point.

———. 2000. *The Amber Spyglass*. New York: Scholastic Point.

Robinson, Phil. 2014. *The Last of the Vampires* [1893]. Cryptofiction Classics.

Rose, E.M. 2015. *The Murder of William of Norwich: The Origins of the Blood Libel in Medieval*. Oxford: Oxford University Press.

Ruickbie, Leo. 2014. "Memento (Non)Mori: Memory, Discourse and Transmission During the Eighteenth-Century Vampire Epidemic and After." In Simon Bacon and Katarzyna Bronk, eds, *Undead Memory: Vampires and Human Memory in Popular Culture*. Oxford: Peter Lang, 21–57.

Ruggari, Amanda. 2016. "The World's Most Powerful Corporation." *BBC*. 30 March. http://www.bbc.com/capital/story/20160330-the-worlds-most-powerful-corporation. Accessed 20 May 2020.

Sakurazaka, Hiroshi. 2004. *All You Need Is Kill*. San Francisco: Viz Media.

Serviss, Garrett P. 1947. *Edison's Conquest of Mars* [1897]. Los Angeles: Carcosa House.

Showalter, Elaine. 1992. *Sexual Anarchy: Gender and Culture at the Fin De Siecle*. London: Virago.

Slate, Joe H. 2002. *Psychic Vampires: Protection from Energy Predators & Parasites*. Minnesota: Llewelyn Publications.

Stableford, Brian. 1995. *Opening Minds: Essays on Fantastic Literature*. San Bernardino: Borgo Press.

Stecopoulos, Harry. 1997. "The World According to Normal Bean: Edgar Rice Burroughs Popular Culture." In Harry Stecopoulos and Michael Uebel, eds., *Race and the Subject of Masculinities*. Durham: Duke University Press, 170–91.

Stoker, Bram. 1997. *Dracula* [1897]. London: Signet Classics.

Taylor, Dorceta E. 2014. *Toxic Communities: Environmental Racism, Industrial Pollution, and Residential Mobility*. New York: New York University Press.

Thweatt-Bates, Janine. 2012. *Cyborg Selves: A Theological Anthropology of the Posthuman*. Farnham: Ashgate.

VanderMere, Jeff. 2014. *Annihilation: A Novel*. New York: Farrar, Straus, and Giroux.

Viereck, George Sylvester. 2007. *The House of the Vampire* [1907]. Teddington: Echo Library.

Weaver, Matt. 2001. "Urban Regeneration—The Issue Explained." *The Guardian*. 19 March. https://www.theguardian.com/society/2001/mar/19/regeneration.urbanregeneration1?CMP=Share_iOSApp_Other. Accessed 20 May 2020.

Weinstock, Jeffrey. 2012. *The Vampire Film: Undead Cinema*. New York: Columbia University Press.

Wells, H.G. 1995. *The Time Machine* [1895]. New York: Dover Publishing.

_____. 2014. "The Flowering of the Strange Orchid" [1894]. Scotts Valley: CreateSpace Independent Publishing Platform.

_____. 2018. *The War of the Worlds* [1897]. https://www.gutenberg.org/files/36/36-h/36-h.htm. Accessed 20 May 2020.

Wild, Johnathan. 2017. *Literature of the 1900s: The Great Edwardian Emporium.* Edinburgh: Edinburgh University Press.

Wills, Matthew. 2018. "What the War of the Worlds Had to Do with Tasmania." *JSTOR Daily.* 3 December. https://daily.jstor.org/what-the-war-of-the-world-had-to-do-with-tasmania/. Accessed 20 May 2020.

Wilson, Colin. 2013. *The Space Vampires* [1976]. New York: Random House.

Wyndham, John. 2008. *The Day of the Triffids* [1951]. London: Penguin.

Yarboro, Chelsea Quin. 2014. *Hôtel Transylvania: A Timeless Novel of Love and Peril* [1978]. New York: Open Road.

Index

Abhuman 56, 65
abjectivity 4, 12, 127
Africa 12, 160
African American 69, 70, 79, 80, 121, 131, 179
alien: contagion 17, 68; craft 29, 30, 42, 49, 53, 67, 153; double 6, 13, 152; entity 6, 20, 26, 56, 68, 69, 72, 75, 99, 106–7, 109, 114, 144; flora 7, 13, 71, 153; other 3, 6, 24, 55, 119, 161, 176; race 4, 9, 21, 41, 59, 135, 148, 150, 154; vampire 5, 6–10, 11, 17, 21–2, 24, 29, 33, 55, 56–7, 59, 65, 73, 84, 109, 112, 149, 154, 167, 169, 172
Alien (film) 6, 10, 35, 38, 41–3, 44, 50, 53, 55–6, 58, 59, 61, 106, 107, 154, 167
America 4, 7, 17, 18, 19–21, 24, 30, 31, 65, 66, 71, 89, 92, 98, 100, 107, 122–5, 135, 137, 152, 155, 156, 163, 173
angel 15, 31, 61, 99
anthropocene 12, 129, 148
antidote 131, 176, 177
apocalypse 16, 21, 76, 77, 84, 88, 158, 161, 167, 169, 174, 176, 177
assimilation 10, 12, 77, 102, 139, 162–3
asteroid 30, 164
astronaut 4, 10, 52, 58, 59, 64, 65–7, 80, 109, 142, 143, 164
augmentation 20, 34, 37, 45, 46, 103, 130

bacteria 18, 68
bat 1, 19, 20, 23, 123, 129
bath 26, 45, 66, 73–4, 102, 113, 162
Bathory, Countess 93, 94
battle 31, 32, 36, 37, 106, 108, 114, 122, 131, 137, 138, 141, 166
becoming 56, 129–32, 165, 179
biology 4, 9, 12, 24, 25, 30, 35, 46, 67, 100, 109, 130–1, 149, 161; energy 8, 39, 41, 44, 45, 61, 141–2, 161
bio-weapon 23, 39, 44
black hole 4, 8, 12, 110, 112, 142, 143, 144
blood 1, 6, 9, 10, 12, 24, 33, 36, 37, 39, 51, 55, 57, 71, 84, 90, 99, 154; contamination 26, 29, 32, 69, 118, 127; drinking 3, 4, 6–8, 12, 15, 24, 45, 63, 65, 69, 80, 87, 92–3, 117, 120, 122, 123, 124, 148, 149, 150, 151, 153, 175; transfusion 23, 32

boundaries 2, 114, 118, 140
burial 5

capitalism 80, 81
carnivorous 19, 157, 158
castle 1, 42, 79, 85, 119, 130, 133
cat 55, 75
Central America 106
children 16, 27, 28, 30, 48, 60, 66, 68, 85, 86–91, 95, 98, 99, 119, 120, 143, 171–3, 176–9
chimera 157
city 29, 40, 47, 72, 79, 80, 81, 84, 100, 104, 112–5, 117, 126, 128, 132, 134–5, 164, 167, 170, 171, 172
climate 13, 141, 148
clone 29, 30, 34, 35, 46, 47, 74, 103, 131, 133–4, 152
Cold War 7, 21, 24, 59, 65, 71, 149, 160, 173
colonialism 3, 12, 13, 15, 17–20, 21, 37, 39, 40, 71, 115, 123, 125, 127, 135, 127, 155, 157, 158, 174, 178; post 11, 149
colonization 3, 37, 76, 126
consumerism 5, 9, 15, 37, 41, 44, 46, 52, 53, 114, 163, 179
contagion 17, 18, 29, 53, 86, 132, 150, 163
containment 25, 126, 164
cyberspace 11

Dark City (film) 3, 11, 26, 109, 112–5, 135
darkness 6, 11, 13, 51, 52, 55, 57, 76, 112, 133
death 4, 5, 11, 18, 24, 37, 45, 48, 53, 54, 55, 64, 66, 81, 82, 83, 93, 94, 95, 100–1, 105, 108, 131, 134, 137, 140, 143, 146, 154, 157, 169, 171, 173
demon 66, 67, 85–7, 89, 90, 98, 122–5, 145, 170, 172, 173
desire 25, 36, 37, 44, 52, 58, 65, 75, 107, 139, 142, 176
despair 85, 87, 178
devolution 3, 6, 17, 115
devil 66, 67, 99, 100
dimension 2, 3, 77, 88, 90, 91, 98, 111, 143, 144, 145–7, 159, 173–4; inter 2; vampiric 4, 11, 112
disease 18, 68, 87, 117, 128, 131, 148, 159
dog 24, 87, 150, 151
doppelgänger 6, 11, 21, 95, 116, 122

189

190 Index

Dracula (1931) 119, 156
Dracula (novel) 2, 3, 9, 17, 27, 49, 52, 65, 83, 106, 115, 126, 146, 164, 179
Dracula, Count 1, 2, 5, 7, 8, 10, 15, 16, 19, 22, 25, 29, 32, 44, 48, 51, 68, 74, 89, 91, 97, 120, 129, 130, 133, 133, 155, 156, 163, 165, 170, 178

Earth 1, 2, 3, 4, 5, 9–10, 12, 15–6, 17, 19–27, 29, 30, 34, 36, 37, 38, 39, 41–53, 57–66, 68–71, 74–8, 83, 84, 100, 107–10, 112–3, 125, 127–8, 132, 135–7, 139, 141–2, 144–7, 149, 151–5, 158–9, 161, 164–7, 169, 170, 172, 176, 178
Earthling 31, 34, 51, 59
ecoimmune 38, 69
ecology 9, 12, 21, 35, 36, 37, 75, 95, 148, 152, 160; dark 62, 151
ecosystem 13, 37, 71, 160, 174
eggs 6, 54, 55, 76, 154, 157
emasculation 54, 104
energy 3, 5–6, 8, 10–1, 13, 19, 25–7, 34, 35, 45, 52, 62, 67, 69–70, 74, 75, 84, 90, 93, 96, 101, 102, 106–8, 112, 114, 115, 135–9, 141–2, 144, 148, 156, 159, 163, 167, 169–70
environment 4, 12, 13, 17–9, 21–2, 26–8, 32, 34, 35, 37, 39, 40, 53, 57, 67, 71, 75, 76, 85, 87, 88, 96, 100, 102, 103, 107, 109–10, 112, 114, 120, 127–9, 134, 144, 146–50, 152, 156, 161, 174, 177
eternal 32, 78, 92, 132, 134
ethnicity 11, 116, 121
evil 17, 20, 58, 90, 92, 93, 115
evolution 5, 8, 13, 17–9, 20, 22, 28, 30, 46, 47, 61, 70, 75, 115, 127, 130, 148, 151, 155, 157, 166, 168, 177
excessive states 2, 10, 11, 26, 41, 97, 98, 100, 110–2, 116, 157, 161, 166, 169, 170–1
exoskeleton 10, 15, 27, 28, 31, 34, 37, 49, 64, 67, 76, 99, 103, 128
extraterrestrial 1, 6, 24, 29, 30, 41, 43, 66, 68, 149, 160

faith 98, 99, 100, 171
farm 45, 125, 127, 128, 142, 158, 160–1, 167; human 9, 29, 46, 109, 148, 151
fascism 119, 120, 121
fear 6, 7, 10, 11, 18, 26, 50, 60, 71, 85–8, 91, 93–6, 144, 153, 170
female 24–5, 39, 77, 104–5, 119, 122, 146, 153, 154, 162
femininity 25, 39, 66, 166, 178
feminist 38
feminization 17, 39
flesh 15, 27, 32, 49, 58, 76, 101, 103, 162, 166, 176, 179
fungus 12, 87, 98, 100, 102, 157, 174, 176–9
future 3, 5, 11, 12, 13, 15, 17, 19, 20, 22–3, 34, 40, 44, 47, 50, 51, 52, 63, 74, 75, 77, 103–7, 109, 115–6, 119, 122, 126, 128, 130, 141, 143–5, 150–2, 161, 164, 166, 172, 176, 178–80

galaxy 4, 45, 46, 53, 109, 135, 143
gaze 29, 125
ghost 5, 10, 38–40, 48, 49, 50, 51–2, 57, 58, 94, 100, 102, 122, 142–3
glamor 29, 153, 154
god/s 9, 17, 18, 44, 45, 46, 59, 81, 99, 107, 115, 117, 155, 164
gothic 2, 53, 55, 56, 140, 156

haunt 10, 48, 51, 55, 57, 67, 86, 89, 94, 96, 111
heaven 67, 73, 152
hell 67, 98, 99, 112, 161
history 8, 11, 18, 33, 39, 41, 44, 79, 109, 110, 116, 119, 124–5, 153, 155, 156, 167
hive mind 30, 114, 127, 154, 163
human 1–13, 16, 20–30, 32–48, 49–53, 55–60, 63–78, 84, 88, 90, 96, 98, 99, 100, 102–9, 112, 114–22, 124–9, 131–4, 137–41, 145, 147–53, 154, 157–9, 161–70, 172, 173, 174–9; antihuman 6, 71; nonhuman 6, 65, 106, 148; posthuman 28, 106
humanity 3–4, 9–10, 13, 16–7, 22, 24, 27, 34–6, 41, 43, 45, 65, 70, 74–5, 78, 101, 105, 108, 126–8, 141, 143, 151, 178–9
humanoid 8, 28, 42, 43, 45–8, 49, 54, 97, 106, 154
hunger 20, 25, 75, 164
hybridity 12, 13, 26–7, 30, 32–4, 37, 39, 48, 62, 65, 102, 107, 109, 115, 119, 124, 127, 129, 149, 157, 161, 163, 164, 165, 176–9
hypnosis 78, 81, 120, 154

I Am Legend (1954) 16, 30, 36, 141, 158, 178
identity 10, 20, 21, 40, 49, 79, 91, 107, 113, 123, 130, 163, 179
immune system 12, 24, 34, 38, 45, 47, 75, 111, 168
imperialism 3, 17, 18, 33
indigenous 11, 13, 18, 34–6, 38–40, 71, 125, 127
infect 29, 32, 38, 39, 40, 41, 49, 69, 70, 74, 75, 76, 85, 87, 96, 99, 118, 127, 129, 141, 146, 155, 162–3, 174, 176, 177, 178
influence 21, 29, 49, 57, 67, 68, 82, 86, 98, 154
insect 4, 30, 31, 132, 154, 157
invaders 2, 3, 5, 9, 15, 18–21, 27, 28–30, 35–7, 39–40, 51, 55, 71, 74, 75, 125, 127, 148, 152, 157, 164, 168
invasion 12, 16–8, 20, 24, 27, 31, 33–4, 149, 167, 170, 173–4; narrative 18

Japan 31, 122–5
Jewish 119–21
Jouissance 12, 37, 39, 41, 44, 61, 116, 161, 163–4
Jupiter Ascending (film) 9, 21, 40, 45–8

king vampire 23, 32, 33, 82, 134, 174

laboratory 60, 63, 70, 128, 157, 173, 177–8
Lifeforce (film) 8, 10, 84, 89
London 1, 2, 16, 21, 87, 117, 120, 129, 160, 161, 177

Index 191

Los Angeles 25, 28, 30, 107
love 30, 73, 78, 92, 125, 134, 136, 143, 144, 157, 167, 179

machine 26, 28, 34, 41, 45, 55, 80, 94, 96, 103–6, 137–41
map 41, 42, 133
Mars 1–3, 9, 10, 13, 15, 19, 20, 37–40, 50–2, 59, 60, 135–7, 148, 152, 153
Martian 3, 5, 6, 7, 8, 9, 12, 15–24, 26, 28, 32, 34, 39–40, 44, 47, 50, 52, 59, 62, 64, 100, 103, 105, 115, 126, 127, 128, 135, 137, 148, 151, 157, 158, 178
masculinity 66; hypermasculinity 39, 104, 107, 108; nonmasculinity 178
Matheson, Richard 16, 30, 141, 158
memory 1, 39, 40, 58, 65, 74, 77, 81, 92, 113–5, 133, 134, 165
Metropolis 28, 104, 114, 115, 170, 177
military 29, 31, 32, 34–5, 37, 43, 69, 70, 103, 106, 121, 123, 134, 177
mind 9, 28, 30, 40, 76, 85, 89, 114, 133, 170, 173, 176; control 29, 48–9, 68, 74, 89–91, 146, 163, 174
mirror 2, 6, 11, 12, 49, 61, 82, 92, 93, 95, 96, 110, 115–6, 117, 120, 121, 145, 165, 173, 174, 179
miscegenation 6, 10, 15, 18, 27, 65, 107, 118, 119, 127, 157, 179
mist 1, 8, 20, 40, 51, 54, 57, 58, 71, 129, 165, 170
monster 2, 4, 51, 52, 55, 64, 71, 80, 95, 98, 100, 107, 124, 145, 147, 149, 150, 151–2, 156, 157, 159, 162, 165, 168, 172, 174, 176
monsterization 7, 126
moon 34, 53
the moon 109, 152, 153
murder 45, 46, 47, 50, 100, 101–2, 112, 113, 117–8, 120, 170
mutation 4, 27, 70, 109, 133, 164

nanotechnology 44, 69, 129
Native American 35, 39, 40, 125–7, 135
New York 1, 28, 66, 78, 79
Nosferatu (film) 3, 6, 12, 51, 53, 54, 100, 120, 132, 148, 159
Not of This Earth (film) 3, 9, 21, 22–4, 26
nuclear 40, 44, 69, 70, 138, 139

The Omega Man (film) 36, 40, 131, 140
orbit 4, 41, 60, 61, 71, 109, 142, 143, 144, 145, 158
organic 11, 25, 28, 30, 36, 37, 38, 44, 62, 97, 98, 100, 159, 163–4
organism 60, 62, 69–71, 148, 161
Orlok 6, 51, 55, 96, 97, 100, 120, 127, 159
outer space 2, 3, 4–5, 10, 12, 21, 25, 29, 46, 52, 57, 59, 61–6, 71, 107, 141, 144, 147, 149, 155
outsider 2, 12, 27, 65, 108, 127, 137, 157, 158, 172

pandemic 150
parasite 30, 58, 59, 67, 75–8, 114, 115, 137, 163–5, 176
past 5, 7, 11, 12, 15, 36, 36, 39, 47, 51, 56, 60, 74, 77, 79, 103, 106, 108, 109, 112–5, 122, 124–5, 143, 145, 150–1, 155–6, 171–3, 174, 179
patriarchy 39, 103, 129
penetration 22, 39, 54, 60, 64, 76, 149, 162, 164, 178
pilot 4, 29, 54, 61, 63, 66, 110, 142
plague 18, 41, 46, 48, 57, 87, 120, 132–3, 140, 178
planet 4, 8, 9–10, 12, 16, 20, 21, 27, 30, 34, 35–40, 41–4, 46–7, 48, 50–4, 63, 66, 70, 71, 73, 75–8, 108–9, 115, 126, 127–8, 131, 135–7, 139, 141–5, 147, 148–50, 152–3, 164
Planet of the Vampires (film) 7, 10, 49, 57–9, 68, 75
predator 6, 36, 101, 154, 159, 167
Predator (film franchise) 6, 11, 21, 41, 43, 53, 103, 106–9
purgatory 81

quantum 143
quarantine 13, 56, 60, 70, 118, 119, 164
queen 12, 55, 126, 127, 149, 152
Queen of Blood (film) 72, 152–4, 163
queer 30

racism 79, 120
rat 27, 55, 60, 157
religion 18, 98, 117, 135, 136, 172
Renfield 17, 22, 44, 49, 65, 108, 110, 146, 156
repetition 26, 32, 33, 65, 95, 158, 160
replication 65, 67, 69, 117, 152, 166
reptile 26, 36, 101
resistance 5, 9, 27, 30, 31, 39, 57, 63, 64, 74, 75, 76–8, 92, 103, 129, 132–4, 139–41, 148, 153, 154, 175
resurrection 39, 134
robot 11, 34, 37, 42, 69, 103–6, 137–8, 144
rural 79, 98, 100

Satan 7, 67, 68, 102, 156
satellite 68, 69, 158
scavengers 88, 137
science 3, 15, 45, 149, 150, 158, 159
science fiction 59, 155
sex 2, 6, 8, 24, 26, 38, 54, 66, 71, 73, 90, 104–5, 107, 116, 153–4
sexuality 11, 15, 25, 55
shadow 6, 11, 29, 51–2, 54, 55, 57, 75, 89, 96, 116
slavery 20, 79, 80, 92
snow 5, 12, 60, 88, 107, 146, 149–51, 167
solar 109, 138, 141, 160, 164, 177
Solaris (film) 71, 143, 144
Son of Dracula (film) 1, 19, 92
South America 12, 155, 176
space 2–5, 7, 10–2, 16–7, 20–1, 22, 25, 26–7,

29–30, 34, 41–2, 44, 46, 49–61, 63–7, 71, 76, 79, 80, 84, 85, 88, 90, 105, 107–10, 112, 114–5, 130, 141–4, 146–7, 149–53, 155, 159, 164, 166–7, 172, 177
specter 52, 115
spectral 55, 57, 89, 94
spies 7, 24, 42, 152, 273, 175
spirit 2, 38, 39, 48, 49, 67, 93
spirituality 35, 38, 40, 87, 117, 136
Stoker, Bram. 1–3, 6, 8–10, 12, 15–6, 32, 52, 54, 65, 83, 106, 110, 115, 119, 126, 129, 135, 148, 156, 157, 166
strangers 8, 71, 113–5, 135, 162
sun 2, 18, 58, 64, 96, 115, 141, 142, 145
supernatural 52, 54, 93, 94, 95, 100, 116, 119, 122, 155, 165, 173
symbiotic 34, 38, 40, 58, 89, 100, 150, 161, 164–6, 176

terror 86, 150
terrorist 24
time 3–5, 7, 8, 9, 13, 17–9, 21, 25–7, 31–3, 41–2, 45–7, 50, 56, 57, 63, 65, 67, 70–1, 74, 77, 78, 79, 81, 85–6, 88, 92, 95, 100, 101, 103–4, 106, 108, 110, 115, 119, 123, 141–4, 147–8, 150–1, 173
transformation 1, 5, 6, 25–6, 27, 40, 49, 56, 65, 67, 97, 103–4, 105, 109, 129–30, 133, 135, 139, 161, 162, 164, 177
Transylvania 1, 2, 3, 32, 129
trauma 15, 39, 81, 82, 85, 88, 111, 115, 160

undead 1, 5, 12, 34, 44, 52, 80, 119, 131, 134, 148; memory 39, 40, 49, 172
underground 11, 12, 27, 32, 39, 53, 69, 107, 114, 116, 129, 139, 149–50, 151, 167, 174
urban 11, 85, 100, 112, 114, 128; legend 11, 91, 93, 95, 96, 97–8, 156

vagina 25, 55
vampire 3–4, 6, 9, 11–3, 15, 19–20, 22–3, 25, 27, 30, 32, 38, 41, 42–3, 45–6, 50–4, 56–7, 59–60, 62–3, 67–9, 71–2, 74–9, 80, 82, 83, 87–91, 92, 93, 98–100, 102, 105–7, 108, 109–12, 114–6, 117–8, 122, 123, 127, 129–33, 135–6, 138–41, 144–5, 147–8, 151, 155–8, 163–6, 170, 174–6; alien 8–10, 17, 20, 21, 26, 33, 56, 65, 72, 84, 89, 112, 167, 169, 172; energy 8, 26, 62, 67, 75, 90, 96, 108, 144, 170, 171; psychic 114; real 2, 122, 174; space 5, 7, 29, 46, 49
Van Helsing 1, 56, 91, 175
Venus flytrap 8, 12, 132, 148, 153, 159
victim 5, 8, 10, 23, 26, 28–9, 45, 49–51, 52, 55–6, 58, 65, 69, 74–5, 81, 89, 91, 96, 97, 100, 105, 111, 114, 120, 124, 129, 144, 148, 152, 154, 155, 157, 159, 162, 163–4, 167, 170, 177
violence 26, 30, 37, 55, 57, 60, 65–7, 75, 76, 80, 92, 100, 102, 106, 107, 109, 111, 127–8, 140, 150, 158, 160, 164, 169, 176, 178
virility 1, 3, 18, 19, 20, 21, 129, 137
virus 9, 29, 30, 71, 75, 96, 118, 121, 128, 131, 139
voracity 115, 165

War of the Worlds (film) 21, 36, 148
War of the Worlds (novel) 1–3, 5, 6, 8–9, 12, 15–20, 29, 34, 42, 44, 47–8, 51, 58, 59, 71, 74, 75, 98, 102, 107, 115, 148, 151, 160, 168, 174, 178, 179
warrior 11, 36, 108, 124, 135
weapons 3, 20, 23, 30, 31, 36, 39, 44, 51, 66, 70, 107, 129, 130, 131, 133, 135, 138, 158, 168, 169
wells, H.G. 1–3, 6, 8–10, 13, 15–21, 23–4, 26, 27, 28, 29, 30, 31, 32, 36, 37, 40, 44–5, 49, 51–2, 62, 64, 75, 100, 103, 104, 105, 115, 128, 137, 148, 151, 154, 156, 158, 168
whiteness 18, 36, 40, 78–83, 95, 127, 129, 131, 139, 155, 160, 179
wolf 1, 20, 129, 165
world mirror 2, 6, 11, 12, 93, 96, 115, 116, 120, 121, 145, 173, 174, 179
world parallel 6, 7, 10, 11–12, 22, 91, 116, 120, 124, 125, 133–4, 147
wormhole 109, 110, 142–5

xenomorph 6, 8, 42, 43, 44–5, 50, 55, 60–1, 109, 120, 154, 167

zombie 79, 80, 161, 178

www.ingramcontent.com/pod-product-compliance
Ingram Content Group UK Ltd.
Pitfield, Milton Keynes, MK11 3LW, UK
UKHW042011140426
5217IPUK00015B/1106